THE
SOCIALIST
MANIFESTO

THE SOCIALIST MANIFESTO

THE CASE FOR RADICAL POLITICS
IN AN ERA OF EXTREME INEQUALITY

BHASKAR SUNKARA

BASIC BOOKS
New York

Basic Books
Hachette Book Group
1290 Avenue of the Americas, New York, NY 10104
www.basicbooks.com

Printed in the United States of America

First Edition: April 2019

Published by Basic Books, an imprint of Perseus Books, LLC, a subsidiary of Hachette Book Group, Inc. The Basic Books name and logo is a trademark of the Hachette Book Group.

The Hachette Speakers Bureau provides a wide range of authors for speaking events. To find out more, go to www.hachettespeakersbureau.com or call (866) 376-6591.

The publisher is not responsible for websites (or their content) that are not owned by the publisher.

Print book interior design by Jouve.

Library of Congress Cataloging-in-Publication Data
Names: Sunkara, Bhaskar, author.
Title: The socialist manifesto : the case for radical politics in an era of extreme inequality / Bhaskar Sunkara.
Description: New York, NY : Basic Books, 2019. | Includes bibliographical references and index.
Identifiers: LCCN 2018039872 (print) | LCCN 2018055833 (ebook) | ISBN 9781541674004 (ebook) | ISBN 9781541617391 (hardcover)
Subjects: LCSH: Socialism. | Socialism—United States. | Equality. | Equality—United States.
Classification: LCC HX73 (ebook) | LCC HX73 .S86 2019 (print) | DDC 320.53/10973—dc23
LC record available at https://lccn.loc.gov/2018039872

ISBNs: 978-1-5416-1739-1 (hardcover), 978-1-5416-7400-4 (ebook)

LSC-C

10 9 8 7 6 5 4 3 2 1

For my brothers and sisters, Jayaa,
Priya, Sumant, and Sunil

CONTENTS

PREFACE

I T'S OBVIOUS THAT things are changing. When I was in high school and I told people I was a socialist, they looked at me as if I were crazy. When I tell people I'm a socialist today, they just nod and go about their day—not a hint of physical revulsion.

I discovered socialism largely by chance. My parents immigrated to the United States from Trinidad and Tobago with four children shortly before I was born. My mother worked nights as a telemarketer, my father, a declassed professional, eventually as a civil servant in New York City.

After hopping around for a bit, they rented in a suburban town with a good school district. Even though we didn't have much, I had enough—a decent home, a great education, basketball courts, and a public library where I spent way too much of my youth. My life was far more comfortable than the world my parents were born into, or even that of my older siblings. It was clear to me why—certainly the tireless efforts of my family, but even more than that, the environment around me. And that environment wouldn't have been possible without the state.

We have social democracy in the United States—but it's exclusionary and funded by regressive property taxes (renting, in my parents' case, was a bit of a loophole). Even at the age of thirteen, I saw the difference that access to quality public goods made and thought of myself as a committed liberal, in the best American sense.

My turn to socialism may have been organic, but it certainly wasn't an awakening. Like many a middle-class kid before me, I found radicalism through books. My local library had heaps of socialist literature, most of them donated by red diaper babies and Jewish cultural associations. By chance, I picked up Leon Trotsky's *My Life* the summer after seventh grade, didn't particularly like it (still don't), but was sufficiently intrigued to read the Isaac Deutscher biographies of Trotsky, the works of democratic socialist thinkers including Michael Harrington and Ralph Miliband, and eventually the mysterious Karl Marx himself.

I hear from people who say they're socialists in their hearts but, growing pragmatic with time, moderate liberals in their heads. I might have been the opposite. I saw the importance of day-to-day reforms and was myself the beneficiary of those victories—Marxism, though, was in my head. The 9/11 attacks and the subsequent "war on terror" only reinforced these tendencies, as I and many people of my generation were introduced to mass protest through the antiwar movement.

Marxism provided a framework for understanding why reforms won within capitalism were so hard to sustain and why there was so much suffering in societies filled with abundance. I eventually combined my social-democratic heart and my still inchoate Marxist brain into the politics I espouse today: a radicalism that is aware of the difficulty of revolutionary change and, at the same time, of how profound the gains of reform can be.

What follows is a book I wanted to write when I was 68. I'm writing it forty years too soon, and I may one day want to revise much of it. What I am certain about is that we live in a world marked by extreme inequality, by unnecessary pain and suffering, and that a better one can be constructed. That conviction won't change, unless the world does—which is to say, unless we are able to change it.

Our current politics don't seem to offer much of a future at all. The choice before us appears to be between, on the one hand, a technocratic neoliberalism that embraces the rhetoric of social inclusion but not equality and, on the other, a right-wing populism channeling anger into the worst directions. To be a socialist today is to believe that more, not less, democracy will help solve social ills—and to believe that ordinary people can shape the systems that shape their lives.

ONE

A DAY IN THE LIFE OF A SOCIALIST CITIZEN

I'M WRITING THIS book in 2018, so if you're picking up a dusty copy some day in the future, you should know that Jon Bon Jovi is the most popular and critically acclaimed musician of this era. With that in mind, let's try a thought experiment.[1]

Say you're a big Bon Jovi fan (and really, why wouldn't you be?). You're looking for a job, and you write Jon Bon Jovi a letter with your resume attached, and he's kind enough to give you a reference to work for his family's pasta sauce company. Now, as contemporary readers will no doubt know, Bongiovi Brand pasta sauce is widely regarded as the finest pasta sauce. You take your position there bottling such Italian American favorites as "Classic Curry" sauce with great pride.

You're paid $15 an hour and work from nine to five every day. It's not great, but you have bills piling up and weird hobbies to pay for. It's certainly better than being unemployed and stealing Wi-Fi from your neighbor Fred, a twice-divorced pediatrician who cried at the end of *The Blind Side*.

Despite the unrivaled quality of their product, Bongiovi is still a small firm. You're quickly trained in the most efficient way to bottle and seal pasta sauce. It's mind-numbing stuff, but otherwise things are okay. You take a liking to your coworkers and make friends.

Over the months, you become better and better at your job. It might sound silly, but you take pride in the work. You believe in "Classic Curry" and its capacity to bring joy and satisfaction to people across the world. You also get along great with your bosses—it's a pasta sauce factory, not some Dickensian sweatshop. When you look sad, your foreman asks you what's wrong and tries to cheer you up. When you make a mistake, you're not fired, but given some friendly feedback. Mr. Bongiovi even occasionally treats his employees to a Trenton Thunder minor league baseball game after work.

On your one-year anniversary at the company, you get to counting. You used to bottle 100 pasta sauces a day—now you average about 125. Proud of yourself, you tell your bosses. They say they're aware of how great you've been doing and really appreciate your service. They even nominated you for Employee of the Month. You thank them, but suggest that maybe it would be fair if you got paid 25 percent more to reflect your increased productivity.

Your managers think about it and remind you that the economy is in a recession and many people are looking for work. They also invoke the company's mission statement, about how innovative pasta sauce could one day change the world. Bongiovi Brand isn't a food manufacturer; it's a culture, an ethos, a creed, a way of life.

It's hard to argue with any of that, and you're willing to drop the matter and just get by with your current pay. But luckily your bosses end their spiel with a compromise: they'll pay you $17 an hour, and if you keep up the good work, there's a promotion with your name on it.

You can't shake the feeling of elation. You're so happy that your co-worker Debra says to you, "Hey, you're absolutely glowing!" And you tell her that's because you just got a raise to $17 an hour. She hesitates for only a moment and then congratulates you—but something doesn't feel right.

Later that day, you're passing by the labeling department, and you see Debra crying. Everyone's eyes at Bongiovi are always a bit watery as a result of the vast amount of curry incinerated on the premises, but this seems different.

"Hey, you didn't happen to watch a 2009 sports drama written and directed by John Lee Hancock and featuring a gut-wrenching performance by Sandra Bullock?"

"Yes, but I'm actually crying because I've been working here for three years, and I only make $13 an hour."

Bottling sauce was no harder than labeling it—you're outraged by the disparity. You promise you'll talk to management about it.

The next day you do just that, saying, "Listen, I know I'm kind of a favorite around here on account of my personality, but it's really unfair that Debra is paid so much less than me for doing basically the same work." Your bosses tell you that, actually, you aren't a favorite—in fact everyone thinks you're kind of weird. They explain that the difference in pay is based on the fact that Debra's old job gave her $7.50 an hour, so she was started at $11 here, which was still a big improvement. Plus, she's never asked for a raise the way you did.

All that information seems accurate, so you go ahead and ask if she can also receive a raise. Your managers say that they'd love to do that, but times are tough, and to be honest, Debra isn't as productive as some of her coworkers. They can't give everyone a raise. You learn that a big corporate rival has been winning market share by cutting labor costs and lowering the price of their sauce. "The best thing we can do for Debra is to make sure she has a job for years to come."

You don't see them budging, so you drop the matter and tell Debra you tried your best.

But what happened to Debra becomes a catalyst for change at Bongiovi. First, employees meet together after work to talk about how much they're paid and what conditions are like at the plant. They care about the

company, but they want to receive benefits like paid sick days. The meetings snowball, and eventually workers form a union.

The union helps things for a while, but the next few years are tough
for the curry-flavored pasta sauce market. Competitors in India—a land
of curry, tomatoes, and cheap labor—are well positioned to disrupt the
industry. There are rumors of the company being sold or jobs getting outsourced, but management says nothing. Finally, Mr. Bongiovi addresses
the speculation: we're in it for the long haul, we believe in pasta sauce, but
more than that we believe in people.

Things would have to change to restore Bongiovi Brand to profitability,
but the union contract limits Mr. Bongiovi's options. He loves his employees, but it's sometimes necessary to saw off a leg to save a life. Without the
freedom to unilaterally lay off redundant workers, Bongiovi thinks up another plan: he gets a line of credit from his son Jon and uses it to upgrade
machinery in the factory.

At first you welcome the development—bottling pasta is hard work,
and the new system will be semi-automated. If you turned out a hundred
jars an hour before, you figured you could do two hundred now. But
instead of making your life easier, the changes make your job more difficult. Your bosses are as friendly as ever, but they're under tremendous
pressure themselves. They say everyone needs to produce two hundred
fifty jars an hour for the sauce to be priced competitively, then three
hundred jars. The company even tries to find more time for you to bottle
sauce—first by cutting lunch breaks and then by extending the workday
an hour.

The union stops the latter, but the employees want to avoid disruptions
and prove how productive American labor can be. Plus, it would look terrible for union leaders if a shop closed down just a few years after being
organized—imagine how many workers at other companies would be discouraged from doing the same!

The result is that you feel helpless. Even before the more demanding
work regime, you felt as though you didn't have a say in how things were

run and you got sick of being told what to do every day. You know your company is in a precarious position, but you also know that those in charge are getting paid fifty times more than you. Are they really doing fifty times the work? Couldn't you figure out how to do their jobs too?

At the end of every day you're physically and emotionally exhausted and unable to do the things outside of work you used to love: write, swim, take out loans in the name of Fred's cat. You think about quitting, but without family or savings to rely on, it's impossible.

Who put you in this situation? Jon Bon Jovi? Those curry-loving Indians?

THE ANSWER ISN'T who, it's what: capitalism. Capitalism isn't the consumer products you use every day, even if those commodities (wet wipes, tobacco, hair wigs) are produced in capitalist workplaces. Nor is capitalism the exchange of goods and services through the market. There have been markets for thousands of years, but, as we will see, capitalism is a relatively new development.

The market under capitalism is different because you don't just choose to participate in it—you have to take part in it to survive. Your ancestors were peasants, but they weren't any less greedy than you. They had their little plot of land, and they grew as much crop as possible on it. They ate some of it, and then they gave a chunk of the remainder to a local lord to avoid getting killed. Any leftover product they often took to town and sold at the market.[2]

But you, pasta sauce proletarian, face a different scenario. You might've said that you're into locally sourced, sustainable food on your Tinder profile, but you don't own any land. All you have is your ability to work and various personal effects that I originally listed here in great detail but have since been removed by my editor.

Now that's not nothing. You're an above-average student, a hard worker, and capable of thinking creatively and solving problems. But those skills aren't enough—they don't provide you with the stuff you need to survive. That's where Mr. Bongiovi comes in.

By virtue of owning a place of work, a boss has something any would-be employee needs. Without land to sow, your labor power by itself isn't going to produce any commodities. So you rent yourself to Mr. Bongiovi, mix your labor with the tools he owns and the efforts of the other people he's hired, and in return receive a wage, which is really just a way to get the resources you need to survive.

The power imbalances are obvious when you enter into your employment contract. Though Mr. Bongiovi needs workers, he needs you as an individual employee less than you need grocery money. But that doesn't mean that the arrangement isn't mutually beneficial. Better to be exploited in a capitalist society than unemployed and destitute.[3]

You're allowed to do almost anything you want on nights and weekends. Sure, you can't break the law, but you're living in a democracy and can theoretically influence those laws. But when you're at the pasta sauce plant, you're subject to the dicta of your bosses. They're bound by state and federal labor regulations and even a union contract, but it still feels oppressive.

You endure, in part by telling yourself that reconciling yourself to authority is a necessary part of adulthood. But if you had a reasonable alternative to submitting to someone else's power, wouldn't you take it?

Your cousin Tito used to work at a Subway, but then he saved up and started a Hindu nationalist yoga magazine. Certainly, some people by virtue of chance or talent manage to go from workers to small business owners, who themselves employ labor. But that route can't be taken by everyone—there would be no one left to hire! Without such luck or a trust fund to fall back on, you're stuck subordinating yourself to capitalists who own private property and can make wealth out of your labor.

But that's not to say that money is literally made from your sweat. Profit isn't guaranteed—and entrepreneurial risk is one justification for capitalist profits. The pasta sauce you're bottling has to sell for more than the direct cost of producing it, plus any overhead. After all that, if Mr. Bongiovi wants to stay competitive, he has to invest in new technologies and fix wear and tear on existing machines.

Under feudalism, it's clear that a lord is exploiting a peasant—the peasant is doing all of the labor. Capitalism complicates matters: capitalists contribute to production as managers and conveners of labor, and their efforts are necessary to create new places of work. And, crucially, capitalists themselves are hostage to the market. Mr. Bongiovi is a nice man, and he wants to pay his workers double what they earn now, but he knows rivals will outcompete him if his labor costs are twice as high.

When he's running his business, all the complexity inherent in Mr. Bongiovi—his compassion, his love of bird watching, his good humor—is necessarily subordinated to the pursuit of profit. But he also gets rich in the process, so don't feel too sorry for him

We can do better than this capitalist reality you're stuck in.

IMAGINE YOU WERE born in Malmö, Sweden, instead of Edison, New Jersey. It is a slightly idealized version of Sweden, a mix of what social democracy actually accomplished in that country and what it could (or even should) have. The food is worse than in New Jersey—more preserved fish, less pizza. ABBA is no Bon Jovi. Your neighbor Frederick is naked a lot but otherwise seems okay.

When you were a baby, your parents were able to take paid time off work to take care of you. As a young person, you had access to a range of effective social services—free schools, great health care, affordable housing. After you finish university, you weigh your options. Should you do a PhD in art history (it's free), apply for a state stipend to begin writing the Great Swedish Novel, or just find a job that seems interesting and see what happens next?

You pick up the *Arbetet* newspaper and read the classifieds. Unemployment is low, and there are many well-paid jobs to pick from. One, in particular, catches your eye. It's an ad from a Swedish death metal band, which needs someone to keep its members fully stocked with spiked armor and goat heads for their next tour and to run its Twitter account.

You're really good at social media—like, really. So naturally you get the job—20 euro an hour, 35 hours a week, with six weeks of paid vacation. You start working, and you find that things are okay. Your bosses are too busy making music to supervise you too much, so you have a lot of autonomy. Online ticket sales grow 12 percent in your first year, and you receive a nice raise, but you're not really happy with the work. You quit.

In Sweden, unlike in New Jersey, more spheres of life are decommodified, meaning they're taken out of the market and enjoyed as social rights. Even though you are unemployed—indeed, you would not have quit your job otherwise—you can rely on benefits, engage in civic life, and take some time to consider what to do next.

You could survive beyond a subsistence level on Swedish welfare, but you need an income to prepare for the next stage in your life: having a family, buying your own apartment, and so on. With that in mind, you take a job working at Koenigsegg, a high-performance sports car manufacturer.

After a few wildly successful quarters, Koenigsegg decides to expand into the consumer automotive industry. It builds a new factory, purchasing top of the line equipment. The company hopes it can win an advantage over its two main rivals, Saab and Volvo, by maintaining a smaller workforce and capitalizing on existing brand recognition among car enthusiasts.

Not one for physical labor, you apply for an inventory management position. You don't earn much more than the assembly line workers, who are covered in the same industry-wide bargaining agreement. But you make 30 euro an hour, have plenty of vacation, and no longer need to listen to satanic mixtapes. It's a good deal.

Your first year, the firm isn't profitable, but it produces a well-regarded Volvo S60 competitor, and there's hope that the company's market share will grow. Your own morale wavers a bit. You don't like your managers and what you perceive as a lack of freedom in the workplace. You're paid well, and you have plenty of spare time, but spending sixteen hundred hours a year looking at spreadsheets isn't exactly fulfilling.

At first, personal triumphs outweigh your professional malaise. You meet someone you want to spend the rest of your life with, and even though having children isn't for you, you now have another reason to look forward to your frequent vacations.

Yet as you get settled at home, your work becomes more precarious. The company isn't doing well—it produces quality cars, but there isn't much consumer response. Management pours more money into marketing, but in doing so cuts into razor-thin profit margins. Kept alive by strong earnings from Koenigsegg's traditional sports cars, the company decides to keep working toward a breakthrough in its mass-market operation.

You're relieved, but the union contract that covers most of your workplace is about to expire. The agreement doesn't only apply to your factory, or even Koenigsegg as a whole, but to much of the Swedish automotive sector. Even though Koenigsegg is struggling, other manufacturers are doing well, buoyed by export sales and favorable market conditions.

The national trade union federation takes an aggressive stance, basing its demands on the wages of a more efficient car manufacturer, Volvo. Equal pay for equal work is the federation's principle. Saab and other, even more efficient companies than Volvo are easily able to pay the new wages and use the remaining profits to expand, but the increased labor costs spell disaster for Koenigsegg. You thought you were getting a raise; instead you can't sleep at night. Sometimes it's the thumping Eurodance coming from Frederick's parties keeping you awake, but more often it's your fears about your future.

Those fears are soon realized. Koenigsegg decides to halt production on its Volvo S60 competitor. The company survives, but it can't accommodate its entire existing staff. Your severance is generous, but it's only enough to keep you going for a year.

If you were a white-collar worker in America—much less a humble bottler of curry pasta sauce—you'd be in trouble. As a Swede, however, you land on your feet, owing to the generous welfare state. More important than the unemployment assistance, you and your other laid off coworkers are provided with state-funded retraining. The companies that survived the wage hike are investing in labor-saving technology, but they're also expanding, meaning there are new jobs to fill.

What now? Maybe you end up working at Volvo, in a more senior position even. It doesn't solve all of your problems; you're not content with your life in every way. But you're living in the most humane social system ever constructed. For a species that spent the better part of its existence hiding in trees from predators or huddled for warmth in caves, you could do worse than social-democratic, only partially fictional Sweden. But is there another alternative, one superior to our idealized social democracy?

IT'S HERE THAT you have to start using your imagination. Say you're once again a pasta-sauce bottling New Jerseyan, and that the state is the epicenter of a radical political upheaval. Your problems can't be solved through action at the Bongiovi plant alone, but there's hope for change through a broader movement.

That struggle goes national with its rhetoric of democracy and fairness. Soon, a new left-populist movement fronted by Bruce Springsteen wins the presidency and a majority in Congress (Bon Jovi sticks to music, because he has too much respect for his craft). With the help of a rank-and-file resurgence in the labor movement, the president and Congress usher in the kind of reforms your doppelgänger in Sweden already enjoys. Health and education become social rights; child care and housing are made affordable.

Social democracy is so good that even Fred doesn't mind working at a public hospital. But not everyone is pleased. A lot of people benefited from the old system—the corporate health care industry, for example, put up a mighty struggle when the US National Health Service was created, and is still trying to make a comeback by providing "personalized" outpatient services. And the economy is still driven by private enterprise. Capitalists resent the higher taxes they have to pay, don't want to comply with new environmental regulations, and hate dealing with more empowered and restive workplaces.

Especially during downturns in the business cycle, capitalists can make a credible argument to voters: the whole economy only works if we're making money, and we'll only take risks in bringing new products and services to market if there's a large enough reward to justify it. Plus, those bankers you keep handcuffing give us the financing we need to keep the whole machine humming.

Luckily, for most of the next decade, the new working-class political coalition—labor unions, feminist and anti-racist social movements, environmental activists—coheres a political program capable of beating back the capitalists. Still, there are divisions among Mr. Springsteen's supporters. Some, like The Boss himself, want to preserve gains already won by making tactical concessions to capitalists. With a baseline of profitability protected, he and like-minded politicians argue, a segment of the elite can be persuaded that they benefit more by sticking with American social democracy than closing up shop or moving abroad. Others are less compromising, but though they push the system to its limits, they don't believe it can be transcended. They settle for as much socialism as capitalism can take, supporting cooperatives and helping enlarge the public sector to mitigate the power of big corporations. Finally, there are radicals who want to break from capitalism entirely and create an even more democratic and egalitarian society.

These ideas and debates swirl around, while circumstances provide an opening for the radicals. Not only does a sizable minority of the nation make clear a desire for more left-wing reforms for ideological reasons (opposition to hierarchy and exploitation, even in a tempered state), but others come to support the socialists for practical reasons. You're among the latter, believing that to even preserve the gains already made, capital flight and the continued political resistance of outnumbered but still powerful elites need to be taken on directly.

The nation is convulsed by strike waves matched in their intensity by owner lockouts. Social movements make heard long-muted demands for justice and equality, and people entirely new to politics hit the streets. Workplaces are occupied, and bosses are even kidnapped by radicalized workers. Even Fred finds a socialist group willing to have him (the six-member International Workers' Committee for the Sixth International). Religious organizations and others concerned with the instability call for a return to law and order.

But in the end, a socialist coalition has a mandate to change society. It does not have a precise blueprint, and there will be need for improvisation and new thinking. But it does have the benefit of both the recent lessons of Springsteenist-left governance and those from the often tragic twentieth-century experience of socialism in power. History doesn't usually offer second chances, so what would we do with one?

FOR YEARS PRIOR to this moment, there have been arguments within the modern American socialist movement—of which you are now part—about what exactly we oppose in capitalism and what we can live with. Capitalism is a social system based on private ownership of the means of production and wage labor. It relies on multiple markets: markets for goods and services, the labor market, and the capital market.

The left wing of the Springsteenist movement opposes private ownership of production and wage labor because of the power it gives some people over others. Its members believe socially created wealth shouldn't be privately expropriated. Where the movement stands on markets is less clear.

Outside of theory, there's no such thing as a "free market"—capitalism requires both planning and a regulated market. But the question about what role each would play under socialism is an open one. You spend long nights eating Hawaiian pizza and discussing it with Fred. As a doctor who sees how well the government-run health care system works, and as an avid *SimCity 2000* fan, Fred proposes that markets can be done away with and replaced with central planning. In this system, regional or national planners decide what the economy should produce and then ask firms to turn out a certain amount of goods. They might have discretion in how they do so, but they have to hit their quotas.

You bring up the failure of that system in the Soviet Union. But Fred insists this will be different. Unlike in the old USSR, civil society would be free, and the plan could be formed democratically.

You're skeptical, as you know that in the past planned economies went hand in hand with authoritarianism and corruption. Beyond that, they had trouble with "informational" problems. Backward countries using command economies were able to rapidly industrialize. Yet problems grew over time, as more and more goods had to be produced, all of which required prices to be set by planners without the range of consumer feedback that markets provide.

These planned economies had "strong thumbs, no fingers": they were great at routinized tasks like carrying out vaccination campaigns, educating citizens, or mass-producing tanks, but couldn't adapt to local conditions or unexpected changes.[4]

Consider a commodity like an iPhone. It is composed of hundreds of parts, each requiring dozens of raw materials, all of them mined, produced, and transported by thousands of people. How would we coordinate all of them? Now multiply that dilemma to an almost infinite combination of consumer preferences, goods, and services.[5]

"Why wouldn't factory managers wastefully use raw materials, requesting more than they needed for production, out of uncertainty, like they did in the Eastern Bloc?"

"Look at Walmart and Amazon!" Fred counters.

"I thought you 'only shopped local,'" you reply.

But he has a point. If Walmart was a country, it'd have a larger GDP than the whole of East Germany in 1989, and much of its activity is consciously planned, without crippling inefficiencies.[6]

You remain skeptical, but reply that even if new technologies solved calculation problems and markets could be simulated and responded to by planners and producers, incentive problems would still exist. In a condition of relative scarcity, and with robots unable yet to do all the work for us, wouldn't we need inefficient firms to fail? Wouldn't we need to compel each other, in some way, to innovate and work productively? Markets already have answers to these questions.

Yes, a democratic planning board could, with oversight from civil society, close the worst firms and provide perks to the most efficient workers, but this process seems vulnerable to political lobbying or worse. As you see it, in Fred's idealized version of central planning, too much seems to be riding on the general population developing a socialist consciousness.

Still, among some socialists, more democratic, local, and nonmarket ways for people to communicate their consumer preferences are being discussed. Neighborhood councils could lay out their consumption needs and reconcile those demands with what democratic workplaces are willing and able to produce. But these councils run the risk of being tedious, the sort of things only people who like endless meetings would enjoy. That's not to mention the complexity of trying to negotiate among all parties in such a system.[7]

Your debate with Fred plays out across society. On ideological grounds, it's legislated that workers should control their firms and that they should no longer receive a wage (though there would still be minimum incomes based on job classification), becoming real stakeholders in their companies instead.[8]

Two key markets under capitalism are thereby done away with: the traditional labor market and capital markets. But markets for goods and services remain. Too many informational problems exist for them to be done away with. Companies will also still have to compete with each other—inefficient firms will collapse (though the fall for individual stakeholders in a firm would be cushioned by the welfare state, even more so than it was in our idealized Sweden).[9]

These measures provoke turmoil as capitalists muster desperate acts of resistance. But in the end banks are nationalized, and the state takes over all private firms. You see firsthand how things play out at the pasta sauce plant.

YOUR WORKPLACE HAS been more stable than most. Since you had a union, wages at the firm were already higher than industry average before Springsteenism, so Bongiovi had less trouble dealing with the new national living wage legislation. Only three days were lost to work stoppages in the past year, a miracle considering the turmoil elsewhere.

The cooperative sector was at first just a minor competitor to the private, capitalist one. Congressional legislation was passed to socialize shuttered businesses or those already occupied by workers. But the policy proved popular, and it was a way to erode the power of capitalists still trying to roll back reforms. It was expanded to firms employing more than fifty workers, Bongiovi's included. Along with other shareholders, he was expropriated with compensation on a prorated basis. Indeed, he received more than others by agreeing to cooperate with the transition.

It wasn't that Mr. Bongiovi was supportive of the process; he was simply resigned, worn down by years of inroads into his property rights. With his payout, he was able to retire comfortably and reconcile himself to the new order. Other capitalists were more resistant. They were free to organize in civil society, but moderate social democrats constituted a far more powerful opposition to the governing radicals. A tiny minority of elites, including an eccentric George W. Bush grandson, even sincerely adopted the socialist cause.

It's May 1, 2036, and things have been slowly shifting around you for years. But on this day, everything will decisively change. The final shares of Bongiovi Brand pass into state ownership. Don't worry, though: you're not trading a set of unelected private managers for distant government bureaucrats. Collectively you and your coworkers now control your company. You're more like citizens of a community than owners. You just have to pay a tax on its capital assets (the building and the land it's on, machinery, and so forth), in effect renting it from society as a whole. (To preserve the value of the capital stock in your care, a depreciation fund must be set up for repairs and improvements.)[10]

Your tax goes into a public fund, which invests in new endeavors. More about that later. But the tax you pay also solves the problem of different production processes having wildly different capital-labor ratios. If workers simply collectively owned their firms' capital, those in capital-intensive industries would earn far more profits than those in labor-intensive ones. Having different "rents" prevents that. You also have to pay a graduated income tax, as you did before, on the income you take home. This funds social services and other state expenditures.[11]

A meeting is convened at the start of the day, and everyone looks differently at the worn-down factory that you came to despise but that now belongs to you and your colleagues. The sense of pride quickly subsides as practical business begins.

Though new laws assert that everyone should participate in management on equal footing, this is implemented in various ways across companies. Because it is a larger enterprise, a representative system of governance is approved at Bongiovi. Workers from each department elect delegates to a proportionately elected workers' council. This council has oversight over the entire business and is tasked with appointing management, including a managing director.

You get yourself elected as a council member and, in choosing the new management, vote for a mix of experienced middle managers and others drawn from the shop floor. Most have already been trained, while the rest have demonstrated themselves to be quick studies. Those selected have a three-year term that can be extended, though they're required to spend at least two weeks a year on the shop floor.

Collectively, the workers' council also writes a new firm-operating agreement and suggests pay differentials, subject to approval from the general membership and to annual revision. In the new system, workers don't get a wage; instead they get a share of the profits. However it is decided that people should receive more compensation for roles that involve more stress, responsibility, or training. On the other side of the spectrum, jobs that are seen as undesirable are paid well enough to ensure they're adequately staffed. Here's a compensation table you help come up with:[12]

Title	Required Education	Skill/ Experience	Authority	Responsibility	Physical Effort	Mental Effort	Working Conditions	Total
Managing Director	100	170	150	200	10	100	10	740
Technical Director	130	140	140	160	10	90	10	680
Production Manager	90	130	100	100	10	90	30	550
Foreperson	80	100	50	50	10	40	40	360
Sales Agent	100	100	0	50	10	50	10	320
Bottlers	40	40	0	30	40	30	50	230
Custodians	20	10	0	10	50	10	100	200
Labelers	40	20	0	30	30	20	50	190

It looks a bit arbitrary, but the scale was set after extensive discussions and study. Along with the operating agreement, it is approved by

70 percent of the workers. Before Springsteenism, the average CEO-to-worker compensation in the nation was 354:1; after, it dropped to 89:1. At your workplace the most extreme differential is now 4:1. It's similar at others, as well.

Work gets better, but it doesn't feel as if something monumental has happened. You get paid more, you have a bit more say in what goes on at work, your job is secure, your managers are responsive, there's more office camaraderie, but still, at the end of the day, everyone just wants to leave.

That's not because things are bad at work, but because things are better where they are going—to homes no longer ripped apart by financial burdens, where household work is more equally shared (better-paid women have the power to negotiate a different compact with their spouses), and to communities where entertainment, sports, and leisure are accessible to all. It's a transformed world, where life isn't perfect, but where millions have more spare time and less stress.

This newfound freedom comes from expansive social services and public guarantees. Under capitalism, the heads of enterprises constantly fought back against social reforms. But now these policies are in sync with the values of wealth-generating, worker-controlled firms.

Of course, just as there are still plenty of social problems to confront, there are still issues at work. Receiving a share of profits rather than a fixed wage motivates most people at the firm, but a few of your colleagues struggle. Your bottling partner Kiran shows up late often and neglects important assignments.

You gently nudge him to pick it up, but the stakes don't seem very high. Kiran is a friendly person, and how much damage can one worker do? Yet management takes notice of his behavior. One day, Kiran is written up for safety violations, caused by his laxness. He resents being told how to do his job, one he's clearly tiring of.

"Capitalism is the exploitation of person by person; socialism is the exact opposite," he laments.

It's understandable that someone would be sick of work that, no matter the degree of worker control, is still work. But from the unit supervisor's perspective, she has the duty to make sure everyone is doing their share. And unlike management back when the plant was privately owned, if someone thinks a supervisor is acting improperly or wants things to be run differently, they have democratic recourses to do something about it.

In this case, Kiran is clearly at fault, and his behavior doesn't change. He's not dehumanized, but rather dealt with much as he would be in a highly unionized social democracy. Kiran is protected from discrimination and wrongful termination by robust state legislation. He goes through a progressive disciplinary process—first comes a warning, with concrete suggestions for improvement, then a suspension with pay, then finally, dismissal with three months of severance.

It's when Kiran leaves Bongiovi that the difference between New Jersey 2019 and New Jersey 2036 is most obvious. In the past, Kiran would've been desperate without work, his entire existence dependent on convincing an employer to give him another chance. Now, he can get by on the state's basic income grant and supplement it by taking a guaranteed public sector job, doing socially necessary work. He has access to all the core necessities of life, and when he decides to become a barber, it's his choice.

A real choice, not a "work or starve" choice. People don't merely have a voice in their workplace; they have the freedom to leave. Why don't more people decide to opt out of the labor market? The chance to make more money, which could allow them easier access to consumer goods or exotic travel, plays a role. But others truly take pride in their jobs and enjoy collaborating at work.

Meanwhile, back at Bongiovi, you see that plant democracy is more than symbolic. Back in 2019, labor-saving technology had everyone working faster. Now, when new technology is brought in, your coworkers have a different calculus. If they can produce 20 percent more per employee, why not decrease the workweek to twenty-eight hours? (For all sectors, legislation dictates the required workweek cannot exceed thirty-five hours.)[13]

There is still market competition, and firms still fail, but the grow-or-die imperative doesn't apply when your enterprise's goal is no longer to maximize total profits but rather to maximize profit-per-worker. And instead of a race to the bottom, there's pressure to make sure janitorial and other "dirty jobs" are well compensated. In time, many of these tasks will be automated. People used to fear that machines would bring about mass unemployment, but now you and most others look forward to the social impact of technological innovations.[14]

At this point, you've been bottling sauce for twenty years; you've seen the firm adapt to new consumer preferences and maintain a steady market share for much of that time. Though the future looks bright, you decide to do something else with your life. Through work rotations and meetings, you have a sense of Bongiovi's entire operation and can probably run for a management role. But the whole industry kind of bores you. You didn't get into the curry pasta sauce hustle because you loved the game. Back in 2018, you just needed some money.

Now, with half your life still ahead of you, you have options. One day, while hanging out with the now retired and increasingly tolerable Fred, you come up with a design for medical utility suspenders. How would you go about securing capital for a new venture under socialism?

Unlike in capitalism, start-ups aren't fueled by private investment, but rather the capital goods tax mentioned earlier. The funds are invested into the economy in a variety of ways. National planning projects—like renovating the energy grid or high-speed rail networks—are the first priority. What's left is given to regions on a per capita basis. Under capitalism, people were forced to abandon cities to chase jobs in expanding markets. Now people still move around, but they won't be compelled to do so by capital flight.[15]

The funds are channeled by regional investment banks (public, of course) that engage in more local planning and then apportion the rest to new or existing firms. Applicants are judged on the basis of profitability, job creation, and other criteria including environmental impact. If there aren't enough profitable enterprises starting up or expanding, some of the money can always be directly transferred back to taxpayers to stimulate demand.[16]

All of these outcomes entail trade-offs, and these trade-offs are political decisions. Citizens in one area might pursue a different policy balance than those in another, and adjustments would be made constantly, with successful experiments emulated.

The partners you bring into your firm will be just that—they'll be shareholders, not your employees. But since you're starting the firm, you have some discretion in setting the initial operating agreement. In order to attract workers, you need to keep income differentials relatively flat. But in the end it's worth it to you—you and Fred are rewarded for your new invention with a small amount of state prize money, and you do end up earning more as an elected manager at your new job than your old one. But what's more significant is the fact that your suspenders catch on and become a fashion statement outside of the medical profession. You've finally left your mark on the world.

The decades pass on, and you eventually retire, cared for by the society that you contributed so much to, while enjoying the love of friends and family. Looking out at the broader world, you see that things are as dynamic as they were in 2036. With more decisions in the hands of ordinary people, civil life is full of political debate and new ideas. Even distributional questions are still not settled: a center-right party advocates for more market incentives and a reduction in the basic income; a center-left party questions traditional metrics of growth, proposing a happiness index instead; an internationalist left calls for more vigorous support for the workers' movement abroad and more extensive democratic planning at home. And yes, there is a Right calling for the restoration of capitalism, but its support diminishes over time, much like monarchism slowly lost supporters in the nineteenth and twentieth centuries.

It's a starting point, then, for a better society, not necessarily a happy ending. You'll live long enough to see whether or not, as abundance and automation spread, there will be less need for material incentives. You'll see whether markets can be eroded further, and you'll ask, as many others will, if that would be desirable.

There's a greater sphere for participation, as democracy has been radically extended to the social and economic realms. That carries with it some risks. Struggles against racial disparities and further battles against the sexual division of labor will be needed. Informed citizens will have to watch out for new forms of exploitation and oppression and small inequities spiraling into bigger ones. But these are the perils of democracy, and a small price to pay for living in the world's first truly democratic society.

THOUGH HARDLY APPROACHING "rich Instagram kids on a yacht" levels of privilege, in all these examples you're doing okay to begin with. Even under capitalism you enjoyed a solid education and found employment. You even had leisure time. Millions today living in the richest societies in history, however, can claim no such luck.

For these people—much less billions in the Global South—the struggle for reform is urgent. Capitalist growth has produced wonders, and, especially when harnessed by strong states, it continues to. But it also has proved itself to be no natural friend of democracy, civic freedom, the environment, or the lives of those it doesn't have a profitable way to exploit.

At its core, to be a socialist is to assert the moral worth of every person, no matter who they are, where they're from, or what they did.[17] With any luck, future generations will look back at the time when life outcomes were accidents of birth with shock and disgust, the same way we look back on more extreme forms of exploitation and oppression—slavery, feudalism, and so on—that have already been done away with. If all human beings have the same inherent worth, then they must be free to fulfill their potential, to flourish in all their individuality.

In order to realize this kind of expansive freedom, we need to guarantee at least the basics of a good life to all. And given the opportunity to thrive, people can contribute to society and create the conditions in which others can do the same. Freedom for working people today, however, means limiting the freedom of those who benefit from the inequities inherent in class society. Socialism is not so much about trading in freedom for equality but rather posing the question, "Freedom for whom?"

Now imagine what a change it would be for a young black American to grow up in a society where they didn't have to settle for the worst schools, the worst health care, the worst jobs, or possibly be subjected to the worst carceral system on Earth. Imagine what it would mean for women if they were more easily able to leave abusive relationships or escape workplace harassment with the help of strong welfare guarantees. Imagine our future Einsteins and Leonardo da Vincis liberated from grinding poverty and misery and able to contribute to human greatness. Or forget Einstein and Leonardo—better yet, imagine ordinary people, with ordinary abilities, having time after their twenty-eight-hour workweek to explore whatever interests or hobbies strike their fancy (or simply enjoy their right to be bored). The deluge of bad poetry, strange philosophical blog posts, and terrible abstract art will be a sure sign of progress.

But if we're already in our idealized version of Malmö, Sweden (one that might have been close to reality back in 1976), why would we want to go further? A good social democracy checks a lot of the boxes mentioned above, and presumably where it falls short it could be improved without completely doing away with private ownership.[18]

There is an ideological motivation for a more radical socialism, the moral idea that the exploitation of people by other people is a problem in desperate need of a solution. Capitalism both creates the preconditions for radical human flourishing and prevents its ultimate fulfillment. For socialists, to the extent that some hierarchies linger, they have to be constantly justified and held in check. Think about the authority a parent wields over a child. By most people's lights (including most socialists'), this authority is reasonable, but it is also regulated by law. You can't beat your child, and you can't keep them out of school or prevent them from leaving home when they become adults.[19]

Today almost everyone would agree that extreme forms of exploitation, like slavery, should be prohibited. The socialist argues that wage labor is in fact an unacceptable form of exploitation, too, and that we have alternatives that will empower people to control their destinies inside and outside the workplace. But even I have a hard time imagining that the abstractions of ideology will be enough to encourage a risky leap from a humane social-democratic world into an unknown socialist one. If it happens, we will probably only be driven down the path to socialism by practical necessity, by the day-to-day struggles to preserve and expand reforms.

Indeed, as we'll see in the historical tour of socialism that makes up the first part of this book, social democracy bolstered the power of labor to degrees few thought possible, but still left capital structurally dominant. With the power to withhold investment, with the economy still reliant on their profits, capitalists were able to hold democratic governments hostage and roll back reforms. Their economic power translated into enduring power over the political process.

Social democracy is a step in the right direction, then, but ultimately not enough, owing to its vulnerability. Of course, we should be so lucky to find ourselves living under social democracy today. Neoliberalism is the watchword of our age. Most people are saddled with debt, have few job protections, can't comfortably afford health care and housing, and don't believe that their children will fare any better than they do. In this new gilded age, they're unwilling philanthropists, subsidizing the lavish lifestyles of the rich.

Socialism can do better—but I don't claim that it can fix everything. Even under socialism life would still be filled with plenty of lows. It will still sometimes feel overwhelming, you'll probably get your heart broken, and people will still die tragically from accidents and suffer bad luck. But even if we can't solve the human condition, we can turn a world filled with excruciating misery into one where ordinary unhappiness reigns. Maybe we could even make some progress on that front. As Marx put it, with our animal problems solved, we can begin to solve our human ones.[20]

BOOKS LIKE THIS often start by telling you, the reader, what's wrong with the world today. For much of capitalism's history, radicals have been sustained less by a clear vision of socialism than by visceral opposition to the horrors around them. Instead of making the case for socialism, we made the case against capitalism. I have tried to do something different by presenting what a different social system could look like and how we can get there.

Naturally, it's easy to compare an existing, complicated society with one that only lives in our imagination. In Marx's day, utopian socialists did little but write "recipes for the cookshops of the future." But today, it's a crucial task to win people over to the idea that things can be different, even if we can't precisely say what future generations will decide to construct.[21]

The first part of this book charts the history of socialism from Marx to the present day. Every would-be socialist, and anyone interested in socialist ideas (even if only to know how the other side thinks), needs to engage with the many threads of this story. Often maligned as utopians with eyes only on the future, socialists in fact have from the beginning been students of history. Today's socialists must follow in the same tradition.

In a matter of decades, socialists went from fringe believers to masters of much of the world. I tell that story, from the emergence of capitalism and the creation of a working class, to the maturation and then implosion of working-class politics in the parties of the Second International. Then there's the rise of the Bolsheviks in Russia. The authoritarian collectivism their experiment produced not only claimed millions of lives but came to be associated with any challenge to capitalism. I do not shy away from considering what went wrong in the Soviet experience, which jettisoned the democracy and civil liberties at the core of the socialist dream.

Elsewhere, socialists did eventually win power in capitalist democracies, constructing societies that allowed millions to live decent, fulfilling lives. Despite not being able to bring about a successor system, their reforms had radical implications. We'll see why social democracy failed but also how it opened up new avenues to a socialism beyond capitalism. We'll consider checkered attempts by those in the Third World, namely Chinese revolutionaries, to use socialism as an ideology of national development. Finally, we arrive at socialist politics in the United States, which have appeared episodically and supported important reforms but have not taken root as they have elsewhere.

The twentieth century, for both good and ill, left socialists with plenty of lessons. The history that follows is not comprehensive but selective, aiming to draw out those lessons, from both the revolutionary and the reformist wings of socialism, for the present day. We can learn from this history that the road to a socialism beyond capitalism goes through the struggle for reforms and social democracy, that it is not a different path altogether. We can also learn that we can't rely on the professed good intentions of socialist leaders: the way to prevent abuses of power is to have a free civil society and robust democratic institutions. This is the only "socialism" worthy of the name.

Today there is much talk of "democratic socialism," and indeed I see that term as synonymous with "socialism." What separates social democracy from democratic socialism isn't just whether one believes there's a place for capitalist private property in a just society, but how one goes about fighting for reforms. The best social democrats today might want to fight for macroeconomic policies from above to help workers. But while not rejecting all forms of technocratic expertise, the democratic socialist knows that it will take mass struggle from below and messy disruptions to bring about a more durable and radical sort of change.

In the second part of this book, I discuss the world today and why there are new opportunities for this better sort of socialism to take root. As we'll see, Britain's Jeremy Corbyn and the United States' Bernie Sanders have pursued a "class struggle" social democracy, unleashing popular energy that has revitalized the Left as a whole. I offer a tentative strategy for taking advantage of this unexpected second chance and explain why the working class can still be an agent of social transformation.

Even in the bleakest chapters in this book, an urgent commitment should be clear: if there is a future for humanity—free of exploitation, climate holocaust, demagoguery, and the war of all against all—then we must place our faith in the ability of people to save themselves and each other.

PART I

TWO

GRAVEDIGGERS

Cⁿ APITALISM SEEMS LIKE our destiny. Ever since we started beating animals to death with stones, we've been trading their furs. Adam Smith wrote about humanity's "propensity to truck, barter, and exchange one thing for another." We've been doing that in markets for millennia.

Have the seeds of capitalism always existed, not just in our societies but in our souls? A close look at the system's rise reveals something else. Namely, that it was an accident.

In most accounts, capitalism appeared sometime between the fourteenth and sixteenth centuries, as our tendency to seek market opportunities finally saw people begin to break free of the shackles of feudalism, and as Florence, Venice, and other disruptive city-states traded and innovated Europe out of the muck of the Middle Ages. But this story isn't right. Capitalism didn't come about because markets grew to a certain point. Instead, what we understand as capitalism resulted from a societal shift, as we went from using markets from time to time to producing for the market as our all-consuming task.[1]

And capitalism didn't start in the grand cities of the Italian Renaissance, but in some soggy fields on a backward island. England, by virtue of a few distinctive facts about its agriculture, became the world's greatest power and later the first home of the industrial proletariat whom Marx and generations of socialists placed their faith in.[2]

Before capitalism, feudalism was the dominant system across much of the world. Under it, people were divided between the majority who worked the land to survive and the small minority who appropriated the majority's labor through political coercion. Peasants had access to their own land, thus access to the means of their survival. However, lords used laws and force of arms to extract a portion of their yield. With these proceeds they purchased luxuries the producers couldn't afford and expanded their military power. This helped them not only cement their standing in relation to other lords and their realm's monarch but also fend off peasant revolt. The system didn't encourage growth or innovation—peasants knew that if they produced more for exchange, much of it would go to their lords. They also mostly grew a variety of subsistence crops, rather than specializing in a cash crop.[3]

Feudalism faced periodic demographic crises, none more significant than the Black Death, which ravaged Eurasia in the 1300s. As much as 20 percent of the world's population perished, and close to half of all people in Europe. As soon as it recovered, the continent plunged into warfare and revolt.[4]

The ruling class reasserted its control in Eastern Europe, where peasants had their autonomy stripped through an even more extreme system of feudalism, called serfdom, which by the mid-1600s bound them to estates and criminalized flight. In France, by contrast, the peasants managed to secure de facto ownership of their land and gave less of their yields to lords. The French lords themselves increasingly became functionaries of a centralized, absolutist state.

A middle ground prevailed in England. Peasants stopped their ruling class from extracting a greater surplus from them through brute force, but they failed to win legal land rights. English lords, searching for new ways to produce surpluses beyond exploiting the depleted peasantry, laid the groundwork for a shift from peasant-proprietor production to a tenant system. Tenants received one- or two-year leases and had incentives to be ever more productive, since they kept all the surplus after their rent was paid. Landlords had every reason to support these developments, which allowed them to create a market for land leases (the more productive the farmers, the higher the leases could go). Tenant farmers were compelled by the market to maximize production in a way peasants weren't. These farmers, in turn, began hiring landless peasants and others as wage laborers.

It may sound like a small shift, but in fact it was an epochal transformation. More and more land in England came under this system. The process created a highly productive agriculture sector able to sustain a large population not engaged in farming. It also meant that there was a majority without property that could be essentially forced into wage labor and become a market for cheap consumer goods.[5]

For the first time in history, a society became subordinated to markets and elites ruled by, as Karl Marx put it, "the dull compulsion of economic relations" rather than political coercion. There had been markets before, indeed going back thousands of years, but early modern England was the world's first market society. The old customs and obligations that held people together cracked, as did the stability that hereditary access to land and communal rights offered. Most people resisted their conversion to wage laborers, preferring even vagrancy to the odd new way of life. The state tried to cut off other avenues of survival by banning poaching, hunting, fishing, and foraging from formerly common lands. The 1744 Vagrancy Act offered stern punishment for those "who refused to work for the usual and common wages." A series of Enclosure Acts privatized communal property, further eroding the possibility of living off the land.[6]

Spurred by the accident of capitalism, the English population increased sevenfold between 1520 and 1850, and the proletariat's number multiplied by twenty-three. The losers in this process would in time be transformed into an industrial working class with incredible latent power.[7]

OTHER COUNTRIES SOON began to emulate England's astonishing productivity increases. But it still had tremendous advantages over its competitors.

Even before the Industrial Revolution, England was home to major technological advances. Newcomen's steam engine revolutionized mining, and in 1721 Lombe's silk mill—Britain's first factory—foreshadowed the radical shifts to come. The 1780s witnessed the start of what became known as the Industrial Revolution. New manufacturing methods emerged. Starting with mechanized spinning, the textile industry was one of the first to be transformed, processing raw cotton harvested by the Americas' slaves. Eventually, hand production in other sectors gave way to machines.[8]

That Britain was at the helm of industrialization was never in doubt— in 1800 it produced ten million tons of coal, while its nearest rival, France, produced only one million. Even before the Industrial Revolution, more than half of Britain's population was engaged in labor other than agriculture, but it took several more decades for the landscape to be truly transformed by railroads, steamships, and heavy industry. Capitalists used the new technologies to create great factories that required a disciplined, centralized workforce.[9]

But the would-be urban proletariat had to be lured to cities first. Fortunately for the capitalists, the agricultural revolution and consequent population boom left many in poverty. Fleeing the countryside for the city was one way out. Wage labor was just as unappealing for them as it was for the old peasantry, but the impoverished had little chance of survival otherwise. They were joined in the new factories by Irish immigrants fleeing the devastating Great Famine.

Once in cities workers had to be radically retrained. The capitalist clock was nothing like the seasonal labor many were used to in the countryside or the less methodical pace in artisanal workshops. Harsh discipline and low wages remolded humans—many of them women and children— into creatures who did little but labor. When not chained to machines for twelve-hour shifts, they lived amid smog and dust in cramped, disease-filled quarters.[10]

Visiting mid-nineteenth-century Manchester, a center of English industry, the French sociologist Alexis de Tocqueville remarked, "Here humanity attains its most complete development and its most brutish, here civilization works its miracles and civilized man is turned almost into a savage." Around the same time, Friedrich Engels described an English capitalist (decent and respectful, a good husband with private virtues) who listened politely to complaints about workers' conditions before replying, "And yet there is a great deal of money made here."[11]

Engels was a figure every bit as remarkable as his famous collaborator, Karl Marx. He was born in 1820 to a wealthy merchant family and at seventeen was sent to Bremen—one of Germany's largest commercial cities—to work as a business clerk. Engels rebelled against his father, a "fanatical and despotic" textile manufacturer, and sought to free himself through radical philosophy. When he later served in the Artillery Guards of Berlin, Engels proved to be a terrible soldier but a sharp and energetic mind. In the city's beer halls, he associated with a rambunctious group of Young Hegelians and was drawn to a kind of democratic republicanism, Jacobin (which is to say, radical) in its spirit.[12]

His father endeavored to cure him of his political sentiments by condemning Friedrich to middle management at a textile mill he owned in Manchester. The city had recently risen to prominence as a hub of the Industrial Revolution. Without schooling or access to basic sanitation, the workers attracted to Manchester feared losing their jobs, knowing that utter destitution was never far away. Little of the great wealth they helped create went to them. For his part, Engels saw them as destined for something greater than poverty.[13]

From 1842 to 1844, he investigated firsthand the nature of capitalist production by day and at night explored the city's underbelly. He "forsook the company and the dinner-parties, the port-wine and champagne of the middle-classes" and made genuine connections with workers by discussing their grievances and acting in solidarity with their struggles.[14]

Engels lived a double life in the sense that he had fine lodgings in a nice part of town but spent most of his time in rented rooms in working-class districts. His allegiances, however, were never in doubt. In Manchester, Engels met and fell in love with an Irish woman, Mary Burns, who had been doing factory work since she was a small child. Mary and other friends were his guides to the city's south side, where tens of thousands of Irish workers lived, and to other neighborhoods few other bourgeois people even set foot in.

At just twenty-four, Engels wrote *The Condition of the Working Class in England*. The bland title did not convey that it was a work of both insight and anger: Even more than Charles Dickens, Benjamin Disraeli, and other social critics of the time, Engels captured the life of the industrial proletariat. He described a London slum's living quarters, where "filth and tottering ruin surpass all description" and "no doors are needed, there being nothing to steal." He wrote of garbage and ash, foul liquids oozing on the street, and residents "losing daily more and more of their power to resist the demoralizing influence of want, filth, and evil surroundings." A clearly outraged Engels reminded readers that all this was taking place in "the richest city of God's earth." The same barbarity was evident in Liverpool, where forty-five thousand people lived packed into fewer than eight thousand badly ventilated cellars, and in the overwhelmingly working-class Glasgow. But the most vivid passages in the book concerned the horrors of Manchester, whose three hundred fifty thousand working people were "robbed of all humanity, degraded, reduced morally and physically to bestiality." Inside the factory that made his family rich labored "women made unfit for childbearing, children deformed, men enfeebled, limbs crushed, whole generations wrecked, afflicted with disease and infirmity."[15]

And yet Engels thought the stunted, oppressed class he came to know could have great political power. Not all workers were passive in the face of poverty and abuse. "Luddites," the machine-breakers maligned in the popular imagination, fought against the acceleration of work, in the recognition that technological advance didn't mean progress for them. In 1830, agricultural workers in Kent destroyed grain threshers and sent letters to local elites demanding wage increases under the ominous pseudonym "Captain Swing." Less provocative but even more threatening to capitalists were early efforts at trade unionism and Chartism, a movement that arose in 1838 and sparked struggle for universal suffrage. Unrest simmered across much of Britain and was brutally put down by state authorities.

In January 1851, the *Economist*, a magazine founded to promote free trade, rhapsodized that it was "a happiness and a privilege to have had our lot cast in the first fifty years of this century," a period that had "witnessed a leap forward in all the elements of material well-being such as neither scientific vision nor poetic fancy ever pictured." The periodical's assessment of the Industrial Revolution was partially true. But capitalism, that accident of history, had conjured a dangerous combination: immense, lucrative industries and a deprived and discontented class of people locked within them. This was the reality in which Marxist theory was first constructed.[16]

JORDAN AND PIPPEN, Sonny and Cher, Marx and Engels. One of history's great partnerships was forged with a week of drinking and conversation in Paris. Like Engels, as a teenager Karl Marx wanted nothing more than to escape the boredom and conservatism of the Rhineland. He did have the advantage of a liberal father, who only offered mild rebukes of his brilliant son's dueling and boozing. Though respected by his peers, Marx kept radical company at university, attracting the attention of Prussian authorities and sinking his chances at an academic career. He turned elsewhere, marrying the rebellious aristocrat Jenny von Westphalen and traveling to Paris to pursue a career in journalism.

Marx was fortunate enough to meet Engels in the French capital. Through his new friend he learned about the realities of industrial capitalism and shifted his attention away from philosophy and toward political economy. Even more important, Engels was willing to be his benefactor as he pursued writing and politics. Kicked out of Paris for their writings, they lived in Brussels between 1845 and 1848, where they joined the Communist League and organized German-speaking workers. They also continued quarreling with more prominent radicals, including Karl Grün, Pierre-Joseph Proudhon, Wilhelm Weitling, and the followers of Louis Auguste Blanqui. Marx and Engels consistently advocated for a democratic politics, driven by the mass of workers themselves, to the point that the day's insurrectionists could call them moderates. Their talents, however, still commanded respect, and the pair was commissioned by the Communist League to write *The Communist Manifesto*, which was published on the eve of the 1848 Revolutions.

The final draft drew on the ideas of both men, but it was composed entirely by Marx. The bourgeoisie, the *Manifesto* argued, "has been the first to show what man's activity can bring about. It has accomplished wonders far surpassing Egyptian pyramids, Roman aqueducts, and Gothic cathedrals; it has conducted expeditions that put in the shade all former Exoduses of nations and crusades." Driven to expand and find new markets, the capitalists described by Marx are revolutionaries, dissolving "all fixed, fast-frozen relations, with their train of ancient and venerable prejudices and opinions." (It's a better description, perhaps, of what capitalism has accomplished by 2018 than of its record in 1848.)

For all their wonder at these new developments, Marx and Engels claimed that the system's contradictions were only mounting as it matured. Along with modern industry, the bourgeoisie produced "its own grave diggers"—the proletariat. These workers had a reason to overthrow capitalism and replace it with a production system governed in their interests.

Though it has been debated and scrutinized like no other work since the Bible, *The Communist Manifesto* was a short document written on the eve of an international revolution to popularize a political program. Its most important legacy was in laying out definitions of capitalism and communism ("an association in which the free development of each is the condition for the free development of all") and describing the working-class agent at the heart of future transformations. Prior socialisms had embraced the underclass, sought the philanthropy of elites, crafted utopian schemes, or gazed backward to the agrarian past. Marx and Engels instead proposed galloping forward alongside modernity.

Marx and Engels hoped that the Revolutions of 1848 would be "the immediate prelude to the proletarian revolution." Unrest had started in France but quickly spread to Germany, then Italy, Hungary, and a half dozen other European countries. The contagion even reached Colombia and Brazil. But the "specter of communism" wasn't haunting the capitalist world—radical republicanism was. Workers, artisans, and even some peasants demanded reforms such as minimum wages, suffrage, and state-provided education. Even when their demands were focused around challenging the aristocracy, they nevertheless found few allies in the bourgeoisie. If anything, Marx's mistake was in overestimating the political interest of capitalists to sweep away the old vestiges of feudalism. In the aftermath of 1848, he advocated that workers fight for their rights in new organizations, sometimes allied with, but fundamentally independent of, the erstwhile "liberal" bourgeoisie.

Some governments were toppled, but many of the regimes survived or reemerged. While other socialists responded to the defeats of 1848 by receding into conspiratorial radicalism, in the years that followed Marx wedded himself sincerely to workers' causes. He engaged with the Chartists and later helped found the International Workingmen's Association (IWA). When trade unionism spread in the 1850s and '60s, Marx saw potential in the movement. The Russian anarchist Mikhail Bakunin and others rejected the often politically conservative unions, but Marx interpreted them as a sign of an increasingly self-organized and class-conscious movement—prerequisites for the struggles that could lift workers out of misery.

AT THE SAME time, Marx, Jenny, and their growing family were miserable themselves, an "infernal mess" of poverty and woe. He was living in London on whatever Engels sent him and the pittance he earned from his journalism for the *New York Daily Tribune*. Marx was hounded by bill collectors and suffering from ill health when he began writing his masterwork, *Capital*, in 1852.[17]

By then his thinking had matured. He was a historical material-ist, which meant that he thought various forms of society reflect differ-ent material possibilities and constraints. Modes of production moved in stages, and each stage yielded a certain set of social relations. As Marx wrote in *The Poverty of Philosophy*, "the hand-mill gives you society with the feudal lord, the steam mill society with the industrial capitalist." Like previous modes of production, capitalism would eventually become a fetter on development and would have to be replaced by another. This wasn't necessarily a determinist argument. Marx believed that "men make their own history, but they do not make it as they please; they do not make it under self-selected circumstances, but under circumstances existing al-ready, given and transmitted from the past." Agency, through class strug-gle, was the motor of history, though it was molded by context. In "Theses on Feuerbach," Marx criticized the "vulgar materialism" of the Young Hegelians, who downplayed the role of political actors in changing so-ciety, and described history as an interplay of circumstance and human activity.[18]

Even without the insights of historical materialism, anyone living amid the Industrial Revolution knew that their era was profoundly unlike previ-ous ones. In *Capital*, Marx explained more convincingly than anyone else how it came about, as well as its defining features. The effort took him fif-teen years. All the while, he recalled "The Unknown Masterpiece," his favorite Honoré de Balzac short story. In it a painter, Frenhofer, spends a decade perfecting a portrait meant to be "the most complete representative of reality." When he discovers that all he has produced is a woman's foot and a confused swirl of colors, he destroys his painting and dies.[19]

When it was finally released in 1867, the first volume of *Capital* won no great fanfare. Like Frenhofer, Marx must have despaired, thinking him-self a failure. But as the late scholar Marshall Berman pointed out, and

Balzac had no way of knowing, the painter's "great work is in fact a perfect description of a twentieth-century abstract painting." *Capital* received its widest acclaim after Marx's death, and it certainly reads like a modernist work, in that it's made up of layers upon layers of satire, metaphor, and allusion. If you search through its web of footnotes, you'll find denunciations of "dwarf" economists and references to Don Quixote and Sophocles.

All of this might have made the volume more confusing than it needed to be, but the core of *Capital* is a clear demystification of capitalism. Marx showed how natural resources, capital, and human labor had been harnessed through organization to create great wealth.

Under earlier modes of production, people bartered by exchanging commodity (C) for commodity (C). Later, money (M) helped us mediate those transactions: we sold commodities in return for money that we used to purchase another good (C-M-C). Capitalists, however, relate to exchange differently. They used money from commodity sales to invest in production in order to make more goods that they were then compelled by competition to sell at a profit (M-C-M'). Much of the resulting yield was thrown back into making more commodities in the "restless never-ending process of profit making." If capitalists ever slowed down or showed any mercy, they would get swallowed up by their rivals.[20]

But Marx, of course, didn't just see markets and commodities when examining capitalism. He saw the labor of millions ensnared by it. In all but the most primitive societies, labor beyond a subsistence level created a surplus, and any surplus was appropriated, consumed, or otherwise directed by elites. Under feudalism, exploitation was obvious. If peasants had to give 40 percent of their yield to their lord, they knew that out of the fifty days they labored in the fields, they were only reaping the rewards of thirty. Marx pointed out that similar dynamics existed under capitalism. Workers couldn't just be employed for the "necessary working time" required to ensure their existence. Capitalists kept their firms profitable by extracting "surplus value" through extending the working day or increasing the pace and efficiency of production.[21]

It's easy to understand this concept on production lines. If you're bottling a hundred curry pasta sauce jars an hour, sixty of those might be necessary to pay your wages and other overheads, but every jar after that is surplus. Some goes directly into a capitalist's pockets, but much of it is reinvested into production to keep firms competitive. Socialists call this phenomenon "exploitation."

Marx believed there were ways to diminish exploitation short of ending capitalism completely. He was a vigorous advocate of the United Kingdom's Factory Act of 1847, because it restricted the working hours of women and young people in mills to ten hours a day. It was a politically imposed limit on the extent of capitalist exploitation and thus a "triumph of the political economy of the working class."[22]

Capital was presenting a theory, and like all theory its goal was to simplify an almost infinitely complex reality to arrive at certain truths. It was a critique of the ascendant political economy of the time, not a completely fleshed out, alternative body of political economy, and it was concerned with the broad contours of capitalism, not its fine-grained details. Still, *Capital* remains a profound accomplishment. Marx wrote of a system prone to crises, always close to spiraling out of control, but still incredibly dynamic. He brings to light conflict and the subordination of person to person, but also the subordination of all people to the market. We can recognize the same forces acting on us today whenever we stress over bills, worry about our relationship to our bosses, or wonder why so many of them seem to be sociopaths. The market demands it. Marx's hope, however, was that a system with people at the core could be consciously changed.

WHAT A SUCCESSOR system might look like, Marx only vaguely indicated. He didn't want to fall into the same trap of the utopian socialists, such as France's Saint-Simon and Britain's Robert Owen. They spent their energy writing detailed blueprints for the future but had no strategy to realize them besides the goodwill of elites. What's more, they suffered from a profoundly antidemocratic sensibility. Marx believed that socialism came from the struggles of workers, not the plans of a few intellectuals.

In *The German Ideology*, Marx did describe an "end of history": communism. He wrote of a world without states and with class divisions overcome, in which "society regulates the general production and thus makes it possible for me to do one thing today and another tomorrow, to hunt in the morning, fish in the afternoon, rear cattle in the evening, criticise after dinner, just as I have a mind, without ever becoming hunter, fisherman, herdsman or critic." This passage is often ridiculed for its utopianism, but it's a provocation to imagine a future where abundance reigned and people were freed from social constraints.[23]

Marx recognized the need for a transition period—socialism, or what he called the "dictatorship of the proletariat." This would come about after the ruling class was dispossessed but also with the world "in every respect still stamped with the birthmarks of the old society from whose womb it emerges." As opposed to postpolitical communism, socialism essentially meant radical democracy. The use of the word "dictatorship," which has left the phrase open to critique, meant something specific in Marx's usage. The meaningful distinction, to Marx, was between personal dictatorships and social dictatorships, in which an entire class had a say in governance. Broadly, the task of a dictatorship of the proletariat would be to introduce new economic and social measures and slowly lay the groundwork for the communist future.[24]

Though Marx introduced the concept in his writings on the 1848 Revolution, most of his ideas about working-class rule appear in his discussions of the Paris Commune. The Commune was a radical government that briefly flowered in 1871 after the collapse of Napoleon III's regime. "The Commune," as Marx wrote, "was formed of the municipal councilors, chosen by universal suffrage in the various wards of the town, responsible and revocable at short terms." It was "a working, not a parliamentary body, executive and legislative at the same time." It was not, in other words, an authoritarian dictatorship; Marx described an egalitarian, participatory

democracy. When the Paris Commune was brutally crushed by the Ver-
sailles government, Marx eulogized it, writing that it would be "forever
celebrated as the glorious harbinger of a new society." He lamented that
the Communards hadn't gone far enough in destroying the capitalist government or taking control of more levers of economic power.[25]

In *The Communist Manifesto* and elsewhere, Marx presented an immediate set of demands for the socialist movement. If successful, they would
have resulted in a society where a radically transformed, democratic state
held formerly private property and used it rationally under the direction
and to the benefit of the people. How this would work in practice was beyond the scope of Marx's ambition, and anyway, the question never came
close to relevancy in his lifetime.

Marx could not have been expected to see perfectly into the future. But
he proved remarkably farsighted. Adam Smith wrote *The Wealth of Nations*
in 1776 and died in 1790. He only saw the very beginning of capitalism. It
was Marx who gazed at the great factory cities, steamboats, and railroads,
and guessed that more marvels were to come. It was also Marx who never
lost sight of the human cost of progress. His moral outrage made him a
socialist, but he spent far more of his life examining capitalism than envi-
sioning an alternative to it.

HUMANITY MIGHT HAVE always been trucking, bartering, and exchanging,
but we've also been dreaming of cooperation and equality at the same time.
In Buddha's rebellion against the caste system, in the Hebrew Bible's ire
against those who rob "poor ones of justice," in Christianity's revolutionary humanism, and in generations of peasant revolt, we've seen egalitarian
ideas appear and take hold. The French Revolution of 1789 trumpeted the
Enlightenment dream of "liberty, equality, and fraternity." Its appeal has
never been extinguished, but it has been frustrated by capitalism—the
very system that creates the riches to make it achievable.[26]

Despite his prescience, and despite his belief in capitalism's capacity
to transform and adapt, Marx could not have foreseen the welfare states

of the twentieth century or how ordinary workers could rise out of poverty and even become consumers of luxury goods. But the core of the system he described is little changed. Capitalism is crisis-prone, is built on domination and exploitation, and for all its micro-rationality has produced macro-irrationalities in the form of social and environmental destruction. It's also a truly universal system. When Marx wrote in the *Manifesto* that "all that is solid melts into air" before capital's might, it had barely spread beyond the West. Now, finally, capitalism reigns supreme in all corners of the world.[27]

More improviser than prophet, what Marx left us wasn't scripture but a method of looking at the world and a set of concerns to animate us. Over the years, he revised and constantly questioned his own thought, but remained consistent as a democrat and a believer that the majority had an interest in its own self-emancipation. If we can fault him for anything, it's for how unqualified that faith was and for underestimating how capitalism could find ways to mitigate, if not solve, its contradictions.

Marx's fate over the past century has been a sad one. He once said his favorite motto was "Doubt all things," but under authoritarian regimes, Marxism was turned into a science that allowed no room for doubt. "Dialectical materialism" became rigid, a dogmatic caricature used to produce insights on everything from genetics to theater art. But Marx should be saved from being rendered toothless by today's academics, too. He wasn't an innocent bystander just trying to understand capitalism.

"Philosophers have only interpreted the world," Marx famously wrote. "The point is to change it." True to his word, Marx was just as much a pamphleteer and an activist as he was a theorist. He left behind thousands of pages of notes, correspondence, and passionate political interventions. There was a reason Marx was chased from country after country by state agents. In 1883, as his friend was being buried, Engels reminded mourners that "Marx was before all else a revolutionist. His real mission in life was to contribute, in one way or another, to the overthrow of capitalist society and of the state institutions which it had brought into being, to contribute to the liberation of the modern proletariat."[28]

Marx's sprawling ideas were meant to be taken and made useful for future struggles—vulgarized, necessarily, perhaps, but still true to their radically democratic essence. In the twelve years between Marx's death and his own, Engels helped refine and propagate the "materialist conception of history" among movements of workers who were turning to socialism. No movement was larger, more influential, or more loyal to Marxism's founders than the social democrats of their homeland.

THREE

THE FUTURE WE LOST

ROSA LUXEMBURG WAS already a distinguished theorist when she started teaching activists and trade unionists at the Social Democratic Party's (SPD) Berlin school. In one classroom photo from 1907, she's smiling and standing not far from where Friedrich Ebert, the future German president, sits. Another student of hers, Wilhelm Pieck, is in the same row, even closer. He also went on to be a German president.

Ebert, a Social Democrat, helmed the prewar Weimar Republic; Pieck, the Communist postwar East German state. Each of their paths led to power. Rosa Luxemburg's led to the bottom of a canal.

On January 15, 1919, the same day she was martyred, her comrade Karl Liebknecht was wheeled into a morgue, riddled with gunshot wounds. Liebknecht's father was cofounder of the SPD, a party that Luxemburg had joined twenty years earlier.

They both intimately knew the men blamed for their deaths—Friedrich Ebert and Gustav Noske. In 1891, all four of them had been at the pivotal Erfurt Congress, where they laid the groundwork for a generation of working-class politics. SPD leader August Bebel spoke at the meeting with widely shared confidence, "I am convinced that there are only a few people in this hall who will not experience the great day [of socialism]." As

Luxemburg recounted, "a warm, electric stream of life, of idealism, of security in joyful action" swept through the delegates.[1]

In the years that followed, Europe's socialists had plenty of cause for optimism. In election after election, their parties saw vote totals climb as newly enfranchised workers turned out for them. It seemed natural—not least to terrified industrialists—that working-class political rights were translating into a shift in the balance of power. But the pressures that would ultimately kill many of the democratic revolutionaries, corrupt those who survived, and turn others into defenders of law and order were already emerging.

The socialist movements of the nineteenth and early twentieth centuries never ended up inheriting the world. Not just poorly led, they ran into a recurring problem of collective action. Though workers could only win gains through class struggle, they had more than their chains to lose in revolutionary politics. They relied on capital to survive and could not so easily break with the system that oppressed them and marched them off to war.

Still, as we will see, the Second International era gave birth to mass working-class parties that for the first time threatened to take state power from capitalists. The debates and political forms that emerged during this period have shaped the Left ever since—as have questions about how the twentieth century would have played out if these organizations had taken a different course.

BY THE MIDDLE of the nineteenth century, Germany was undergoing a chaotic transformation into an industrial powerhouse. The country's Junker class of aristocratic landholders were paradoxically committed to breakneck modernization. The emerging capitalist class, for its part, didn't fully commit to the Revolution of 1848, leaving political power mostly in the hands of the old elite and increasingly ceding the fight for democracy to workers.

Like thousands of others, the future leader of German social democracy, August Bebel, went from trade union politics to socialism after reading the work of Ferdinand Lassalle. Lassalle was an unlikely founder of the General German Workers' Association (ADAV). At barely twenty years old, he had won fame defending the Countess Sophie von Hatzfeldt in a protracted divorce. His first instinct was to challenge her husband to a duel, but after he was turned down, he pursued an eight-year legal battle fought in thirty-six different courtrooms. Ultimately, Lassalle triumphed, winning the countess and himself a large fortune.

Soon enough, he secured a more permanent place in history. After 1848, German workers began to see liberalism as inadequate to their interests, and Lassalle took up their cause. At a time when veteran German socialists were in an uneasy alliance with the middle-class Progressive Party, Lassalle used his considerable talents to sway the movement in a different direction. In 1863 he helped found the ADAV, which adopted as its platform his sprawling treatise that argued for universal suffrage and state support for producer cooperatives.

In pursuit of these demands, Lassalle attempted to forge an alliance with Otto von Bismarck, building on their shared opposition to liberalism. The bid for support failed, and the just thirty-nine-year-old Lassalle died in a duel soon after.

Intellectually, Lassalle drew on Marxism but found fierce critics in Marx and Engels themselves. (Though the penniless Marx used to sometimes ask him for loans.) He saw the state as autonomous rather than an instrument of class rule, and his belief in an "iron law of wages," the idea that nothing could prevent wages from falling below subsistence levels, led him to downplay the possibilities for trade union victories within capitalism. More importantly, Marx and Engels rejected his bid for reform from above, instead advocating mass struggle to achieve change. Yet after Lassalle's death, even his famous detractors had to concede that his efforts had "woken up the German working class" to a destiny distinct from liberalism.[2]

With its newly anointed leader suddenly dead, the future of the German workers' movement was uncertain. Bebel eventually moved toward more conventional Marxist thought and together with Wilhelm Liebknecht, a personal friend of Marx's, founded the Social Democratic Workers' Party (SDAP) in 1869. Unlike the ADAV, the party's program was clear, built on ten defined demands and six general principles that laid out the injustice of the present situation, the goal of working-class liberation from the wage labor system in particular and class society as a whole, and a commitment to political freedom and democracy.

The seeds of what would become Second International Marxism were apparent in the SDAP program. But when the party merged with the ADAV six years later to form the twenty-thousand-strong Socialist Workers' Party of Germany (SAP), the new organization's founding document had a distinct Lassallean flavor. It predictably drew the ire of Marx. The text claimed that "labor is the source of all wealth and all culture" (what about nature?, Marx objected) and established a resolute principle of working-class independence: "The emancipation of labor must be the work of the laboring class, opposed to which all other classes are only a reactionary body." The Gotha Program, as the SAP's manifesto was called, sought "the free state and the socialist society, the destruction of the iron law of wages, the overthrow of exploitation in all forms and the abolition of all social and political inequality."

In addition to his continued theoretical opposition to the Lassallean "iron law of wages" thesis and the idea that even other oppressed classes were a "reactionary body," Marx rightly questioned what this desired "free state" was. Only a decade had passed since Lassalle's failed overture to Bismarck, and he thought it vital for the SAP to have a clear view of the state. As he wrote in *The German Ideology* (1846), "the executive of the modern state is nothing but a committee for managing the common affairs of the whole bourgeoisie." A party whose socialist ideas were more than "skin-deep" would have to overcome that state and fight for a transition period "in which the state can be nothing but the revolutionary dictatorship of the proletariat." Marx did not spell out the implications in his *Critique of the Gotha Programme* nor elsewhere in his writings, besides in his brief commentary on the Paris Commune. That omission—what form politics should take under socialism and how should the socialist state's institutions be structured?—would be significant in the next century. At the time, however, Marx's polemics aside, the Socialist Workers' Party grew and evolved in the newly unified German nation.[3]

Bismarck, now the German Empire's first chancellor, was well aware of the party's organizing efforts. He might have recalled his early meetings with Lassalle and thus how willing some workers were to embrace statist reforms. He implemented a carrot-and-stick approach toward the restive workers' movement.

The stick came first: the new SAP won 9 percent in the 1877 elections, a modest amount but a threefold increase over the total ADAV/SDAP vote in 1874. Soon arrived a pretext to clamp down on the party: two attempts in 1878 on the kaiser's life by presumed leftists. It was more than enough for Bismarck to convince the Reichstag to pass *Sozialistengesetz*, a series of acts banning social-democratic agitation. The SAP could still stand for elections, but campaigning was effectively impossible. Party meetings were forbidden, newspapers were shuttered, and members sometimes arrested. Factory owners across the country made their workers sign vows that they were not Social Democrats.

Then came the carrot, as Bismarck began to offer workers a kind of socialism from above: health insurance and social security schemes, believing that "the real grievance of the worker is the insecurity of his existence." The Social Democrats weren't fooled, even by the regime's selective nationalizations. They realized that capitalism need not be laissez-faire, and pejoratively labeled Bismarck's plan "state socialism." Voters for their part saw the situation quite rationally: the concessions were made because of the SAP's strength, which only served to vindicate it. Bismarck discovered that winning concessions often emboldens rather than placates the oppressed.

The SAP continued to radicalize. At its first congress in exile in 1880, it removed a Gotha Program clause vowing to struggle only by legal means.

Three years later, delegates went further and called their party a "revolutionary one" without parliamentary illusions, and proud of its roots in the "great master Marx."

SOCIAL DEMOCRACY WAS becoming a force beyond Germany, as well. The Second International—the successor to the International Workingmen's Association of Marx's day—was founded in Paris on Bastille Day, 1889, one hundred years after the start of the French Revolution. The hall at Salle Petrelle chosen for the gathering was draped in red cloth and filled with red flags. Above its presidium, in gold letters, read the parting exhortation of *The Communist Manifesto*: "Workers of the world, unite!" The venue proved too small for the four hundred delegates from nineteen countries, and hasty preparations had to be made to host the rest of the proceedings elsewhere.

Often with the Germans as their model, parties sprouted up across Europe claiming fealty to Marxism. It is easy, then, to conflate the triumph of Marxism (or even socialism more broadly) with the general rise of workers' movements. But objective and subjective factors were equally important. Socialists were able to credibly explain the injustices of the capitalist system, convince people that it could be done away with, and describe an agent with an interest in its overthrow. But they wouldn't have been able to do this without mass discontent amid rapid urbanization and industrialization. The process of creating a shared working-class identity and a politics to match it required brilliant feats of adaption and organizing.

Throughout most of the nineteenth century, radical movements were dominated by non-Marxists—first "utopian" socialists, who sought to build harmonious societies through creating a "new man" in communes, then intransigent anarchists who posed a maximalist opposition to both capitalist domination and the state itself. It was Marxist-influenced, "scientific" socialism that provided a more credible account of the difficult world workers found themselves in and a plausible way out.[4]

Parties across Europe met various roadblocks on the road to socialism. Most of the Second International, aside from the Russians, had more favorable conditions to organize in at home than did the Germans. At the Paris Congress, Bebel warned his colleagues to burn papers before returning to Germany and look out for state agents in their midst. It was a reminder that their early success was not without its hardships, with party leaders in exile or under constant threat of arrest. They soon experienced some relief, as Bismarck's 1890 resignation coincided with the expiration of the antisocialist laws. SAP campaigning was once again legal. By then, the newly renamed Social Democratic Party had amassed a considerable base of support—one in five German voters backed it in 1890.

This didn't translate into political victories. Germany was intensely federalized, and different states had different suffrage laws. Where social democracy was strongest—such as in Prussia—representation was also less democratic, and conservative rural districts were heavily favored. Thus, though the largest party by popular vote, the SPD ended up with the fifth largest Reichstag contingent. With over 1.4 million votes, the party won only 35 seats, while the German Conservative Party received 73 from 895,100 votes.

What's more, though it had a parliament, Germany remained a semi-autocratic monarchy. The emperor held sway in foreign policy and directly appointed a chancellor, who had great power over domestic affairs. And in the Reichstag itself, a conservative Junker could win rousing applause after saying, "The King of Prussia and German Emperor must always be able to say to a lieutenant: take ten men and shoot the Reichstag!" (That same representative would play a role making Hitler chancellor in 1933.)[5]

Not surprisingly, the SPD tended to see German democracy as a sham. It still sought democratic victories, but for the most part the SPD adopted a stance of "pure opposition." Elections were mostly measures of strength and for propaganda purposes. Even when the party won seats, legislative bodies were treated primarily as arenas to clarify class lines.

Social Democratic legislators voted against state budgets; the movement had no interest in managing the capitalist state, only in organizing the working class, with an eye to a future period in power.

The party's theory reflected its isolation. Its 1891 Erfurt Program was a considerably more radical—and Marxist—document than the Gotha Program. Written by Eduard Bernstein and Karl Kautsky, two theorists who would shape the SPD for years to come, the text portended the collapse of capitalism, describing an era of devastating crises and the "ever more stark opposition between exploiters and the exploited." Private ownership, once the revolutionary force described in *The Communist Manifesto*, was now presented as a fetter on economic development. The solution proposed by Erfurt was the socialization of all private production. As Bernstein and Kautsky wrote, such a "transformation amounts to the emancipation not only of the proletariat, but of the entire human race."

The immediate tasks of the day were laid out in a section largely drafted by Bernstein: "Without political rights, the working class cannot carry on its economic struggles and develop its economic organization. It cannot bring about the transfer of the means of production into the possession of the community without first having obtained political power." The Erfurt Program also shifted away from Lassallean illiberalism to a declaration that the party "fights not only the exploitation and oppression of wage earners in society today, but every manner of exploitation and oppression, whether directed against a class, party, sex, or race."

The program concluded with a list of demands, ranging from proportional representation and universal suffrage to political freedoms and free medical care to the replacement of Germany's standing army with a militia. It also advocated workplace reform such as the eight-hour day, an end to child labor, and the prohibition of night work.

There is an obvious gap between the radical, almost apocalyptic vision of capitalism in crisis and the comparatively modest immediate demands put forth by Bernstein and Kautsky. There was also a more subtle tension in the program, between the urgency of the crisis described and the relatively passive role assigned to the working-class party: "It is the task of the Social Democratic Party to shape the struggle of the working class into a conscious and unified one and to point out the inherent necessity of its goals." This is a concept of the party that Kautsky, in particular, would return to—one that prepares for but does not make revolution.

But, for the time, the Erfurt Program worked. Its marriage of maximalism and incrementalism proved practical for a broad party. All members of the SPD thought that reforms should be sought. The debate within the party was over how that should happen (class independence or alliances, rupture or compromise). All agreed, too, that the proletariat should look toward the socialist horizon.

More than anyone else, Kautsky embodied the Erfurtian synthesis. The quintessential German Marxist was actually born in Prague and grew up in Vienna. Unlike the proletarian Bebel, Kautsky was from a middle-class family that encouraged his interest in art, history, and philosophy. As a teenager, the 1871 Paris Commune stirred his imagination, but so did books like George Sand's *The Sin of M. Antoine*, a mid-century work filled with romantic, radical sentiments. But the intellectual climate that Kautsky and others were born into was anything but idealist. This was an era of scientific advance, highly rationalist in its outlook. The young Kautsky studied Charles Darwin and biologist Ernst Haeckel. Marxism was not positivist, but it was able to draw in intellectuals with both its clear moral opposition to capitalist exploitation and its claim to know the laws of history and where it was headed.[6]

Kautsky joined the Social Democratic Party of Austria when he was twenty-one, allying himself with the most radical (verging on anarchist) wing of a fractious formation. Even then, he was more of an intellectual than an organizer, and in 1880 his work took him to Zurich, a city teeming with socialist exiles from across Germany and Russia. He met Eduard Bernstein there. Bernstein was just a few years older than Kautsky, and they quickly became "of one heart and one soul." Together they studied Engels's *Anti-Dühring*, a thorough rebuttal of the ethical, cross-class (as opposed to class-struggle-driven) socialism promoted by Eugen Dühring. The experience won them both over to Marxism.

Through Bernstein and Bebel, Kautsky started a correspondence with Engels and ventured to London in March 1881 to visit him and Marx for several months. Engels took to him, while Marx, nearing his final days, thought Kautsky a "very talented drinker" but intellectually a "mediocrity with a small-minded outlook." In sum, that made him "a decent fellow in his own way."[7]

Throughout the 1880s, Kautsky would make trips to London, growing close with Engels. The friendship would endure until Engels's death in 1895, after which Kautsky was widely accepted as his heir. It was through Kautsky, not its two founders, that Marxism first captivated a mass audience.

KAUTSKY WAS AN industrious and intermittently brilliant theorist, but his success had much to do with timing. He founded the widely read socialist theoretical journal *Die Neue Zeit* in 1883. Coupled with his connection to Engels and the support of Bebel, Kautsky became an authoritative voice within the SPD without ever having run for a party post. After the Second International was formed and with his Erfurt Program emulated by party after party, Kautsky was without irony considered the "pope of Marxism." During his day, socialism broke from its relative isolation and merged itself with a broader workers' movement. For the first time they could be spoken of as one and the same.

The fact that Kautsky was in Germany, the epicenter of social democracy, was key to his prominence. The Social Democratic Party reached new heights every year—from 352,000 votes on its founding in 1874 to 1.4 million in 1890 to 3 million (nearly one-third of the electorate) in 1903. Social Democratic workers weren't just voting for the party; they were enmeshed in its institutions and emotionally committed to its cause. Despite the working class's growing importance, it was isolated from mainstream

German culture. The SPD wasn't just a party: It was an alternative culture, where workers could educate themselves in a day school or through reading seventy-five affiliated papers, play in sports leagues or gymnastic clubs, and find friends and lovers at picnics and party taverns. This sense of collective belonging was cemented by lectures, rallies, and rituals.[8]

At times, Bebel's rhetoric seemed to mimic the messianic appeal of Christianity. Christians knew that Christ would come again in his glory to judge the living and the dead. Social Democrats knew that every moment drew them closer to salvation on Earth.

But more concretely, social democracy's network of cooperative businesses and credit unions offered advancement to some workers, and for many others its clinics and other services filled gaps in the Bismarckian welfare state. For a party unable to deliver legislative victories, these material gains translated into legitimacy. More loftily, in theory, the "state within the state" was providing workers with the training and experience they would need when the "great day" finally came and they were to govern.

In practice, it may be that these institutions fostered moderation and integrated workers into mainstream German society rather than offering an alternative to it. But those who already had power—not just in Germany but across Europe—looked nervously at the social democrats among them, growing more numerous by the day.

THERE WERE THOSE within the movement, however, who were beginning to question its foundation. This was perhaps to be expected—from the start, the modern Left had been divided over countless questions—but in this case, its source was not: Eduard Bernstein, coauthor of the party's Erfurt Program, began to drift away from its orthodoxy in the mid-1890s.

Though largely unschooled, Bernstein was supremely talented. Both Marx and Engels regarded him as the superior intellect to the younger Kautsky. After his short stint in Zurich, Bernstein spent over a decade living in London, engaging with another rising workers' movement, but one that had less time for Marxism. Bernstein arrived in England with impeccable Marxist credentials, but in the same British Library where Marx had labored, he spent long days struggling to "stretch his teachings, to bring them in accord with practical realities."

The usually gregarious Bernstein distanced himself from friends and grew irritable, tormented by an intellectual dilemma. Capitalism was thriving and proving itself malleable, and he didn't foresee "a collapse of the bourgeois economy in the near future."

Not explicitly rejecting Marx, but instead using ambiguities in his thought to defend his new positions, Bernstein radically questioned orthodox Marxism. In a series of *Neue Zeit* articles, he posited that capitalism had morphed in a way Marx and Engels did not anticipate. For one, society wasn't "splitting up into two great hostile camps...Bourgeoisie and Proletariat," as *The Communist Manifesto* claimed and the Erfurt Program echoed. Instead of disappearing, intermediary classes played a vital role in the modern economy. The 1891 program had also said that production was increasingly becoming "the monopoly of a relatively small number of capitalists and large landowners," but as Bernstein pointed out, smaller firms were alive and well. As for workers, though they were certainly exploited and suffering, their material standing was slowly improving rather than deteriorating.

Bernstein ventured furthest from his previous views when he insisted that capitalism had found ways to self-regulate and avoid crises, and that the working class had won the means, in the form of parliaments, to shape its development and slowly legislate reforms. His final broadside against the doom and gloom and revolutionary posturing of his party's mainstream was his proclamation that "the ultimate aim of socialism is nothing, but the movement is everything."

Though he was wrong about capitalism's ability to prevent crises, Bernstein perceived that though it was filled with internal contradictions, capitalism also had mechanisms for stabilization and adaption. There is a reason none of capitalism's many crises have proved terminal. More importantly, Bernstein offered a solution to tensions in the Erfurt Program. "The fault," Bernstein wrote, "lies in the doctrine which assumes that progress depends on the deterioration of social conditions." The party claimed that capitalism was collapsing, but its immediate tasks seemed neither to hasten its demise nor to forestall it. Bernstein saw capitalism stabilizing itself, and he was glad for it, as it was in this environment that workers could win gains. His view that "the ultimate aim of socialism is nothing" didn't mean that he abandoned socialism, but rather that he saw the path to it as gradual rather than through revolution. Fittingly, the English-language collection of his work was titled *Evolutionary Socialism*.

Bernstein's insistence that social democracy would reach new heights when it freed itself from "obsolete phraseology" and was "willing to appear what it really is today; a democratic-Socialist reform party" foreshadowed postwar social democracy, when new opportunities appeared to manage the capitalist state in the interests of workers. In his own time, Bernstein's status as a leading Marxist intellectual meant the *Neue Zeit* articles caused worldwide controversy.[9]

Bernstein was right to question the teleology that ran through Second International Marxism. Borrowing from Kant, he believed that socialism was something that morally and ethically *ought to be*, not something that was necessarily *destined to be*. But Bernstein missed the fact that the confidence that history was on their side gave socialists strength. It also helped paper over differences between revolutionaries and reformists within social-democratic parties.

Kautsky at first hesitated in response to his friend. Not only was personal affection at play, but he seemed genuinely unsure what to make of the work. When its political implications became clear, however, the challenge couldn't be ignored. The future of the entire movement seemed to rest on their doctrinal dispute. When Kautsky entered the fray, he did so vigorously, both privately and publicly. Writing Bernstein directly, he complained that his "Marxism had collapsed" and that Bernstein was trying to "become a representative of English socialism" with his moderate turn.

(Engels had also once worried about Bernstein's affinity for Britain's moderate Fabian socialists but dismissed it as a symptom of health troubles he was dealing with at the time.) Bernstein, for his part, simply asserted that English capitalism was further along the same road as Germany and other industrial nations.

At his most damning, Kautsky even said that his friend had ceased to be a social democrat at all and didn't have a place in the SPD. The theorist had already traded barbs with Bavarian reformist Georg von Vollmar, who went further than Bernstein and favored the SPD's transformation from a workers' party into a broader "people's party." Kautsky responded that such a development would mean going from "a party of the fighting proletariat into an eclectic swamp of frustrated fellows."

But the most powerful riposte to Bernstein came from Rosa Luxemburg, who wrote a series of articles called "Social Reform or Revolution?" They represented the finest synthesis of Marxist orthodoxy yet written. Luxemburg argues that far from stabilizing capitalism, the growth of finance capital and industrial cartels would exacerbate the system's crises.

The young, Polish-born radical didn't reject the daily fight for reforms or the importance of trade unions, seeing them as vital to building class consciousness. But she argued that a socialist society would emerge only after a decisive rupture with capitalism. She likened the struggles of those who tried to gradually bring about change within capitalism to the plight of Sisyphus. They make progress up the hill, only to have to start again when their reforms are rolled back. In other words, without the structural leap to socialism, all that is won is the momentary "suppression of the abuses of capitalism instead of suppression of capitalism itself."

There was a difference in emphasis between Luxemburg's "hammer blow of revolution" and Kautsky's more passive role for the party, but for the moment the two thinkers were in accord. Kautsky would trumpet "Social Reform or Revolution?" and help bring more attention to Luxemburg's work. The larger distinction, after all, was between the radicals like them and the reformists (or "revisionists," as they were known) like Bernstein.

Toward the end of 1898, the SPD officially intervened into the growing theoretical dispute at the party's Stuttgart Congress. Ultimately, the leadership joined the radicals and repudiated Bernstein. But the revisionists would eventually have their moment.

THE 1903 ELECTION witnessed the SPD extend its appeal for the first time to the middle class. The revisionists tried to use the occasion to force the party to take its parliamentary work more seriously, by forming tactical coalitions with liberals to win reforms.

The radicals beat them back at the Dresden Congress that year, however, buoyed by Kautsky's broadsides against the moderates and again with the support of Bebel and much of the party executive. In January 1905, SPD radicals found additional encouragement abroad. Russia's 1905 Revolution showed the power of working-class mobilization: the Romanov dynasty, which had seemed unassailable, was almost driven from power. Labor militancy also rose within Germany, with strike activity increasing dramatically. The conditions—lockouts, increased employer organization, and cost of living increases—that led to caution among trade-union leaders fostered militancy in the rank and file.[10]

Debates within the SPD over the mass (or general) strike had gone on for several years, but the events of 1905 gave them more urgency. Instead of localized work stoppages at one plant or in one sector, mass strikes were political tools to force drastic concessions across industries. In the United States, the Philadelphia General Strike in 1835 called for wage increases and a ten-hour workday. Similar strikes occurred in 1877 in St. Louis and in 1892 in New Orleans. But the mass strikes debated in Germany were those by Belgian workers hoping to secure universal suffrage. Luxemburg thought the Belgians too timid, tactically, and the revolution in Russia proved how far the general strike could go. While the revisionists saw a path to reform through the existing parliament and liberal coalitions, radicals, armed with this new weapon, could present a vision of democratizing the state through street action.

In 1905, Kautsky was the voice of the radicals. His analysis of the 1905 Revolution, in particular his warnings about the mendacity of Russian liberalism and his commentary on the radical potential of the empire's peasantry, was admired by Lenin and eventually proved prescient. It was his ally Luxemburg, however, who saw the Russian experience as replicable in Germany. When the revolution broke out, she traveled in disguise and took part in the movement in Poland, where she witnessed ordinary workers radicalize in the span of weeks.

In her 1906 book, *The Mass Strike, the Political Party and the Trade Unions*, Luxemburg endorsed general strikes. But unlike anarchists, Luxemburg didn't equate the tactic with revolution, "in contradistinction to the daily political struggle of the working class," but rather saw it as a tool to raise class consciousness and exert power.

Luxemburg reminded readers that "economic" and "political" struggles were inseparable. Rather than trade unions launching limited economic strikes for better conditions and wages, indefinite, general strikes could win political ends, including suffrage and democratization. These gains wouldn't preclude parliamentary action, but rather turn parliament into a vehicle that could actually pass radical reforms. Unlike for Bernstein, the movement was "not everything" for Luxemburg; it had a distinct aim: "the dictatorship of the proletariat," a task "accomplished during a long period of gigantic social struggles." And unlike Bebel, Luxemburg didn't see the mass strike as a one-off event, directed by the party, but a grassroots form of struggle that couldn't be turned on and off by command.

By breaking down the barriers between economic and political struggles, Luxemburg was attempting to stall the growing separation of the trade union movement and social democracy. Though in theory unions had no official power within the party, in practice a "theory of equal authority" was gaining favor. Unions would use workplace strikes tactically, and the SPD would use parliament to win political reforms. But with the path to reforms blocked by the antidemocratic Reichstag and many rank-and-file workers discontent with their economic situation, the need for a more radical approach was obvious to Luxemburg.

LUXEMBURG'S ENTHUSIASM FOR the new wave of worker militancy might have led her to underestimate the strength of the status quo. At the turn of the century, Social Democratic Party membership was surging, but its affiliated unions were growing at an even faster clip. It was among organized labor that Bernstein's ideas found warm welcome.

Fueled by a booming economy, the unions evolved from fringe, radical bodies to the mass guarantors of economic security. They organized 1.7 million workers by 1906, while the party itself could only boast 400,000 members. Unions won tangible gains for their membership not by following the SPD's tack of "pure opposition" but by negotiating with employers.

Labor wrestled concessions by threatening to disrupt production if demands were not met. But the logic of capitalism sets limits on the nature and extent of those demands: Workers need their firms to be profitable to stay employed, which tempers wage demands. And though capitalists need workers in order to stay in business, the relationship between the two sides is asymmetrical, as the unemployed stood ready to fill in for unruly workers. Achieving real gains, then, required both steady offensives and also the shrewdness to know when to retreat. It was an environment that fostered moderation, not revolution.

The stakes involved in this balancing act were high, and many in the union movement came to resent the more symbolic political demands of social democracy. For example, thirty thousand workers were locked out by their employers in 1906 after observing the traditional May Day strike. Such provocative political actions threatened to deplete union funds needed for economic strikes, and to open the way for a broader employer counteroffensive.

Divisions emerged between the more moderate trade union members and the more radical SPD general membership, but unions were themselves increasingly dominated by a conservative leadership. Growing trade union membership meant more staff to manage their affairs. This was no doubt necessary, but it created a bureaucratic layer of people who worked in the name of the working class but were increasingly alienated from its day-to-day experience.

The mass strike debate, in particular, was a persistent headache for the trade unions. The challenge, after all, wasn't just from radical intellectuals but from some rank-and-file unionists, such as the Ruhr basin's coal miners. The union leaders decided to deal with the problem preemptively.

At the Cologne labor conference in May 1905, Theodor Bömelburg, head of the masons' union, denounced the "literati" and its radical pretenses, and organized opposition to the mass strike tactic. It was an effort to inoculate the unions against the results of the SPD's coming Jena Congress, in which debates about the mass strike would loom large. The unions not only rejected the tactic but forbade discussion of it. Delegates insisted on peace in the labor movement to allow for unions to consolidate and grow. Their reply to outraged leftists would soon become familiar: "Go back to Russia."

Just a few months later, however, at the Jena Congress, the mass strike was endorsed by the party as a legitimate tactic, though with plenty of qualifications. It was a tension typical of the time: the general membership would push through radical measures, trade unions would either defeat or neuter those measures, and the executive would engage in rhetorical gymnastics to appease all sides.

But the sides were not of equal strength. The party leadership—though in theory disputing the revisionism that much of the union bureaucracy endorsed—in practice came to side with them. Crucially, in 1906, trade unions were granted veto power if the party wanted to declare a general strike and they disagreed.

Even if they had reservations, the SPD's leadership reasoned that the growing power of allied unions meant that they had to be placated for the sake of unity. If they had any doubts about this course, figures like Bebel could look to the negative example of Britain, where the Marxists of the

Social Democratic Federation were a marginal, isolated group, while a non-Marxist, reformist Labour Party enjoyed mass support.

While revisionists were challenging the revolutionary goals of the Erfurt Program, the radicals were seeking new tactics to make those goals a reality. All the while, the SPD executive struggled to preserve Erfurt's hard-won merger of the workers' and socialist movements. Yet its institutional needs would lead it to develop its own conservatizing bureaucracy. As it turned out, in a case study of the fragility of building a socialist movement within capitalism, the center would not hold.

FRIEDRICH EBERT ARRIVED at the Social Democratic Party's Berlin office right after New Year's 1906 to find it in chaos. Record keeping was abysmal, and the party was failing to collect desperately needed dues. To the outside world the SPD was already without rival, the first mass party, but internally, it was as if nothing had changed from the lean years underground.

Ebert was just the man to turn things around. He wasn't a sterling orator or thinker, nor was he much to look at: one writer was kind enough to describe him as "a short fat man, with short legs, a short neck, and a pear-shaped head on a pear-shaped body." But Ebert was disciplined and systematic, and quickly set about renovating the party's operations.[11]

He had been waiting for this opportunity for some time. The son of a tailor, Ebert was attracted to social democracy early in life, but he never joined its most radical wing. After struggling to survive as an artisan saddle maker, like Bebel he found material security through his political work. His administrative talents became apparent during his time as a member of Bremen's city council and as its local SPD labor secretary. It was a surprise, but no great one, when he was selected to join the party executive in 1905.

Despite its explosive growth, the SPD had retained the structure it had adopted at Gotha in 1875. A five-member executive (expanded to seven in 1900) was tasked with managing day-to-day business, drafting the party congress agenda and carrying out its decisions. This body's work was overseen by a small control commission, while the leadership's links to branches throughout the country were maintained by volunteer liaisons elected out of locals. Combined with a handful of editors and staff from the party press, the central office only encompassed a few dozen people.

The SPD was highly fragmented, reflecting both the composition of the German state and the legacy of anti-SPD legislation, and dependent on its volunteers. The pressure to change came initially from the radicals. Some local branches, like those in Bavaria and Baden, pushed for reformist politics that better matched conditions in areas where smaller-scale industry prevailed and agriculture was still dominant. The radicals, feeling confident after the 1905 Jena Congress, saw centralization as a way to discipline these regional tendencies and create a more coherent revolutionary organization. The idea was a mirror image of what trade union leaders were trying to do.

As in the unions, the SPD's bureaucracy emerged mainly out of necessity. Throughout the 1890s, as the party grew, its structure became more complex; district and state party organs were added to the existing local ones. The central organization's tiny staff was meant to coordinate a half million members and support hundreds of electoral races. All wings of the SPD, whether they favored centralism or federalism, recognized the need for a larger bureaucracy.

After years of delay, in 1905 the party eventually added more paid secretaries to its executive. The number of "political" officials was capped at four—two chairs elected by the party congress and two members selected by the control commission—but the number of secretaries was left open. Ebert was the first elected secretary, and he used his newly created secretary-general position to revamp the party's office. He updated administrative protocols and introduced typewriters and filing cabinets. Records that were never kept—lest they fall into state agent hands—were now harnessed. Ebert's goals were to increase membership dues, expand the party press, develop its electoral machine, and, vitally, generate data with which to evaluate progress toward these objectives. Local volunteers were overwhelmed with questionnaires the new infrastructure sent them. They naturally deferred more and more to the growing network of paid professionals.

Ebert fulfilled his administrative mandate exceptionally, but his role was far from apolitical. His efforts brought him into contact with all of the party's local officials. While Kautsky thought in terms of epochs and continents, Ebert worked toward immediate solutions. He wasn't a revolutionary, but neither was the daily work of the party. He can hardly be faulted for building an administrative machine and targeting wavering voters from other parties. Even if he hadn't spent a decade as a moderate in Bremen, this work would've pushed Ebert into a tactical alliance with reformists. Bebel and other formerly radical members of the executive had met the same fate. For their part, Luxemburg and the other SPD radicals operated under the mistaken assumption that reformist party leaders would be forced out when a major political or economic crisis came.

The radicals were right about one thing: a more sophisticated bureaucracy could have both improved the SPD's efficacy and supported rank-and-file militancy. Member engagement, greater oversight, term limits for secretaries, or any number of reforms could have checked any conservatizing tendencies. In the absence of these measures, however, the fact that the bureaucracy grew at a time when the trade union leadership and other dynamics were pushing the SPD rightward all but guaranteed the victory of more conservative forces.

SOCIAL DEMOCRATIC WORKERS were isolated from the rest of German society. This was a major reason they flocked to the SPD, with its clubs and welfare programs, in the first place. They were poorly educated, they lived in cramped, dirty housing, and their bodies were warped by overwork and fatigue. They were distinct, too, in their views on war. Other Germans cheered the patriotic cause during the 1870–1871 Franco-Prussian War. The working-class parties and trade unions opposed it. The society that had given them so little would get "not one man, not one penny!"

In the early days, the SPD was split, with the Lassalleans more accom-modating of the "national interest." But throughout the 1890s, the party was the Reich's only significant antimilitarist force, seeing the army as the tool of a rival class rather than of the nation as a whole. If there was any doubt, they could look at the institution's structure: generaled by Junkers, overseen by bourgeois officers, but manned by workers. It had the same class structure as the rest of Germany.[12]

In place of the old Prussian military system, the SPD proposed a citi-zens' militia. The Erfurt Program's demands go far beyond those found in democratic republics: "Education of all to bear arms. Militia in the place of the standing army. Determination by the popular assembly on questions of war and peace. Settlement of all international disputes by arbitration." In practice, support for a militia system was justified on economic grounds more often than on moral ones. The Social Democrats used the issue to appeal to the popular classes, who disproportionately footed the bill for the military through indirect taxes. In this way the fight against the Junker-controlled army and navy were tied to the struggle for fiscal reform. The approach made tactical sense, as taxation was one of the few areas the Reichstag had discretion over, but hardly challenged the moral right of a ruler to plunge a nation into war.

As internationalists, socialists believe that workers across nations share more with one another than with elites who speak the same language as they do. In practice many social democrats opposed an autocratic form of militarism but failed to present a radical alternative to the rotten system itself. Electoral considerations also forced the party into a balancing act that saw it talk of internationalism yet still make clear a concern about na-tional defense. This would pose a problem when World War I broke out and all belligerents claimed to be fighting a defensive war.

Karl Liebknecht was among the most striking figures trying to push the party in a more radical direction when it came to questions of war and nationalism. Despite the fact that he was the son of an SPD founder, he was a persistent foe of the leadership. An impatient man, guided by his morals above all else, Liebknecht saw the question of war and militarism as the central issue of the time, arguing that peace was only possible if the whole military machine was abolished. He pushed for revolutionary agitation among German military recruits.

For the SPD's leadership such provocations were a danger to the party's steady advance, an advance that would yield many of the transformations radicals like Liebknecht desired anyway. Tensions arose at the Second International's Stuttgart Congress in 1907. In the prior decade, German naval expansion and the two Morocco Crises—in 1905–1906 and 1911—had made continental war a real possibility. Over days of debate, SPD delegates were pushed by British and French socialists to adopt an explicitly antiwar stance.

Earlier, many radicals in the SPD had avoided such a resolution, thinking it naive that social democracy could mobilize to *prevent* war between capitalist states, rather than just responding to a war with socialist revolution. But now they adopted the stance of Liebknecht and Kurt Eisner, who had long sought a more proactive approach. From the party's right wing, they were challenged by those like Gustav Noske, who had insisted in parliament that Social Democrats weren't "vagabonds without a fatherland," but Germans.[13]

Though Noske's rhetoric was an extreme example, most of the German delegation opposed the radicals. Half of them came from the more conservative trade union movement, and many of the remainder were revisionists. They stressed the limited power of the International in domestic affairs and tried to prevent any resolution favoring the mass strike as a weapon to prevent war. Despite German resistance, however, the Stuttgart Congress took a clear antiwar stance, with the caveat that the "International is not able to determine in rigid forms the anti-militarist actions of the working class which are naturally different in different countries."[14]

THE HESITANCY ON the part of the German delegation was not just ideological. The federal election earlier that year had been a disaster for the SPD.

Their vote share only declined 2.7 percent, but the party lost nearly half its Reichstag seats.

The election was seen as a referendum on empire, and the Social Democrats—as the sole opposition to the prevailing imperial foreign policy—were vulnerable. The poor result took on a magnified role, because so much of the party's legitimacy was wrapped up with it moving from strength to strength, in its apparent unstoppable march toward power.

How to proceed next was the question. For radicals, there was no need to break with the strategy of "pure opposition" to bourgeois society: Kautsky thought the 1907 election was proof that the class struggle was sharpening and that the middle class were unstable allies. Mistakes had been made, but they were tactical rather than strategic in nature. To the revisionists, however, the setback was caused by excessive radicalism in all spheres. The working-class vote was intact, but middle-class, progressive voters who had supported the party in 1903 had jumped ship. Throughout 1907, even Bebel felt the need to join Noske in assuring bourgeois critics that the party was not antinational. The Stuttgart Congress had the potential to undo this work.

What made the situation in 1907 especially difficult was the fact that the tactics of the SPD had found imitators on the right. New membership organizations won support for imperialism, as a more populist German nationalism competed with social democracy for the allegiance of workers.

The SPD was largely anticolonial, another of its unique features in the prewar German landscape. The bloody atrocities during the German conquests of its African territories and New Guinea, and later the suppressing of the Herero (1904–1908) and Maji Maji rebellions (1905–1907), were condemned by the party. It is true that Bernstein, editor Joseph Bloch, economist Max Schippel, and a host of other prominent revisionists came to support imperialism, often adopting the idea of a "civilizing mission" popular at the time. But mainstream SPD opinion on the matter was closer to Luxemburg's staunch anticolonialism, and that's how contemporaries perceived the party.[15]

Domestic politics was still the main source of division within the SPD. In the aftermath of the 1907 election, Kautsky staked out consistently radical positions, but he became even more acutely aware of the dangers of a split in the party. By 1910, he began defending the Erfurtian synthesis from challengers on both his left and his right flanks. Luxemburg and likeminded activists on the left had a more active conception of what it would take to win power—that is, through the instigation of class struggle especially through mass strikes, even if it resulted in short-term defeat. Class consciousness was forged and cemented, after all, through action. Kautsky, wary of what failure could bring, thought time was working in social democracy's favor and wanted to postpone the final conflict until victory was certain.

His views, then, were still distinct from the revisionists, who didn't see a need for that conflict, but he moved closer to them on certain parliamentary questions. Whereas after 1907, Kautsky defended the party's radical isolation, after the 1912 elections he saw potential to work with liberals in the Reichstag. Still believing himself the defender of orthodox Marxism, he moved more to the center within the SPD. He would tactically reunite with the Left off and on over the next decade—during which the party would fracture and fail.

IT IS REMARKABLE, in retrospect, how consistently antiwar the SPD majority was before World War I. For decades German Social Democrats risked much for opposing the state and its military: Bebel and the elder Liebknecht faced trial for high treason in 1872; Karl Liebknecht was imprisoned for antiwar writings in 1907; Luxemburg was arraigned in 1914. SPD Reichstag deputies, immune from prosecution, were a reliable source of dissent in a political system lacking it.

Far from moving away from these commitments, as war approached the party embraced an even more strident antiwar spirit. In late 1912, responding to the Balkan War, simultaneous rallies were held in Berlin, London, and Paris. In a dramatic display of internationalism, French socialist

Jean Jaurès visited Berlin to speak against the war in German, while German and British leaders went to London and Paris, respectively. The anti-war demonstrations were the largest ever held by the SPD and took place without support from liberal parties.[16]

The manifesto from the International conference that followed foresaw the Great War's devastation: "The proletariat is conscious of being at this moment the bearer of the entire future of humankind." Its message seemed resolute: "To the capitalist world of exploitation and mass murder, oppose in this way the proletarian world of peace and fraternity of peoples!"[17] But still, in December 1912, the SPD and its counterparts elsewhere in Europe showed that they hadn't completely abandoned the language of "national defense." In the Reichstag, Georg Ledebour and Eduard David, though from opposite wings of the party, both insisted that Germany ought not to uphold its military obligations to Austria-Hungary if it invaded Serbia. They did this, however, while supporting the idea of a defensive alliance with Austria-Hungary against Russia. The principles that would dictate the 1914 war debate were set: mass demonstrations would prevent war; if that failed, the SPD would decide its course based on nature of the conflict.

Some Social Democrats may have predicted that millions would be killed in a continental war, but many German elites saw in a war the chance for quick gains at the expense of their rivals, at home and abroad. Between the Austrian ultimatum to Serbia on July 23, 1914, and the Reichstag war credit vote on August 4, the ruling class decided on war. The working-class movement's position was less clear.

The SPD held to its preventive strategy, with the party initially demanding, as it had in 1912, that the German state restrain Austria and negotiate for peace. Tens of thousands met the call for demonstrations, singing "The Internationale" and proclaiming the unity of all workers, but it was a smaller showing than during the earlier Balkan crisis. The people, like the party, were unprepared for how quickly events would move.[18]

On July 30, the day before Russia mobilized for war, the SPD sent members of its senior leadership to Switzerland with the party treasury.

They were prepared for severe repression if war broke out. Perhaps some knew of Engels's 1889 warning that war would entail "unparalleled devastation" and "the compulsory and universal suppression of our movement." Amid a nationalist upsurge he predicted that the movement "would be overwhelmed, crushed, stamped out by violence." Like Kautsky, Engels saw peace as leading to "almost certain victory" for socialism, but what were his disciples to do when war was inevitable?[19]

When the moment came, they capitulated, fearful of the violent destruction of what they had spent four decades building. Bebel spared his legacy by dying in 1913, but the rest of the leadership was not so lucky. There was dispute over where the party should stand: the fact that Austria was the aggressor seemed to support Chairman Hugo Haase and others who said it was social-democratic policy to oppose war in such a situation, but Ebert could just as compellingly point to Russian mobilization as a threat. The party ended up accepting Wilhelm II's claims that German overtures for peace were being rebuffed by Tsar Nicolas II and acted on that basis.

Seventy-eight out of ninety-two SPD parliamentarians supported funding the war, a decision mirrored by social democrats in other belligerent countries. A minority opposed to the stance led by Liebknecht and Haase nevertheless held to parliamentary norms and voted in bloc with the majority, no doubt confusing the party rank and file about the extent of division within the delegation.

As the kaiser proclaimed, "I no longer know parties, I only know Germans," some SPD members saw an opportunity. The faction around Ludwig Frank explicitly viewed the conflict as a chance to extract democratic reform. As they put it, "We will win suffrage in Prussia by waging a war instead of a general strike." But most of the SPD struck a more conflicted tone, hoping for a rapid peace but asserting that the war was one of self-defense, not conquest. Russian revolutionary Leon Trotsky captured the mood of social democracy's Left, describing August 4, 1914, as "one of the most tragic days" of his life.[20]

The decision of the SPD and other social-democratic parties to support war was not predestined. What was unavoidable were the tensions involved in building a mass party opposed to capitalism while operating within capitalism. Workers wanted more than "pure opposition"; they wanted concrete victories, or else they could lose faith in politics. They also needed to build more professional organizations to represent their interests. But in doing so, a conservative union and party bureaucracy arose that had little interest in opposing an initially popular war or following through on the party's stated goals. It turned out that the revolution wasn't going to make itself, and the majority (many rank-and-file workers included) weren't going to risk everything they had already won to make it.

This is not to say that a different approach was not possible. Institutional measures could have been taken to make the party bureaucracy more democratic and accountable. The trade unions should have perceived the way in which their economic gains would be undermined without radical political reform. The SPD built a strong army, drilled its troops, but waited for its opponent to collapse rather than pressing the offensive.

As the Great War dragged on and its horrific nature became clear, more and more Social Democrats opposed it. But it wasn't until March 1916 that a significant number under Haase's leadership formed a Social Democratic Working Group within the party. It would be another year before the decisive break that saw the creation of an Independent Social Democratic Party (USPD), which united leftists and centrists (and even those revisionists like Bernstein who opposed the war).

The war brought domestic repression and the arrest of leading radicals, making political organizing difficult. Unable to match the size and strength of the SPD, the USPD could do little to end a war that killed millions.

The USPD was itself divided. Most of the party didn't pursue the policy of Lenin's Bolsheviks, who saw the conflict as a reason and a means to agitate for the ruin of all belligerent armies and for worker revolution. Instead, Kautsky and others simply fought for peace.

Luxemburg and Liebknecht, for their part, formed the Spartacus League as a faction within the USPD with a more radical outlook. Later they founded the Communist Party of Germany (KPD). But their effectiveness was limited. When a radical surge took place—as when sailors revolted in Wilhelmshaven and Kiel in 1918 or when soviets emerged throughout Germany (a soviet republic was even proclaimed in Bavaria)—they never were able to shape developments as ably as their Bolshevik counterparts in Russia.

During the German Revolution that followed the nation's defeat in the First World War, the Spartacists faced a question: "Bourgeois democracy or socialist democracy?" They were unable to force their preferred answer. Through decisive and cruel measures—including unleashing right-wing paramilitaries on their former comrades, who murdered Luxemburg, Liebknecht, and scores of others—the Social Democratic Party took power and created a democratic republic, a "bourgeois democracy."

Friedrich Ebert held office until his death in 1925, but despite his best efforts the Weimar Republic would become synonymous with failure. Like the future Communist "workers' state" to its east, the Social Democratic workers' state came to be resented by millions of workers. The SPD only held power briefly in the 1920s, attempting mostly to secure the support of other parties for the young republic. (Even that was far too radical a course for Noske, who broke ranks and backed the conservative war hero Paul von Hindenburg in 1925 and 1932.) Under siege from both left and right, Weimar fell to the horrors of Nazism.

After the Second World War, European social democrats, led by the heirs to Eduard Bernstein, developed what they couldn't after the First: a program to successfully govern the capitalist state. At the same time, Soviet-style socialism came to East Germany from above, with the martyred radical democrats Luxemburg and Liebknecht used as icons of an authoritarian order. In its most formative period, isolated in the harsh conditions of Russia, socialism became synonymous with a bloodied collectivism.

FOUR

THE FEW WHO WON

A DEVOUT POLISH CATHOLIC, Felix Dzerzhinsky was once asked why he was sure God existed. "God is in the heart," the teenager replied. "If I ever come to the conclusion that there is no God, I would put a bullet in my head."

A few years later, he realized just how alone humanity actually was. But instead of turning to a bullet, he found a new faith, vowing "to fight against evil to the last breath" as a revolutionary socialist. By age forty, he was clad in black leather, designing a reign of terror as head of the Soviet Union's secret police.

This story of zealotry fits with the popular image of Bolshevism as a conspiratorial sect, singular and ruthless in purpose. The Bolsheviks took advantage of 1917's democratic upheavals, perverting the noble February Revolution into the excesses of October. That Stalinism had its roots in Bolshevism is no surprise. The extremism of men like Dzerzhinsky, confident the utopia they were building was worth any cost, made it all but certain.

This narrative is neat, and seemingly true. The system that emerged out of the October Revolution was a moral catastrophe. But more than that, it was a tragedy—and tragedies don't need villains.

Consider Dzerzhinsky. His socialism was rooted in the humanist idea that the "present hellish life with its wolfish exploitation, oppression, and violence" could give way to an order "based on harmony, a full life embracing society as a whole." The future executioner suffered for his beliefs—he spent eleven out of his twenty years underground in prison or exile—"in the torments of loneliness, longing for the world and for life."[1]

Poor, tortured, imprisoned, and martyred, the revolutionaries of Russia seemed destined to meet the same fate as radicals elsewhere in Europe. Only they didn't. After he'd spent half a decade in solitary confinement, enduring beatings that permanently disfigured his jaw, Dzerzhinsky's last letter from prison was resolute: "At the moment I am dozing, like a bear in his winter den; all that remains is the thought that spring will come and I will cease to suck my paw and all the strength that still remains in my body and soul will manifest itself. Live I will."

Dzerzhinsky, like the Bolsheviks as a whole, did survive, though many people who ended up in their custody had no such luck. In the merciless environment the party found itself in, socialism became about rationing scarce resources and squeezing labor out of workers and peasants. The socialist sense of history—the fact that the movement was consciously striving for a different world—was a source of many of its triumphs. But in the Russian context it became a way to excuse the terrible human cost of development.

However, the equation of socialism with Stalinism—a common rhetorical tactic among centrists and conservatives—is wrong, and not only outside of Russia. As we'll see, throughout the early Russian Revolution more humane and democratic alternatives within the socialist tradition were fought for, and only defeated through force.

BOTH SIDES OF the Cold War painted Vladimir Lenin and his party as special—unique in their brutality or their model for revolution. But even as an underground movement, it is striking just how ordinary the Bolsheviks were. Lenin saw himself as an orthodox Marxist, trying to adapt the

German Social Democratic Party's (SPD) program to a largely rural and peasant country with a weak civil society and mass illiteracy.[2]

The supposed proto-totalitarian smoking gun, Lenin's 1902 pamphlet *What Is to Be Done?*, does have unusual elements. Lenin calls for professional organizers capable of eluding the police and places special emphasis on the role of print propaganda, for instance. But the pamphlet was not a blueprint for a radically different party; rather, these were necessary tactics for a movement barred from the legal organizing and parliamentary elections pursued by social democrats elsewhere. As Lenin saw it, once tsarism was overthrown, backward Russia and its small working class could develop along Western lines. As he put it in 1899, speaking of the SPD, "We are not in the least afraid to say that we want to imitate the Erfurt Programme; there is nothing bad in imitating what is good."[3]

Siding with the radical Karl Kautsky, Lenin took aim at revisionists like Eduard Bernstein for trying to change "a party of social revolution into a democratic party of social reforms." To be a revolutionary, for Lenin, meant smashing the capitalist state—his was a politics of rupture. But his project, unlike the "Blanquists" he also denounced, was intended to create a workers' movement and place it at the center of political struggle. He did not set out to forge a hardened core of putschists. Lenin's frustration wasn't that workers weren't smart enough to flock to the party, but that socialists were underestimating workers. His goal, following the German example, was a merger of the two currents into a militant socialist workers' movement.

Then perhaps, if not by design, the Bolsheviks were forced by state repression to adopt a military-like structure that they would later take into power. But this claim, too, is dubious, as the Bolsheviks maintained a level of transparency and pluralism few organizations in much more favorable conditions have reached.

Take the Bolshevik "economists," a group Lenin criticized thoroughly in *What Is to Be Done?*. He thought that they, like every other faction of the movement, deserved "to demand the opportunity to express and advocate views." Lenin was hardly a genial interlocutor; like Marx, he was a fan of personal invective. Still, the leader had to deal with not getting his way. Between 1912 and 1914, forty-seven of his articles were rejected by *Pravda*, the "party paper."

Dissent cut through Russian social democracy; no one's marching orders were followed without debate. It wasn't just other currents such as the Mensheviks and Socialist Revolutionaries (SRs), but dozens of shades of opinions among the Bolsheviks themselves.

On important political issues, however, the main wings of Russian social democracy were not far apart. When the Mensheviks and Bolsheviks split in 1903, it was over small points of emphasis, not because of Lenin's supposed call for a professional vanguard party. When the 1905 Revolution arrived, all parts of the movement fought side by side. Most Mensheviks, like most Bolsheviks, opposed the Great War, their clarity on the issue matched by few socialists elsewhere in Europe. In the lead-up to February 1917, they differed on the liberal bourgeoisie—the Mensheviks thought they would lead the first stage of the revolution, the Bolsheviks did not—but agreed that the immediate task of Russian social democracy was overthrowing autocracy, not socialist revolution. Only during the February Revolution did the Bolsheviks start down a different path.

LENIN DIDN'T LEAVE social democracy. It left him. When he first received the news that the SPD had voted for war credits on August 4, 1914, he thought it was capitalist propaganda.

His faith was misplaced. Kautsky wasn't a parliamentarian, but he was present at the war credit debate. He suggested that the SPD abstain from the vote, even as he agreed that Germany was waging a defensive struggle against an eastern threat. Within a year, he changed his tune and vigorously denounced the SPD's pro-war leadership and the German state, but the damage was done.

For more than a century following these events, the Leninist narrative was that Kautsky had been an ideal Marxist until almost the outbreak of

World War I, and that it was his stance on war in 1914 and his opposition to the October Revolution in 1917 that transformed him from revered "Pope of Marxism" to a "great renegade." In his 1939 obituary of the German socialist, Trotsky sounds like a scorned lover: "We remember Kautsky as our former teacher to whom we once owed a good deal, but who separated himself from the proletarian revolution and from whom, consequently, we had to separate ourselves."[4]

Kautsky had shared much with the Russian radicals. "Modern society is ripe for revolution; and the bourgeoisie is not in a position to survive any insurrection." Such a revolution would be won by "a well-disciplined minority, energetic and conscious of the goal." They sound like Lenin's, but these words were Kautsky's.

There was, however, a growing gap between Kautsky's ideas and those of his Russian admirers. His notion of the "dictatorship of the proletariat" differed from Lenin and Trotsky's. Kautsky might have used language similar to theirs in the 1880s, just a decade removed from the Paris Commune and with his party still underground. But his thought evolved. He believed workers would win power through free elections, extend political and civil liberties, and radically reform, not smash, the existing state. Meanwhile, Lenin continued to look for inspiration to the Paris Commune of 1871 and the great revolutions of 1848 and 1789. This was the spirit that spawned the communist movement.[5]

A DECADE BEFORE THE Great War and Kautsky's apostasy, the 1905 Revolution in Russia revealed that Lenin was in step with his era. The "great dress rehearsal" came close to toppling tsarism and gave birth to the soviet (democratic worker councils).

Russia at the time was already pulsing with change. The final decades of the nineteenth century had witnessed rapid economic growth and social advances. Industrial production doubled in the 1890s alone. Horses and carts began to give way to vast railroads and, for a time, Russia even led the world in oil production.[6]

But Russia's development was highly uneven. St. Petersburg's modern factories represented little of life in an empire where, even in its European regions, only one in nine people lived in cities. Though Russia was making progress in absolute terms, it was still falling behind Western Europe. In the countryside, agricultural development advanced at a glacial pace, failing to keep up with huge population growth. Land-hungry peasants pushed eastward from their traditional communes into the steppes. Rural poverty was endemic. With economic stagnation in the countryside and growing but still inchoate capitalist industry in a few cities, scarcity reigned and helped politicize Russia's small working class.

The mass worker protests of 1905 caught the Bolsheviks by surprise. In October, St. Petersburg workers established a soviet to coordinate their actions. The body soon became a kind of workers' parliament, with representation from a range of trade unions and committees. It was essentially a functioning local government, in a struggle with the tsarist regime for legitimacy.

Trotsky, not Lenin, shined brightest in 1905. Neither Menshevik nor Bolshevik, but respected in both camps, he immediately grasped the revolution's significance. During the St. Petersburg Soviet's brief life, the twenty-six-year-old delegate emerged as an unparalleled orator and theorist. By the end of November, he was elected its chair.

The situation by that point was untenable. As feared, Tsar Nicholas II crushed the revolution and reneged on concessions promised to liberal forces. By April 1906, fourteen thousand people had been executed and seventy-five thousand imprisoned.

But the revolutionaries now had a taste of real power. The transformation of Russian social democracy was stunning. Immediately before the 1905 Revolution, the Bolsheviks had just eighty-four hundred members. By the following spring, they could count thirty-four thousand. The Mensheviks also drew thousands to their ranks.

The revolutionary movement finally had something Lenin had been aspiring to for years: a mass base of workers. Attempts to mend the divide between Bolsheviks and Mensheviks would fail, but both factions had a sense that they had entered a new era and that the tsar would soon fall.

But no one came as close as Trotsky to accurately guessing what would happen next. Grasping the implications of 1905, Trotsky refined a novel theory of "permanent revolution." Marxists had traditionally thought that revolution would occur in stages. The first would be "bourgeois-democratic," paving the way for peasant land reform and further urban industrialization, and creating a capitalist republic with freedom of speech and assembly. The new situation would allow social democrats to patiently organize for a second, socialist revolution. The Bolsheviks and Mensheviks agreed on theory but argued over the role liberal capitalists would play. Mensheviks thought they would be at the heart of a bourgeois-democratic revolution, while Lenin believed workers could reconcile their interests with those of peasants and drive the process themselves.

Trotsky foresaw a different scenario. Instead of a bourgeois-democratic revolution, the peasants would defeat the gentry in the countryside, and the workers would conquer capitalists in the cities. This "proletarian-socialist" revolution would merge democratic and socialist ambitions. In underdeveloped Russia, however, after the defeat of the exploiting classes, there would be no material basis for large-scale socialist construction. As a result, the revolution's goals would have to be furthered by an international revolutionary process.

The dramas of 1917 saw Trotsky's vision vindicated, with one key exception: the international revolution didn't come.

TWO YEARS INTO the Great War, three million Russians were dead, the empire's economy was in ruins, and yet the army pushed ahead with futile new offensives. In February 1917, the stalemate on the front was finally broken by its victims.

As in 1905, St. Petersburg (now Petrograd) and its working class led
the way. On International Women's Day, February 23, women textile workers began a strike that spread across the city. By day's end, ninety thousand
workers were involved; by the next day, two hundred thousand. A similar
situation unfolded in Moscow, where workers protested against skyrocketing inflation and bread shortages. Nicholas II refused to make concessions
until he was forced to abdicate on March 1. The Romanov dynasty that had
ruled Russia for three centuries was swept away in a week.

The tsar's fall was almost universally celebrated across the empire.
What to do next was less clear. The Bolsheviks' doctrinal dispute with the
Mensheviks over the liberal bourgeoisie would prove important. Though
the Bolsheviks agreed with their more moderate counterparts that Russia
wasn't yet ready for socialism, they wanted workers and peasants to take
power and carry out the revolution's democratic tasks. But most workers
were instead drawn to the Menshevik call to revive the soviets, which would
assert the interests of the oppressed but not seek to take over the state.

Liberals established a provisional committee to fill the void, but it had
little popular support. On March 1, the day of the tsar's flight, soviet and
liberal leaders came to an agreement for the creation of a new Provisional
Government that would implement a wide range of reforms. Russia would
have full civil liberties, with political prisoners released and the police and
state apparatus transformed.

Important questions about the war, land reform, and elections remained
unresolved, but the February Revolution was among the most sweeping the
world had ever seen. Yet tensions quickly appeared. Sovereign authority
could now be claimed by the worker and soldier soviets *and* by the Provisional Government. Moderate socialists struggled to bridge the gap, believing they had to keep the bourgeoisie within the February consensus.

Russia, after all, seemed far from ready for socialism. It was too underdeveloped, and its working class was a tiny minority. Socialism wasn't
meant to be a way to bypass capitalism but a successor built from its highest point. But those finally released from tyranny weren't going to wait

patiently for Marxist schema to mature. Workers seized factories, and peasants divided up estates. Popular committees sprang up across the country: rank-and-file soldier committees resisted their officers, and peasant organizations oversaw unsanctioned land expropriations. Authority in all its forms was questioned: the aristocracy was gone, but though it was supposedly a "bourgeois revolution," the bourgeoisie was reeling.

In February 1917, there were twenty-four thousand Bolsheviks; within months they were a mass organization ten times that size. For the time being, however, the democratically elected soviets were still dominated by Mensheviks and Socialist Revolutionaries (SRs). Many saw those bodies as having more legitimacy than the Provisional Government. It's not hard to understand why. Prince Georgy Lvov, a link to the old regime, was the nominal head of state, and the conservative Kadets and Octobrists who ran the government were terrified by the revolution that brought them to power. They could pass decrees, try to restore order, and continue the war effort, but few would listen to their commands.

On March 1, the Petrograd Soviet of Workers' and Soldiers' Deputies published its famous Order Number One. It declared that military orders from the Provisional Government were to be carried out "except those which run counter to the orders and decrees issued by the Soviet of Workers' and Soldiers' Deputies." With Order Number One, the soviet demanded a key component of sovereignty. Yet it did not claim to be the functioning authority in the country.

Moderate socialists still had faith in the Provisional Government, which had been recently reconstituted to include more left-wing forces, including Alexander Kerensky, himself a Socialist Revolutionary. The hope was that this alliance would promote calm throughout the country, creating an environment in which socialists could press democratic demands and negotiate an end to the war. For now the fighting would continue, but it was to be strictly "defensive and without annexations."[7]

The Bolsheviks themselves were split on how to relate to the Provisional Government. Returning from Siberian exile in March, Lev Kamenev and Joseph Stalin believed the new republic would stand for years, if not decades, and adjusted their expectations accordingly.

Lenin, still in Swiss exile, was shocked by his party's complacency and organized a return to Russia. The day after his sealed train arrived at Finland Station, he presented his April Theses, in which he reaffirmed his uncompromising antiwar posture and essentially embraced Trotsky's theory of permanent revolution. Like Trotsky, Lenin thought that rather than let the revolution consolidate into a parliamentary republic, socialists should instead push it forward and build "a republic of Soviets of Workers', Agricultural Labourers', and Peasants' Deputies." This wasn't empty rhetoric, given that the soviets had more popular legitimacy than the Provisional Government.

Arguing against the tamer position of Kamenev and Stalin, Lenin said, "No support for the Provisional Government; the utter falsity of all its promises should be made clear." The die was cast—there would be another revolution in 1917.[8]

Trotsky was also in exile when the February Revolution broke out, rousing the "workers and peasants of the Bronx" on the other side of the world. After a perilous voyage home, he was prepared to join the Bolsheviks and play a pivotal role in the events to come.

The reception to Lenin's April Theses among many Bolsheviks was cool at first, but it did immediately find some popular support. Lenin also had an ally in the young Nikolai Bukharin, then on the left of the party.

The Bolsheviks were still split, between those like Lenin and Bukharin who were planning for insurrection and those like Kamenev, Alexei Rykov, Viktor Nogin (who had long wanted to reunite with the Mensheviks), and Gregory Zinoviev who had a more moderate perspective. The latter wanted to replace the Provisional Government with a broad coalition of socialist parties.

Lenin also didn't want a premature uprising that would leave the Bolsheviks isolated and vulnerable, like the Communards of Paris in 1871.

As late as June 1917, he would stress that: "even in the soviets of both capitals, not to speak now of the others, we are an insignificant minority.... The majority of the masses are wavering but still believe the SRs and Mensheviks."[9]

But the party's radical appeals were taking hold. Workers and soldiers flocked to the cause, and some, inspired by slogans such as "All Power to the Soviets," launched spontaneous armed demonstrations in Petrograd against the Provisional Government in July. A crackdown followed. Trotsky was imprisoned for a time, Lenin fled to Finland, publications were banned, and the death penalty was reintroduced for mutinous soldiers. With the blessing of the Menshevik-SR majority, Kerensky's Provisional Government claimed more power for itself.

During his two months of hiding in Finland, Lenin finished a book he titled *The State and Revolution*. His argument with reformists was premised on a simple point: "the working class cannot simply lay hold of the state machinery and wield it for its own purposes." Like Marx and Engels, he saw the state as a tool of class oppression. A tiny minority used it to rule over a great majority. The state was, unsurprisingly, bloody and repressive. Under the dictatorship of the proletariat and its allies, however, the great majority would repress a tiny minority of exploiters. There would be some violence, but by comparison to the prevailing order it would be minimal.

"We are not Utopians," Lenin writes. "We do not 'dream' of dispensing at once with all administration, with all subordination." But as socialism triumphed, the need for a repressive apparatus would dissipate and the state would wither away. Many have portrayed *The State and Revolution* as a false flag—a libertarian socialist document from the father of socialist authoritarianism. But it was a sincere work. It did, however, indicate how simple Lenin appeared to believe constructing a socialist state (and having that state wither away) would be. In power, the Bolsheviks would learn otherwise and horrifically transform themselves in the process.[10]

In August, it was the Right's turn to revolt. General Lavr Kornilov, sensing the instability of the Provisional Government, attempted a coup. With no one else to call on for help, Kerensky appealed to the Petrograd Soviet. It easily beat back Kornilov through strikes and encouraging desertion among the general's soldiers, with the Bolsheviks playing a decisive role. The party's prestige reached a new highpoint, and Kerensky was forced to release its captured leaders. In late September, Trotsky once again became chairman of the Petrograd Soviet, which was now controlled by a Bolshevik majority. The previously small, radical party could now claim a popular mandate. The stage was set for the October Revolution.

Yet the Mensheviks and SRs had one last chance to head off a Bolshevik takeover. The mood in the country had swung even further to the left. It was clear the Provisional Government had no independent means to defend itself in a country that now had six hundred radicalized soviets. Among the Mensheviks, who were hemorrhaging support to the Bolsheviks, a left wing under Julius Martov was gaining strength. Martov was resolutely antiwar and in favor of more sweeping reforms than the Provisional Government could offer. His position was nearly indistinguishable from that of the moderate Bolsheviks.

The Mensheviks and SRs could have stepped in and seized power as part of a broad front of socialist parties to create a constituent assembly and a framework for reforms. The Bolsheviks could have formed a loyal opposition to such a government, or even joined it, as Kamenev and Zinoviev wanted. Yet instead the Mensheviks and SRs clung to the sinking Provisional Government, and even if they hadn't, the two parties were internally divided on the war. To many workers and soldiers, Lenin and Trotsky's insurrection seemed like the only way forward.

With the Petrograd Soviet now under their control, Lenin finally convinced the Bolshevik Central Committee to adopt his plans. The "single greatest event in human history," as socialists called it for decades afterward, was anticlimactic. On October 24, Bolshevik units occupied rail stations, telephone exchanges, and the state bank. The following day they surrounded the Winter Palace and arrested Kerensky's cabinet ministers. One-sixth of the world had been conquered in the name of the proletariat with barely a drop of blood spilled.

Did Lenin lead a coup? Though certainly not as spontaneous as the February Revolution, October represented a genuine popular revolution led by industrial workers, allied with elements of the peasantry. After the Kornilov coup, the Bolsheviks could claim a mandate for the action. They won support through their straightforward call for "peace, land, and bread." The Mensheviks demanded patience from the long-suffering masses; the Bolsheviks made concrete promises. Following through would be another matter, but the Bolsheviks were the force most militantly trying to fulfill the February Revolution's frustrated goals.

In the first months after October, the character of the new regime was not yet clear. The Bolsheviks didn't initially seek a one-party state. Circumstances, as well as their post-October decisions, conspired to create one. Immediately after the revolution, it fell to the Second Congress of Soviets to ratify the transfer of power from the Provisional Government. From 318 soviets, 649 delegates were elected to the body. Reflecting a dramatic shift in popular mood, 390 of them were Bolshevik and 100 Left SRs (Socialist Revolutionaries who supported toppling the Kerensky government).

Now transformed into a small minority, the Right SRs and Mensheviks attacked the October Revolution. Even Martov denounced the Bolshevik "coup d'état," though he also put forth a resolution calling for an interim all-Soviet government and plans for a constituent assembly. Many Bolsheviks supported the motion, and it carried unanimously. Martov's plan would have created the broad socialist government that many had sought in September—only now, in a more radical moment, it would be pressured into ending the war and bringing about land reform.

But as in September, the Right SRs and the majority of Mensheviks refused to go along. They walked out of the Congress, ceding the revolution's future to the Bolsheviks. Martov still wanted a compromise and tried to start negotiations for the creation of a coalition socialist government. But just two hours later, with the moderates no longer in the hall, the Bolshevik mood hardened. "The rising of the masses of the people requires no justification," Trotsky lectured his former comrade bitingly from the floor. "No, here no compromise is possible. To those who have left and to those who tell us to do this we must say: You are miserable bankrupts, your role is played out. Go where you ought to go: into the dustbin of history!"

Here is Trotsky epitomized—rhetorically masterful but tragically overconfident in the ordination of history. The delegates erupted into applause. Martov began to leave with the other left Mensheviks. A young Bolshevik confronted him on the way out, upset that a great champion of the working class would abandon its revolution. Martov stopped before the exit and turned to him: "One day you will understand the crime in which you are taking part."[11]

Almost exactly twenty years to the day, that worker, Ivan Akulov, was murdered in a Stalinist purge.

"WE WILL NOW build the socialist order." Lenin's words just after the revolution suggested a radical course, but in fact the Bolsheviks moved cautiously. Though they had popular support in a few major cities, they knew it would be a struggle to assert authority across a massive, mostly peasant country.

They tried to make good on their stated aims. Against the old elites' resistance, worker control over production was expanded. Homosexuality was decriminalized; divorce and reproductive rights benefited women. Land rights were expanded to peasants, anti-Semitism was vigorously opposed by the state, and steps were taken to allow national self-determination in the former empire Lenin called "a prison house of nations."

When it came to the industrial sector, Lenin's vision of worker control wasn't syndicalist ("the ridiculous transfer of the railways to the railwaymen, or the tanneries to the tanners"); in the long run, he looked to more coordinated *class-wide* methods of ownership. In the short term, he wrote, "the immediate introduction of socialism in Russia is impossible," and argued instead for worker oversight of management, alongside the nationalization of key sectors. That wasn't the limit of his horizons, though. Lenin was impressed by the wartime economy in capitalist states. If planning in the service of chaos was already a reality, why shouldn't planning in the service of human need—under the watch of democratic soviets—be possible?[12]

The push for mass nationalizations came from the grassroots. A contradictory late November order gave factory committees a legal mandate to have a say in production and distribution, though still asserted management's right to manage. Not surprisingly, it fueled disorder and further hampered production. Workers took over factories on their own accord. In many cases, these were honest attempts to restore production after capitalist sabotage or flight; at other times, workers responded to the chaos by hoarding supplies for private use or sale.

Within months the Bolsheviks would have to clamp down on such actions, as their immediate task was restoring basic productivity and order. It's clear that the government intended to maintain a mixed economy—that is, a continued role for private capital—at least until its rescue by revolutions elsewhere in Europe.

But the confusion of the initial postrevolution months was exacerbated by the fact that Bolsheviks never clearly delineated who held power among the overlapping jurisdictions of factory committees and trade unions and a sprawling complex of soviets, not to mention the central state. Centralization and the blurring of party and state were simple, pragmatic ways to resolve the dilemmas.

On the question of the war, too, the Bolsheviks' plans ran into complications. The situation was urgent. Though fighting was subsiding in 1917, between the February and October Revolutions one hundred thousand Russians died on the Eastern Front. The Bolsheviks put out a call to all the belligerents for a "just and democratic peace." If other nations refused, Lenin was confident that "the workers of these countries will understand the duty which now rests upon them of saving mankind from the horrors and consequences of war."[13]

The decree was ignored by the other Entente powers, and, for the moment, so was the call for revolution. Negotiations with the Central Powers began. Against Lenin's advice, the Bolshevik Central Committee turned down an initial peace offer. Left Communists led by Bukharin wanted to continue the war and fan the flames of revolt across Europe. It was a grave miscalculation. Taking advantage of the strife within the young socialist state, the German and Austrian armies advanced, seizing a huge swathe of land from the Baltic to the Black Sea. The Treaty of Brest-Litovsk that followed involved painful concessions, cutting the Soviet state from key agricultural and industrial regions and putting it in a weaker position to deal with growing civil unrest.

Yet as Trotsky put it, "Having mounted the saddle, the rider is obliged to guide the horse—at the risk of breaking his neck." The Bolshevik government rode on. As they imagined it, the survival of the first workers' state would be a boon to the revolutionary movements that would take power in more advanced countries. These states would then come to the Bolsheviks' rescue and help rebuild the country as part of a broader proletarian confederation.[14]

It wasn't as fantastical as it sounds today: this was an era of upheaval. Not long after the October Revolution, German communists launched a series of ill-fated revolts, trying to follow the Russian example. Newly liberated Finland saw its democratically elected socialist government dislodged in a bloody civil war. In 1919, a Hungarian Soviet Republic briefly took power. Two red years of factory occupations and mass strikes shook Italy. Soviets appeared even in Ireland for a time.

The Bolsheviks still hoped for a breakthrough via the newly formed Communist International (Comintern), an organization that attempted to create Bolshevik sister parties in other countries. Yet it was becoming clear that salvation would not come from abroad. Lenin's party had gambled in the hopes of extending the February Revolution's gains and ending not just one grisly war but all future ones. The gamble failed. Yet the most credible alternatives to their leadership now appeared to be at best a right-wing military dictatorship and at worst a form of Judeocidal fascism. Amid unrest and confusion, the actions the Bolsheviks took to survive would only exacerbate the party's worst tendencies.

ATTEMPTS TO UNDERMINE the Bolshevik government started the day it took power in Petrograd. The White movement was the primary challenger, an unholy alliance spanning the political spectrum from right Mensheviks and SRs to extreme nationalists and monarchists. Thirteen thousand American troops along with British, Canadian, French, Greek, Italian, and Japanese forces joined the Whites to aid their brutal domestic opposition. Facing long odds, Trotsky oversaw the creation of a Red Army and managed to triumph in a five-year civil war that claimed nine million lives.

The moment called for hardened men like Felix Dzerzhinsky. He was installed as the head of the newly formed Russian secret police, the Cheka, and he would order his men to collect information on state enemies from across the Soviet Union. Interrogations were quick, and those who failed to dispel suspicion were stood up against a wall and shot. With Lenin's blessing, the Cheka grew to two hundred thousand strong and led a Red Terror in which half as many were killed.

These horrifying acts were carried out amid history's most destructive civil war and a White Terror that murdered more than a hundred thousand, many of them Jews and other minorities. Many Bolsheviks, too, seemed tormented by their actions. Dzerzhinsky lamented that "I have spilt so much blood I no longer have any right to live." Which is, of course, not to excuse the Cheka's actions or the government that signed off on them. There were few external controls on the Cheka's arrests and executions. Collective punishment, state terror, and intimidation—all these were "exceptional" measures that became the norm during Stalin's reign.[15]

During the civil war, the Bolsheviks blurred the line between actions taken out of necessity and those performed out of virtue. There was no clear bedrock of rights and protections that Soviet citizens could claim once the emergency of war subsided. Open debate within the newly formed Communist Party would continue for some time and included factions pushing for democracy and worker power. But the broader political culture of engagement and contestation—sustained by a network of parties and newspapers—that had survived underground for decades under tsarism would never return.

A central problem was the lack of clear agreement on what the dictatorship of the proletariat should look like. The Bolsheviks focused on seizing power, not exercising it. Aside from vague sketches, they hadn't thought much about politics *after* revolution. With the exploiting classes removed from power, wouldn't the proletariat need a socialist theory of jurisprudence or institutional checks on power? Finding themselves in an unprecedented situation, the revolutionaries made it up as they went along.

COMMUNIST POLICY DURING the civil war reflected both practical necessity and ideological zeal. Years of conflict had disrupted agricultural production. Peasants had minimal incentive to send what little they still produced to the cities: there was a shortage of consumer goods, and grain prices continued to decline in relation to those goods. A black market naturally developed. Like the tsarist state and Provisional Government before them, the Communists tried to stamp it out.

They were even more ruthless, applying their class analysis to the countryside, which they saw as divided between poor peasants, middle peasants, and wealthy kulaks. The Bolsheviks hoped to maintain their support among the two former groups by focusing their actions on the latter, but divisions on the ground were not clear, and the presence of armed requisition squads searching for hoarders only further disincentived production. Despite the state's energetic efforts at repression and banning of private trade, it was largely thanks to the black market that Soviet cities survived the civil war.[16]

Communist industrial policy also shifted in the "War Communism" period (1918–1921). The government nationalized the entire economy, instituted rationing, and imposed strict labor discipline. Not even the moderate visions of worker control survived the return to one-man management in factories. Shortages of parts and raw materials slowed production to a crawl. Highly ideological initiatives, like the attempt to construct moneyless budgets, only contributed to the economic catastrophe. By 1921, Russian industry was less than one-third its prewar size.

The Soviet state's political base was decimated by that point, too. Many industrial workers died in the civil war, while others left starving cities and took their chances in the countryside. How to restore Russian industry, and how to revive the worker-peasant alliance that sparked the revolution—these were the questions of the day.

The New Economic Policy (NEP, 1921–1928) was an attempt at an answer. The state retained control of the commanding heights of the economy—large industries, banking, and foreign trade—but legalized markets elsewhere. A tax on food producers replaced counterproductive forced requisitions, with peasants free to dispose of their goods how they wished once the tax was paid. The goal was to replace coercion with accumulation through gradual, unequal exchange. That would provide the necessary peasant surplus to expand industry. Rather than forced collectivization, many NEP supporters also looked to the voluntary creation of agricultural cooperatives that, in time, would outcompete what they saw as needlessly inefficient traditional peasant production.

Politically, however, the NEP period was one of hardening, not liberalization. Party leaders feared that the peasantry's newfound economic power might morph into political opposition. Not only rival parties but even internal Bolshevik factions were banned in 1921. There was still debate within the party, but the Bolsheviks made clear that they would not step away from power. For the moment, they did not seek to censor or control the arts and intellectual life. But it had been easy to fall into a one-party state during the civil war. Then, with the war over, the task of reconstruction required people willing to pursue decisive action. One such leader, Stalin, rose to party general secretary in 1922.

Lenin was wary of certain developments. But though he decried the party-state elite's abuses and excesses, he failed to see that democratic reform was the only possible counterbalance. Approaching death, he warned specifically about Stalin, encouraging the party congress to remove him, but his wishes went unfulfilled. Once Lenin was gone, Stalin used his position to target the supporters of his rival, Trotsky. Still, Stalin was not yet in total control.

Debate within the party crystalized into three main camps: the left opposition of Trotsky, Stalin's supporters, and those around Bukharin, who now found himself on the party's right.

Trotsky pushed for party democracy and other antibureaucratic measures, faster industrialization and collectivization at home, and aggressive revolutionary exhortations abroad. Bukharin was more cautious, seeking to continue slowly "riding into socialism on a peasant nag." Stalin triangulated between the two positions, displaying a political savvy few knew the Georgian possessed.[17]

Trotsky saw the real danger not in Stalin's bureaucratic centrism but in the risk that Bukharin's program would accidentally bring about the restoration of capitalism. Bukharin, too, took far too long to see Stalin as a threat. Yet even had they united, Stalin might very well have still won out:

he applauded the party men Trotsky criticized. Trotsky's call for industrial rejuvenation also hardly won him goodwill among Russia's peasant majority. And without the support of the bureaucracy or the peasantry—and with so many of the old Bolshevik workers dead or exhausted—on what basis could Trotsky hope to defeat Stalin? Confidence in the dialectic of history wasn't enough.

Trotsky was removed from the Central Committee by Stalin in late 1927 and sent into exile shortly after. Until his murder in Mexico thirteen years later, he remained Stalinism's greatest critic. Yet he couldn't admit that any part of the system he so despised had its genesis in the repression that he had helped engineer during the civil war.

DESPITE ALL THE political turmoil, the NEP worked. By 1926, Soviet industry had surpassed prewar levels—a remarkable turnaround from just five years prior. What to do with this new wealth was hotly debated. Should the nation invest in agricultural improvements and light industry or heavy industry? These choices weren't just technical. For a party that grounded its legitimacy in an industrial proletariat, continuing along the more peasant-oriented NEP route had deep political implications.[18]

With the left opposition eliminated and his erstwhile ally Bukharin marginalized, Stalin was free to answer these questions as he saw fit. For his part, he was growing frustrated with the NEP. Under Stalin's direction, the price of industrial goods increased, yet grain prices were kept low. Peasants, naturally, clung to their stock. Periodic crises of this kind occurred throughout the 1920s, as industrial and agricultural prices fell out of sync.

In the past, these problems had been alleviated through price adjustments and other policy changes. This time, however, Stalin made no such efforts. Instead he sent police to commandeer legally produced and traded grain. Local officials who followed existing laws were dismissed. A new period of coercion against every layer of the peasantry was inaugurated. Stalin wanted a "revolution from above." The first show trials took place, and the first Five Year Plan was introduced. It called for the tripling of industrial output and investment.

And then, without warning, millions were forcefully collectivized in massive farms starting in 1928. Planners thought this would permanently solve food supply issues. It had the opposite effect: production fell dramatically, and scapegoats had to be found. Collective punishment returned, not just against supposedly wealthy kulaks but now also against "ideological kulaks," that is, those who opposed the policy. At least six million perished in famine (1932–1933), and millions more would spend their lives in a vast network of forced-labor camps.

Many resisted the new serfdom. Stalin's own wife, Nadezhda Allilu-yeva, committed suicide in 1932 to protest the policies. But there was no serious challenge to the dictator. Within a decade, a once-vibrant, fractious party became a monolithic sect.

Yet if we can look away from the human toll, if only for a moment, we can see that the Five Year Plan was a success on its own terms. The Soviet Union made incredible advances, largely in spite of forced collectivization rather than because of it. State planning led to a rapid rise in GDP, capital accumulation, and consumption. Of course, the economic breakthrough was accompanied by renewed, and even more deadly, political terror. A campaign of mass murder began in 1936, with thousands purged from the Communist Party, including lifelong Bolsheviks. Many of them were imprisoned as counterrevolutionaries, forced to confess to elaborate plots, and then executed.

Stalin had used a food shortage to transform the Soviet Union from an authoritarian state into a horrific totalitarian regime unlike any the world had ever seen. His Soviet Union did help win the war against Nazism, but for every action Stalin took to defeat fascism, he took another to undermine the antifascist struggle—supporting the disastrous Third Period policy that directed Communists to see social democrats as their primary enemy, purging the Red Army of capable officers, ignoring news of imminent Nazi invasion. At the end of the Second World War, the Soviet regime was deeply conservative, pursuing great-power policies on a scale even the tsars couldn't have imagined, along with episodes of mass ethnic cleansing. Under Stalin, the worldwide Communist movement became a tool of Russian national interests rather than one of working-class emancipation.

Dzerzhinsky, who fell to a heart attack in 1926, anguished over every execution order he signed. He was replaced by men with no such compunction.[19]

AFTER STALIN DIED in 1953, the Soviet system changed profoundly. Stalin's command economy remained intact, but the bureaucrats who now ruled the country remained haunted by the terror that had cut through their ranks. The new order was grey and repressive but capable, for a time, of delivering peace and stability and of making gains for society's most downtrodden. Yet the ruling elite ultimately had no interest in building a free civil society from which socialist democracy might have sprung.

The Soviet Union's centrally planned economy, which had allowed it to catch up with the West, began to show strain. Soviet technocrats were remarkably successful considering the enormity of their task, but the inefficiencies of the system fueled popular resentment. Back in the nineteenth century, Alexis de Tocqueville had argued that the most dangerous time for a bad government was when it tried to mend its ways. Mikhail Gorbachev's years in office revealed the truth of the claim. His attempts to renovate the system only undermined the coercion that held it together.

With hindsight we can see that both the Mensheviks and the Bolsheviks were wrong in 1917. The Mensheviks' faith in Russian liberals to carry out sweeping democratic transformations was misplaced, as were the Bolsheviks' hopes for world revolution and a leap from the kingdom of necessity to the kingdom of freedom. Having seen over ten million killed in a capitalist war, and living in an era of upheaval, the Bolsheviks can be forgiven for trying to chart a course to a better world.

What is less forgivable is that a model built from errors and excesses, forged in the worst of conditions, came to be synonymous with the socialist ideal itself. Rather than a democratic movement ready to deliver on the radical promise of the Enlightenment, socialism became associated with stifling authoritarianism and an increasingly sclerotic planned economy. Across the world, Communist movements, at least when in opposition, did find themselves on the right side of battles over civil rights, social justice, and colonialism. But in power, following the Soviet model, they instituted new forms of oppression.

The mature Soviet system was a form of authoritarian collectivism in a world still largely dominated by capitalist production. But over the course of the twentieth century many of those capitalist societies would see themselves transformed by attempts to deliver doses of socialism *within* capitalism. In fact, a few hundred miles to the west of Moscow, democratic socialism came close to becoming a reality.

FIVE

THE GOD THAT FAILED

I N 1976, SWEDISH prime minister Olof Palme remarked that there were two paths for socialists: "Either to return to Stalin and Lenin, or take the road that joins the tradition of social democracy." As the leader of the state that embodied the latter, his choice was obvious. The Swedish model had such prestige that even a Gaullist like French president Georges Pompidou said his ideal society was "Sweden—with a bit more sun."[1]

But though the divergent paths of socialism could not have seemed starker in Palme's day, it wasn't always so. In the immediate aftermath of the Russian Revolution, significant social-democratic minorities joined communist splits, but most social democrats rejected insurrection and accommodated themselves to the democratic republic as the political form for their ambitions. At the same time, almost all these social democrats were still doctrinally Marxist and shared a horizon of socialism. For most that meant a nationalized economy, where the tyranny of the market gave way to rational planning. They wanted to bring about a successor system to capitalism and doubted how much things could be meddled with while within capitalism.

Social democracy never achieved its desired ends, but the reforms it brought about proved successful far beyond expectation. Sweden in the 1970s was not simply the most livable society in history; it was also the

European country where, after World War II, socialists got the furthest along in undermining capital's power. While capitalists worried about Nikita Khrushchev's shoe-banging promises to bury the West, the greatest threat to free market capitalism was not in Russia but in Scandinavia, where the combination of a universal welfare state, full employment, and centralized unions gave labor enormous power. Swedish trade unions even came out with a proposal for wage-earner funds in 1976 that would have slowly socialized private firms. How Sweden's social democrats got to that point, and why their experiment eventually fell apart, is an unlikely, instructive story.

Yet to understand the success of postwar Sweden, we need to first understand the failures of interwar social democracy and the important lesson they offer about the pitfalls socialists encounter when governing without a plan to achieve economic and political change.

EUROPEAN SOCIALISTS WERE presented with the chance to move from opposition to power more quickly than many imagined. They came out of World War I with a great deal of legitimacy—sometimes, as in the case of Germany, because elites were discredited, in others, owing in part to their wartime support for the national cause. As Karl Kautsky put it in 1924, "We had learned how to be an opposition" before the war. Now "we had to take over Government, and that in the fullest sense; in industry, in the localities, in the State." But his party, like other socialists through the interwar years, ruled only through minority or coalition governments.[2]

Left parties had varying success pushing through democratic reforms. They tried to remove any existing barriers to universal suffrage and democratize upper houses of parliament but stopped short of deeper reforms. Surviving monarchies across Europe were stripped of their political power. In line with his predecessor Jean Jaurès, French socialist Léon Blum saw the republican state as a tool to "define, protect, and guarantee the condition of the working class."[3]

The radical dream—replacing capitalism with a socialist economy operating for the common good—was still alive. In the immediate postwar
years, strike waves created fertile terrain for new demands, and with the
onset of the Great Depression, capitalist collapse became a reality. Na-
tionalizing big firms and new planning measures would be a first step. But
social democrats only had a vague idea of what they wanted to do.

Indeed, outside of France, no firms were nationalized by interwar social democracy (despite socialists participating in eight other West European governments). Instead, socialists formed commissions to study the
subject, grappling for the first time with the technical difficulties of constructing a new political economy. Not much resulted from these commissions, and even Kautsky was forced to admit within a few years that "the
creation of a socialistic organization is therefore not so simple a process as
we used to think."[4]

The 1929–1931 British Labour government under Ramsay MacDonald
was the most extreme example of interwar futility. Labour had long been
more moderate than many of its European counterparts; the party eschewed
Marxism and from the beginning operated within a liberal-constitutional
framework. It was a party driven by trade unions' interests, and it never had
the same radical ideological influences as the German SPD. Labour was refused admittance into the Second International for years for its emphasis on
class collaboration, but it took a turn to the left after the Great War. Clause
IV of its constitution, adopted in 1918, called for "the common ownership of
the means of production, distribution and exchange."

The party's second stint in power was in 1929. In the 1923 general
election, Labour won over a million fewer votes than the Conservative
Party but was able to form a minority government with Liberal support.
The experiment only lasted ten months, and with less than a third of Parliament, MacDonald was unable to pass anything other than minor education, housing, and employment reforms. A minority government always
runs on borrowed time, but Labour also had to contend with a red-baiting

Conservative campaign challenging its mild diplomatic overtures to the young Soviet Union.

In 1929, Labour ran on a platform calling for public works construction and a reduction in the workweek to combat unemployment. It was rewarded with a 136-seat gain, making it the leading party in Parliament, though it was short of a majority. Again Labour was dependent on Liberal Party backing.

MacDonald's second ministry was formed in June 1929, just a few months before the start of the Great Depression. The timing couldn't have been worse for Labour's reform agenda. As unemployment rose, the party leadership clung to a rigid economic orthodoxy rather than expanding a public works program. The leaders wanted to reassure markets, and they faced rising inflation and a growing deficit. Advocating austerity, MacDonald reasoned that inflation was a more acute threat than unemployment, and that maintaining free trade and "the strictest regard" to the prevailing economic wisdom would in time allow the unemployed to be reabsorbed into industry. Their urgent task was to avoid shipwrecking democracy "on the hard rock of finance."

MacDonald himself came from humbler origins than any British prime minister, then or since, but he clashed with the trade unions and saw himself as a responsible steward of an entire society, not just a class. Some Labour parliamentarians closer to the unions opposed cuts to unemployment benefits and welfare, advocating increased state planning and spending instead. Though they had far different political aims from MacDonald's, most of the extraparliamentary Left shared the party leadership's belief that not much could be done through government. "No matter how able, how sincere, and how sympathetic the Labour men and women may be who undertake to administer capitalism, capitalism will bring their undertaking to disaster," an article in the Socialist Party of Great Britain's *Socialist Standard* would say.[5]

The MacDonald government governed without attempting to bring about a socialist alternative and without belief that it could reform the existing system. At best, it reassured workers that they alone would not be asked to sacrifice in an era of scarcity, but that fatalism spelled electoral disaster in the 1931 general election.

It was the economist John Maynard Keynes, a liberal who believed socialists were well-intentioned idiots, who presented the best approach of the time to taming capitalism. The methods laid out in his 1936 work, *The General Theory of Employment, Interest and Money*, once implemented, would help spur employment, ensure productive investment, and mitigate crises. Before the Keynesian revolution, the reigning classical theory claimed that cyclical swings in output and employment would be self-adjusting—as aggregate demand fell, production and employment would decline, along with prices and wages. Lower inflation and wages would then encourage capitalists to make employment-generating capital investments, restoring growth. Any interference in that cycle would only prolong agony for workers. The Great Depression, however, was not going away. Wages were low, but unemployment remained high. Keynes advocated a countercyclical fiscal response: deficit spending, tax cuts, and other measures to stimulate aggregate demand during a recession, and tax increases and spending cuts when times were good.

During the MacDonald government, however, though Keynes was around, there was not yet a developed Keynesian alternative. Just as the Lassalle-inspired workers in the nineteenth century clung to a belief in an "iron law of wages" that limited the gains of trade unionism, it would be a struggle to disabuse the twentieth-century workers' movement of orthodox economics. Two years after its sympathetic remark on the "sincere" effort of MacDonald's Labour Party, the *Socialist Standard* would look back on the experience of government as definitive proof that "it is not possible for the Labour Party or any other party to administer capitalism in such a way that the workers' problems can be solved within the framework of the existing system."[6]

The Popular Front government of French socialist leader Léon Blum (1936–1937) was more determined than MacDonald's to deliver change.

French socialists had lost much of their industrial base to the new communist movement but were still very much Marxists. Rebuilding the party's
infrastructure throughout the 1920s, Blum grappled with the question of
why and under what conditions a socialist would enter government. He distinguished between the "exercise of power" (taking office to prepare the
groundwork for socialism) and the "conquest of power" (the actual disman-
tling of capitalism). In the end, Blum settled for "the occupation of power,"
to keep it out of the grasp of fascists.

When the Jewish radical Blum rose to power in 1936, the anti-Semitic
politician Xavier Vallat complained, "For the first time this ancient Gallo-
Roman land will be governed by a Jew." Just before becoming prime
minister, Blum was dragged from a car and beaten, nearly to death, by a
right-wing mob. A picture of him, heavily bandaged with swollen features,
appeared on the March 9, 1936, cover of *Time* magazine.

Reactionaries hated Blum both for being a Jew and for being a socialist. He could have complained that his immediate ambitions were not so
shocking. The French Communist Party supported the Blum government,
but against his wishes and those of its own leadership, it was pressured by
Moscow to avoid playing a direct role in the government.

Under the sway of the Comintern's Third Period strategy, from the
summer of 1928 until a year or two after the rise of Nazism in 1933, the
Communist parties had seen reformist social democrats as their primary
enemy. They even went as far as to call them "social fascists." But by 1934,
relations between socialists and communists in France had become more
fraternal.

In a dramatic about-face, the Comintern began seeking alliances—
"popular fronts"—with other left movements where possible. The justification for forsaking Blum's government in 1936 was not leftist purity. In
fact, Stalin was worried that Communist involvement would scare away the
centrist Radical Party's support for the Popular Front.

The election of Blum's socialist government, however, unleashed a
massive wave of industrial action. Over two million workers took part in

strikes, occupying factories and paralyzing production. Marceau Pivert, leader of the Socialist Party's radical Left, proclaimed that "everything is possible" in the new environment. Business leaders appealed to Blum to restore order. The result was a series of reforms, the Matignon Accords, which granted workers the legal right to strike, made it easier for them to form unions, and offered large wage increases. French workers enjoyed unemployment insurance and two weeks of paid vacation. Exhausted but overjoyed, millions flocked to the countryside and the sea for the first time that summer. The dignity these reforms afforded to working people was undeniable. Though they were the product of grassroots rebellion, not Blum's program, they couldn't have been implemented without the Popular Front in power.

The reforms also contained the seeds of their undoing. The upsurges of May and June 1936 triggered capital flight and a business counteroffensive over the implementation of the reforms. With political instability growing, Blum's middle-class coalition partners abandoned the fight. The leader had neither the support nor the resolve to pursue more radical measures, or to offer adequate aid to his fellow socialist-republicans fighting a bloody civil war against fascists in Spain. Blum was pushed out of power for the last time in 1938, all the while pleading that he had attempted to be a "loyal manager of capitalism."[7]

BLUM MIGHT HAVE been selling his reforms and radical vision short. But unable to protect its policies, the Popular Front in France was little more successful, in the end, than the first two British Labour Party governments. It was only in Sweden that interwar socialists were able to mount a serious challenge to fiscal orthodoxy. Swedish economists had long pursued heterodox economic ideas, and starting in the 1930s, the Swedish Social Democratic Party (SAP) put them into practice.

Accounts of the rise of social democracy in Sweden often focus on the country's exceptional features. Its civic culture, limited state repression, and even racial homogeneity are commonly invoked. But on the whole, the country's Left faced similar challenges to its counterparts elsewhere; it just managed to find ways to overcome them. One relevant difference was that the nation underwent industrialization relatively late, in the 1870s. It was another decade later before the first trade unions were formed, meaning that advocates of industrial unionism who would go on to form the Swedish Trade Union Confederation in 1898 didn't have to contend with powerful, more conservative craft unions.

The late start meant that Swedish unionism developed under the ideological influence of socialism—the SAP was formed along with the creation of the Second International in 1889. The party's founders were drawn to socialism through the example of movements in Denmark and Germany, and the ideology quickly took root in Sweden. Socialists faced the intransigent opposition of elites, with a 1902 *New York Times* article describing battles between workers and capitalists and fears of the "dreaded red flag" flying in a Sweden that was only rivaled by Russia as "the most feudal and oligarchical country in Europe." Sweden was described similarly in SAP literature as an "armed poorhouse."[8]

Sweden did not grant universal male suffrage until the early twentieth century, meaning that like the Bolsheviks, Swedish socialists were forced to focus most of their initial efforts on the shop floor rather than in parliament. In the political struggle for civil reforms, socialists proved themselves abler than the country's liberals. As in Germany, the limited power of elected office also papered over potential differences between a would-be parliamentarist Right and more radical forces. Yet in Sweden, under the leadership of Hjalmar Branting, the Social Democrats were able to maintain a relatively stable broad tent and engage in productive coalition work with liberal and agrarian forces.

Despite some reformist inclinations, from early on the Swedish movement was built on socialist ideological grounds: it advocated for policies that bridged gaps between craft and industrial workers, and it put emphasis on uplifting the most poorly paid. Social Democrats consistently prioritized universal programs—of benefit to both the poor and farmers—and not just the narrow interests of workers. Instead of pursuing shortcuts in their early years in opposition, Sweden's socialists began to build a hegemony more durable than that of other Second International parties.

By the 1920s, things were going according to plan: the struggle for *political* democracy had been largely successful, and as a result the party had a growing electoral mandate. Early SAP minority governments, however, proved unable to usher in phase two—the winning of *social* democracy. That began to change in 1932, when the party embarked on a near half century of uninterrupted rule. The SAP had campaigned on an expansion of public works and more state intervention in the economy, and after taking power began to implement some of the countercyclical policies forsaken by socialists elsewhere.

The real breakthrough, however, came later in the decade, when the SAP formed a parliamentary coalition with the Agrarian Party, and the Swedish Trade Union Confederation (LO) negotiated a "Basic Agreement" with the country's powerful employers' federation (SAF). Reconciling working-class interests with those of small farmers meant that nationalization was off the table for the time being. Similarly, the LO's agreement with the SAF recognized for the first time management's "right to manage"—to direct the labor process and make personnel decisions without interference. Planning was gradually redefined from state nationalization to public investment and economic forecasting.

The party had made a significant shift from opposition and representing the interests of workers alone to constructing a cooperative "people's home" for the entire population. It recognized that prosperity depended on growth, and that there was no immediate alternative to private enterprise. Way back in 1897, amid pitched industrial battles, Swedish socialists made their stated goal "the fostering and development of intellectual and material culture." Nationalization, at the time, was their assumed means, but the goal was more open-ended. Unlike MacDonald's Labour Party, however, they didn't capitulate to the market as it was but made a radical attempt to change how it operated.[9]

The Swedish model matured after the war. During the gestation period of the SAP's 1944 "postwar" program, finance minister Ernst Wigforss argued that the concentration of economic power was the problem, not necessarily private ownership. It was another acknowledgment that Sweden's main issue was underdevelopment, and that it was better for labor to share part of a growing pie with capitalists than to try to capture all of a small one.

Yet the SAP did not rule out immediate socialization if the tamed private market didn't prove itself compatible with the party's values and goals. The debates at the time show a party that still took its commitment to socialism seriously. Some socialists even shared the expectation of Minister of Social Affairs Gustav Möller that a wave of revolutions might follow the war's conclusion and ripen conditions for a more traditional socialist program.

With the Communist vote tripling to 10 percent, the combined Left had an absolute majority in the 1944 elections. And even in a period with emergency wage, price, and consumption controls, planning had a great deal of mystique. Despite Wigforss's assurances about the continued role of private capital, the 1944 program advocated government takeovers of basic industries and finance and an overarching state responsibility for shaping investment and maintaining full employment. Economist and trade minister Gunnar Myrdal spoke of a "harvest time" for the labor movement, in which the fruits of recent economic development would fall to workers. Yet a push for nationalization found resistance from a capitalist class that could credibly threaten to withhold investment. That climate, combined with the onset of the Cold War, tempered the SAP, which forsook alliance with the Communists in favor of a new coalition with the Agrarians.[10]

With the march toward socialization blocked, the party eventually adopted a 1951 plan created by LO economists Gösta Rehn and Rudolf Meidner. They shared the SAP's desire to promote and influence economic expansion but advocated doing so through centralized labor bargaining rather than direct state intervention. The starting point for the

Rehn-Meidner strategy was a commitment to using that sectoral bargaining between the LO and the SAF to help equalize pay levels for all workers. That didn't mean everyone earned the same, but the gap between higher and lower paid workers was reduced. The "equal pay for equal work" principle also meant that differentiated wages should be determined by the type of work performed, not by a particular employer's ability to pay or an employee's power on their shop floor.[11]

This was done for three reasons. First, because of an ideological commitment to equality: even if wages can't be equal, at the very least we should lift up the incomes of the worst off and limit the advantages of the best. Second, because wage compression was politically useful: it reduced divisions within the working class and promoted solidarity across industries. Third, because it played an important macroeconomic role in the Rehn-Meidner plan.

Wage demands would be set so that firms at an average efficiency level could survive, but less efficient firms would be squeezed and forced to radically restructure or go bankrupt. The most productive firms, however, would benefit from the wage restraint of their workers and garner excess profits. These profits would allow them to expand their productive capacity and thus generate more wealth. The system helped encourage high-wage, capital-intensive industry.

These negotiations were done directly between labor and capital, but the role of the state was crucial: "active labor market policies" helped workers formerly employed in less productive firms get reabsorbed in expanding parts of the economy. Social guarantees—for health care, education, child care, and so on—meant that there was a growing state sector to help ensure full employment. It was a program for "functional socialism," in that it made certain socialist priorities clear but would seek them by shaping the outcomes of capitalist enterprise rather than through nationalization. Such a model, however, was one that capitalists would agree to only under duress. As Meidner put it, "management prefers decentralized bargaining" and "wage differentials as instruments for managerial control."[12]

Even though capitalists benefited from the Rehn-Meidner plan in many respects, it was only implemented because a powerful labor movement and social-democratic party forced its way. Nevertheless, it was a "socialism" jointly administered by a powerful employer federation, which was able to set red lines around how far private ownership rights could be eroded.

This contradiction would only emerge later. Sweden thrived in the post-war period. It had not been ravaged by the war, and a rebuilding Europe needed the raw materials it exported. What was good for Volvo also seemed to be good for Sweden. Under the twenty-three-year tenure of Prime Minister Tage Erlander, companies enjoyed soaring profits, and the spoils of that growth were shared widely.

The dream of constructing socialism through nationalizations was abandoned, and as late as 1976, only 5 percent of Swedish industry was under public ownership. But the results were undeniable. The Rehn-Meidner model combined the dynamic power of capital and free trade, on the one hand, with the might of an organized trade union movement and a social-democratic state, on the other, to ensure egalitarian outcomes. Beyond distributing income more fairly, the system allowed Swedes to meet basic needs *outside* the marketplace through welfare state guarantees. It was what Wigforss called a "provisional utopia."

International observers like Anthony Crosland drew profound lessons from the Swedish example. The British Labour parliamentarian believed that socialism was compatible with the private ownership of industry. His 1956 book *The Future of Socialism* criticized the traditional socialist focus on means—the preference for nationalization, for example—instead of the end goal of social equality. "The worst sort of confusion," he wrote, "is the tendency to use [socialism] to describe, not a certain kind of society, but particular policies which are, or are thought to be, means to attain this kind of society." It was the most influential revisionist work since Eduard Bernstein's *Evolutionary Socialism*, perfect for an era in which capitalism seemed dynamic and the scope for reform within it almost boundless. Crosland was explicit about his intention, telling a friend that he was "engaged on a great revision of Marxism, and will certainly emerge as the modern Bernstein."[13]

Bernstein had inklings of how malleable capitalism was, but Crosland had proof. Despite the Depression and war of the 1930s and '40s, the system had not collapsed but was instead being transformed. Living standards were improving, and private capital increasingly found itself subordinated to both the state and labor. This was the case in Clement Attlee's Britain and even more so in Erlander's Sweden. The taxation of capitalist growth and social spending, rather than outright expropriation, seemed to be sufficient. Going further than Bernstein ever did, Crosland wrote, "Marx has little or nothing to offer the contemporary Socialist, either in respect of practical policy, or of the correct analysis of our society, or even the right conceptual tools or framework." Three years after *The Future of Socialism*'s publication, even the venerable German Social Democratic Party abandoned the Marxist concept of class struggle in its Godesberg Program. The reconciliation to capitalism that social democracy had long made in practice was finally codified in theory.[14]

YET IN 1969, when Olof Palme took over as prime minister of Sweden, the class compromise that underpinned the system was starting to come undone. That Palme came to prominence was no great surprise—that he did so on the back of working-class politics was. He was born into an aristocratic Lutheran family and spent much of his childhood on estates and in the company of private tutors. His uncles were so rabidly right-wing that they fought in the Finnish Civil War as foreign volunteers supporting the brutal White Army. One of them, after whom he was named, was killed by the Reds at the Battle of Tampere in 1918.

Palme might have always had some egalitarian instincts. After his 1986 assassination, an old household servant recalled that he was different from his family members, even as an eight-year-old, "always helping us maids carry the dishes and talking to us as equals." But from what we know of his days in primary school and in the military, Palme was hardly political and even displayed some conservative tendencies. As unlikely as it seems, he was won over to socialism during his time in the United States.[15]

In 1947, Palme received a scholarship to study for a year at Kenyon College, a liberal arts school in Ohio. He came to love America, filled as it was with postwar confidence and a vibrant trade union movement. Palme was a member of a socialist society while at school and studied under progressive professors. He wrote his thesis on the United Auto Workers (UAW) and he even conducted research at a ball bearing factory near Kenyon. That summer Palme also talked with UAW leader Walter Reuther in Detroit, admiring what he saw of the American social-democratic movement.[16]

Free from rigid boarding schools and military discipline for the first time, Palme hitchhiked and took Greyhounds across the country. In the process, he discovered how widespread racism was in Jim Crow America. He recalled sitting in the back of the bus with black patrons in the South. When asked to move to the front by some white men, he refused. As he wrote in a letter home, he probably only avoided a beating because "they took me for a crazy foreigner." By the time Palme returned to Sweden, the young man who not long ago thought the Swedish tax rate needed to be halved was writing articles about *The Communist Manifesto*.[17]

The newly politicized Palme became involved in the SAP and chairman of the Swedish students' union in 1952. Many took notice of his charisma and intelligence, and he was soon brought in as an assistant to Prime Minister Erlander. His role in the administration became so vital that the media would sometimes depict Palme as Erlander's puppet master. The prestige and attention didn't please some members of his family, however. His grandmother, proud of her own children's sacrifices against the "Finnish barbarians," regretted that her beloved grandson was "in the service of a party that is busy destroying our country."[18]

When he became prime minister at the age of forty-two, Palme hoped to take the model built under Erlander and widen its scope. His ambitions were rooted in his own views, but also reflected growing pressure from the LO/SAP rank and file. Decades under a strong welfare state, it turned out, didn't satisfy egalitarian demands but fostered more expansive ones. Following SAP setbacks in local elections, a 1967 conference committed the party to an "industrial policy offensive" that hearkened back to the 1940s planning debate. Previously, Swedish social democracy had engaged in little direct industrial planning, relying on the demands of unions and targeted interventions to shape market forces. But now the government set up a public investment bank and expanded state enterprises and mechanisms for the coordination of those firms. The changes were not necessarily anti-capitalist: business needed labor and state support to adjust to a changing world market. But though capitalists could accept active industrial policy, the push to expand workplace democracy was bitterly resisted.[19]

LO leaders had to contend with a wave of wildcat strikes and were pushed to the left as a result in the early 1970s. The federation began advocating the extension of collective bargaining to noneconomic concerns. The employers organized in the SAF refused any such reform, so labor (both the LO and the white-collar federations) resorted to pushing its demands through social-democratic legislation. With the backing of Palme's Social Democratic Party, employers were forced to negotiate with unions on just about every workplace issue. The terms of the 1938 Basic Agreement were violated, with labor firing the first shots.

The most radical shift was the 1976 LO endorsement of a new Meidner Plan, a proposal for a collectively owned wage-earner fund. Decades of wage restraint in productive firms had curbed inflationary pressures and allowed for expansion. But these policies also led to massive "excessive profits"—the product of centralized bargaining, not weak shop floor power—which weren't always productively invested. Many workers, especially those with valuable skills, felt that the wage increases they had been granted were less than they deserved. Those feelings were compounded by the realization that some of Sweden's largest companies were earning extremely high profits, in large part because of labor's willingness to limit its demands. A Communist parliamentarian, C.-H. Hermansson, could point out that even after years of uninterrupted social-democratic rule, "fifteen families" owned the majority of Swedish industry. The LO proposal, which was not cleared beforehand with the SAP, would address both the ideological and the practical problems of capitalists' unilateral control of socially created wealth.[20]

Wage-earner funds had been floated in Germany, the Netherlands, and Denmark in the postwar years, but the Swedish plan was more ambitious. A small working group set up in 1973 spent two years formulating a strategy to shore up the nation's solidaristic wage policy. They ended up presenting a report that advocated a form of profit sharing: firms with over fifty employees would have to take 20 percent of their annual profit and issue shares to a worker-controlled wage-earner fund. Though the proposal was at first received indifferently by LO leaders, they came to see it as a possible solution to the problems facing the Swedish model. The trade union rank and file's response was more enthusiastic, particularly because of the plan's anticapitalist implications. Within several decades, the funds (controlled by workers through union boards), could wrestle ownership from private capital. As Meidner said in a 1975 interview, "We cannot fundamentally change society without changing its ownership structure." It was a left-wing repudiation of "functional socialism."[21]

For their part, many workers who had been indirectly exercising political power through the Social Democratic Party felt they had the skills and expertise to run their own workplaces without compromising with capital. The resolution's adoption at the 1976 LO convention was followed by a spontaneous rendition of "The Internationale."

The Meidner Committee anticipated strong business resistance and stressed that employers were *not* being expropriated. They didn't lose any existing wealth; they just had to give up a portion of future profits. And since that share of profit wouldn't be taxed, the state was itself subsidizing the funds. The plan could have even promoted further wage restraint and less adversarial relations between workers and management. Yet after some consideration, business leaders saw the plan for what it was: an existential threat.

MEANWHILE, PALME PRESSED his larger project throughout his first seven years in office. He was fond of using poetry to describe what social democracy endeavored toward, a world that acknowledged that "man, not the moon, is the measure of everything. An open city without fortifications is what we are building together, its light shining up against the loneliness of space."[22]

For Swedish women, in particular, social democracy was a great boon in what was once considered the most patriarchal country in Scandinavia. Historically, socialists had acquitted themselves far better on the question of sexual equality than their rivals, as most agreed with August Bebel that there couldn't be a just society without "equality of the sexes." But radicals like Alexandra Kollontai and Vladimir Lenin who recognized the "double oppression" that women faced—both from capital and from sexism—thought the scope for reform was limited within capitalism. (In the early 1900s, Kollontai could dismiss the feminist movement itself as "poison.") Socialists, in general, favored universal suffrage, employment, and other civil rights, but were less proactive in other struggles and were suspicious of cross-class feminist causes.[23]

Sweden showed just how much sexual oppression could be diminished within capitalism. Child allowances, family leave, child care, even the provision of school meals—all eased the burdens placed on women. Beyond such legislation, "equal pay for equal work" and industry-level bargaining that favored the lowest-paid sectors disproportionately helped women. Still, as late as 1966, two-thirds of Swedish women stayed at home. A popular 1961 pamphlet pointed out that now women had the right to compete with men in the labor market but also had to maintain their household duties, making it difficult to do both in practice.[24]

Amid debate over this question, the state took steps to facilitate women's labor force participation. An advisory council on sexual equality working directly with the prime minister's office was created to generate policy that encouraged "free development" for women and challenged traditional gender roles. Palme committed himself wholeheartedly to the effort, writing in a thoughtful essay called "The Emancipation of Man" that women's struggle for equality meant taking on the "pressure of thousand years old traditions."

Swedish women finally won abortion rights in 1974. By that year, *80 percent* of women in the country were in paid employment—the highest rate in the world. Combined with the wider social and economic transformation underway, Swedish society was upturned—traditionalism declined, secularism grew, and new forms of sexual liberation flourished. What was once a hierarchical nation, a culture still yearning for past imperial glories, could now take pride in being a democracy committed to equality at home and anticolonial struggles abroad.[25]

BY THE TIME the 1976 general election came around, the Social Democrats had been in power for forty-four years, longer than most Swedes had been alive. They had faced a stiff challenge in 1973, and then, in 1976, the socialist bloc fell short of a majority. The immediate cause of the defeat might have been a debate over nuclear power. It was favored by the Social Democrats but opposed by the Center Party, which expanded its scope to green politics.

The larger challenge came from the structural dilemma of social democracy. No matter how creatively implemented, it was still dependent on private sector profits and the calculation by business that maintaining the peace with a powerful labor movement was worth the cost. Sure enough, employers enjoyed stability: from 1938 to the start of the wildcat strike wave in 1969, strike levels were lower in Sweden than elsewhere in Europe. But political unrest and the end of the postwar economic boom meant that the truce could not last forever. The Left, as we have seen, began to break with aspects of the 1938 Basic Agreement. In some instances, this was an ideological act, such as in the encroachment on management pejoratives and the push for industrial democracy. In other cases, as with the wage-earner fund, it was a mix of practical and ideological imperatives.

The employer federation for its part radicalized as well. For the first time in decades, the SAF began a media campaign against the core pillars of social democracy. It attacked the Meidner Plan, portraying it as an attempt by union bureaucrats to concentrate power in their own hands. The LO rank and file still rallied behind the plan, but the SAP was never much committed to it to begin with. Nor were white-collar-professional left voters. The charges stuck. Fifty thousand people demonstrated against the Meidner Plan in late 1983.

At the same time, employers began resisting even moderate demands for wage increases. Amid broader economic shifts that resulted in the internationalization of the Swedish economy, and developments including the 1973 worldwide oil crisis, the threat of unemployment and inflation grew. Still tasked with absorbing private sector job losses and maintaining broad welfare supports, the state began growing rapidly, with public expenditure reaching almost 70 percent of GDP.

Social democracy was always predicated on economic expansion. Expansion gave succor to both the working class and capital. When growth slowed and the demands of workers made deeper inroads into firm profits, business owners rebelled against the class compromise.

Neoliberalism—a set of policies to use state power to restore employer profits by rolling back regulations and challenging unions—was one way to solve the crisis of the 1970s. Wrestling control of investment from capital was another. But social democrats were unprepared for this choice. Thinking they had abolished the business cycle through state intervention, they forgot a core tenet of Marxism: that the contradictions of capitalism, and its tendency toward crisis, cannot be resolved within the system.

Perhaps things would have played out differently if Palme and his party had backed the Meidner Plan wholeheartedly in the 1970s. However, they ran into another big dilemma of social democracy: social-democratic leaderships have to win elections and build stable institutions. They didn't necessarily want working-class mobilization outside the voting booth. To maintain electoral stability and their own ability to mediate between capital and labor and to enact reforms, social democrats shied away from leftist solutions to the crisis. In doing so, they ironically ended up undermining their own voting bloc, the true source of their power.[26]

Despite the SAP setback in 1976, the basics of social democracy went unchallenged longer in Sweden than elsewhere in Europe. But in the 1980s centralized bargaining policies and practices began to crumble, and the Meidner Plan was watered down to the point of being inconsequential. Full employment policies were dropped by a social-democratic government during the 1990 financial crisis. Though Sweden still has better social indicators than almost any other nation, its welfare state was reshaped through reforms that privatized key aspects of service provisioning. Entry into the European Union in 1995 further challenged what remained of the Swedish model.

THOUGH OTHER SOCIAL-DEMOCRATIC experiments sputtered and failed, the Left was not in full retreat everywhere. In France, forty-three years after Léon Blum left power, François Mitterrand's 1980s socialist government was an attempt to rage against the dying of the light. His program was the most radical from a mainstream party in decades. "You can be a manager of capitalist society or a founder of a socialist society," Mitterrand could say. "As far as we're concerned, we want to be the second."[27]

By the time Mitterrand took power with Communist support in 1981, France already faced growing unemployment, economic stagnation, and an unfavorable international business climate. Despite his rhetoric, Mitterrand's immediate program was a radical Keynesian one. His "110 Propositions for France" proposed a public works program and the construction of social housing, nurseries, and clinics. The government's early legislative victories expanded shop-floor union rights, along with codetermination measures. Minimum wage and pensions were increased, while the working week was reduced to thirty-nine hours. A 1982 nationalization bill put five industrial groups, almost forty banks, two steel companies, and much of the armaments and aerospace industries under state control. These nationalizations, decried as Bolshevism in the business press, were made not so much on ideological grounds but to help maintain employment and oversee economic restructuring.

Nonetheless, business resistance grew to unprecedented levels, and $5 billion was lost to capital flight. Just a few years after asserting his revolutionary credentials, Mitterrand was pleading with France's business leaders: "This will be one of the ways to end the class struggle. We want to develop a mixed economy. We are not revolutionary Marxists-Leninists." He might have recalled what he had told one of his aides only a few months earlier, "In economics, there are two solutions—either you are a Leninist or you won't change anything."[28]

Mitterrand's program did spark a wave of popular support, but he was unable to harness that energy or to practically deal with employer resistance. His choice of retreat was made easier by restrictions imposed by the European Monetary System, which tied the franc to the Deutschmark and prevented devaluation (today, the eurozone allows for even less monetary flexibility). The bold "110 Propositions" could not overcome the discipline of both domestic elites and the international market. The French socialists were forced into a dramatic U-turn, not just halting their march forward but embracing the politics of austerity.

Olof Palme didn't live long enough to oversee such a retreat in his own country. But within a few years of his 1986 assassination, both state socialism and social democracy were widely pronounced dead worldwide. Social democrats still governed in many places. Since mid-century they had given up the ambition to construct an order after capitalism rather than just doses of socialism within it. Now they ended up, as they had in the interwar period, following the path of the Ramsay MacDonald governments and, at most, marrying redistributive measures to economic orthodoxy.

Tony Blair in Britain, Gerhard Schröder in Germany, and North American counterparts, including Bill Clinton and others in the Democratic

Leadership Council, helped codify the social-democratic retreat into a new ideology. The newly minted Third Way promised "opportunity, not government," and "a politics of inclusion," not welfare. The social democrats who had once demanded a middle way between communism and capitalism, French socialist leader Lionel Jospin lamented, now proposed one between social democracy and neoliberalism. The goalposts had moved to the right. As part of this shift, historic labor parties were transformed into social liberal ones, their appeals designed more for middle-class professionals than their long-neglected working-class bases.[29]

ANTHONY CROSLAND'S *THE Future of Socialism* was at its most poignant in its demands for "not only higher exports and old-age pensions, but more open-air cafes, brighter and gayer streets at night...brighter and cleaner eating houses, more riverside cafes, more pleasure gardens on the Battersea model." The welfare state certainly should not be the end point of human ambitions. But those who embraced Crosland's moderate legacy in bids to modernize their old parties proved better able to enact his dreams of green urban renewal than of social equality.

Does that mean that the decades of effort to build social democracy were in vain? We can recall Rosa Luxemburg's comparison of reformism with the "labor of Sisyphus," the giant in Greek mythology, eternally pushing a boulder uphill, only to see it slide down again when it nears the top. But even after years of slippage, the boulder hasn't come crashing all the way down. In advanced societies shaped by social democrats, key working-class victories have proven durable, and people enjoy protections from the most extreme forms of poverty and insecurity. Democracy prevents capitalism from returning to its "war against all" worst. But for those still aspiring to an age of abundance and solidarity, defending existing victories or negotiating terms of defeat isn't enough.

As we will see, the emergence of the movement around British Labour Party leader Jeremy Corbyn, and to a lesser extent that of Bernie Sanders in the United States, represents a surprising challenge to the Third Way.

What makes Corbyn, in particular, so remarkable is that he doesn't just offer a return to twentieth-century Labourism but rather wants a new "class struggle social democracy" in which the party meeting, union hall, and electoral rally are far from the only acceptable places to practice politics. Yet even if the more combative approach of Corbyn and Sanders succeeds in winning office, the new social democracy will encounter the same structural challenges as the old one, namely its reliance on the profitability of capital and the inflationary tendencies that accompany empowered workplaces and full employment policies. The resolution of these issues will lead us down one of two paths, albeit different ones from those Palme suggested: back to economic orthodoxy or toward a more radical, democratic socialist tradition.

Western Europe and Russia were necessarily the subjects of this and the previous three chapters, as the accident of history that is capitalism— along with its socialist foil—first arose in Europe and only later spread to the rest of the world. However, capital's drive is global, and the resistance it provokes is, too. We now turn to the Third World, where socialists were at the forefront of struggles against colonial oppression and for national development.

SIX

THE THIRD WORLD
REVOLUTION

To M. N. ROY, the Communist International's Second Congress was a revelation. "For the first time," he remarked, "brown and yellow men met with white men who were not overbearing imperialists but friends and comrades."[1]

The young Bengali was already a seasoned activist, having participated in India's radical nationalist movement before being forced to leave the country. Abroad, he discovered Marxism in a New York City public library and even helped found Mexico's Communist Party. The 1920 congress was his first international communist gathering, however. Like the thirty other delegates representing oppressed nations, his views helped shape the proceedings. According to some scholars, Roy's lifetime contributions on the colonial question were as influential as those of Lenin and Mao.[2]

The appeal of socialism in its "Leninist" form was obvious: it foregrounded anti-imperialism, and the agrarian question was just as crucial in mostly peasant Russia as it was across the colonized world. Though Lenin drew mainly on the German Social Democratic Party, he adapted its strategies to Russian conditions, which were closer to what Roy saw in India.

Even more, the Soviet Union already administered a territory of over a hundred nationalities, and debates about self-determination echoed in Africa, Asia, and Latin America.

The old Second International had spent some time examining the colonized world, but while few joined Eduard Bernstein in seeing a "civilizing" silver lining in imperialism, its record was spotty. Notably, the grouping had little representation from oppressed nations, despite being led by parties based in imperialist countries. Even some radicals like Rosa Luxemburg, herself from oppressed Poland, simply opposed all forms of nationalism, including the right to self-determination. A "right of nations," she argued, "is nothing more than a metaphysical cliché of the type of 'rights of man' and 'rights of the citizen.'"[3]

The Communist International hewed closer to Marx's views. Marx had been a longtime advocate of Polish independence and similar struggles. For his part, Lenin often compared the national question to a woman's right to divorce: any good socialist would support that right, but that didn't mean they advocated that all married couples divorce.

In the years after the October Revolution, the Soviet Union had both ideological and practical reasons for encouraging national liberation abroad. Prospects for revolution in Western Europe were dim, but less so elsewhere. "The pariahs are rising," Comintern leaders announced in 1920. "The Socialist who aids directly or indirectly in perpetuating the privileged position of one nation at the expense of another, who accommodates himself to colonial slavery, who draws a line of distinction between races and colors deserves to be branded with infamy, if not with a bullet."[4]

Yet if the Bolsheviks had to grapple with the challenge of leading a highly organized working class trapped in a mostly peasant country, those contradictions were even more significant in the world's less developed countries. Marx had foreseen revolution arising first in the most advanced countries (he later complicated this prediction), the product of a conscious proletariat. Socialism was to be the radically democratic goal of a working class that not only had an interest in its own liberation through the abolition of wage labor but also shared a collective interest in the liberation of all humanity through the abolition of class itself. Such an act required both capitalism creating this working class to begin with and capitalist exchange producing the abundance necessary for socialism to supersede it.

But in the Third World, revolutionaries embraced socialism as a *path* to modernity and national liberation. Adapting a theory that was built around advanced capitalism and an industrial proletariat, they struggled to find "substitute proletariats"—from peasants to junior military officers to deprived underclasses—to achieve these ends. As Roy would later write, "in order to catch up with the time lost, India must live in a few years the life lived by others over a period of a thousand years."[5]

In the twentieth century, socialists played leading roles in the struggle against imperialism. But what made the socialist contribution to movements in the Third World distinct was this emphasis on development. The exploitation of weak nations by strong ones was rejected not only on moral grounds but because it created barriers to improving economic conditions. Nevertheless, attempting to make up for hundreds of years in a "few years" made socialism in the Third World prone to domination by small groups trying to carry out modernization from above. At times they had mass popular support, but these movements ruled over and on behalf of the oppressed, not through them. It was a departure from past socialist claims to represent the self-emancipation of the working class itself.

Nowhere was this dynamic clearer than in the Chinese Revolution, where it played out on a grand scale. The revolution's noteworthy achievements and cataclysmic failures continue to shape the world to this day. But it is telling that Chinese Communism is now at best seen as an overseer of enlightened authoritarianism, rather than a radical socialist force.

WHEN THE Communist Party of China (CPC) held its first congress in 1921, there were only a dozen delegates, representing a grand total of fifty-seven party members. The son of a wealthy peasant, Mao Zedong was among those twelve apostles. As a teenager he had participated in the Xinhai Revolution, which overthrew the Qing dynasty, and afterward began to move from republicanism to socialism. The CPC, which he helped found and which was then led by Chen Duxiu and Li Dazhao, embraced Marxist orthodoxy. It proclaimed itself a "proletarian party" that would help workers "fight for their own class interest."[6]

At the time, China was in disarray. The Qing dynasty collapsed in 1912, after three hundred years in power, but the republic created in its wake was a disaster. Sun Yat-sen's Kuomintang (KMT) only wielded power in the south, and the country was effectively controlled by rival warlords. Dynastic landlords still oversaw massive estates populated by famished peasants. Further blocking the pathway to development was China's status as a semi-colony, vied over by imperialist powers that dominated its major coastal cities. In these cities, a small working class emerged as a result of the influx of foreign capital and industrial equipment, but it represented just 1 percent of China's three hundred million people. The small number of educated militants—people who, like Mao, had participated in the nationalist upheavals of the 1910s—yearned for a united, free, socially reformed China. Many came to adopt socialism to achieve their ends.

Though the CPC saw China's small working class as its true revolutionary force, no one thought it would be able to accomplish much by itself. The party aspired, however, to cement the working class's hegemony over not just struggles against capitalists but those that challenged imperialists and landlords too. Though today mostly associated with the political thought of Italian Marxist Antonio Gramsci, Russian socialists popularized the concept of "hegemony" at the turn of the twentieth century. With it they referred to the process by which the distinct interests of the working class and those of other subaltern classes, such as the peasantry, would be reconciled under working-class leadership. Most Marxists believed that, left to their own devices, peasants would aspire to nothing more than petty proprietorship. They would fight their landlords for their own plots but not for a wider collectivist project. The trick wasn't to force peasants to be something they weren't but rather to harness their impulses as part of a wider socialist project. In the case of the working class, Marxists argued, their self-interest and the collective interests of humanity were aligned.[7]

That was the theory, at least. And seemingly out of nowhere, the Chinese working class began to follow the script. Though that class was still small, it had doubled in size between 1916 and 1922, as railways expanded along with a booming textile industry. The same couldn't be said about the Communist Party. Even as late as 1925, it had just nine hundred members. They were mostly intellectuals—and the Comintern ordered them to become Kuomintang members and find a mass base.

Communists were welcomed into the KMT's executive committee, and Sun Yat-sen relied on Communist efforts and help from Moscow to build his nationalist army. But dissent mounted within the CPC, which, like much of the pre-Stalinist international communist movement, still enjoyed internal democracy. The KMT, central committee member Peng Shuzi argued, was crippled by its association with feudal warlords. Echoing Trotsky's theory of permanent revolution, others, like party general secretary Chen Duxiu, also emphasized the need for organizational and political independence and a battle for change that passed the limits of what the "national bourgeoisie" found acceptable.

Differentiating themselves from the nationalists, the Communists began to focus on working-class agitation and building allied trade unions. Whether spurred by this shift or a fortuitous coincidence, a two-year worker struggle began in 1925 that would parallel the 1905 Russian Revolution. Strikes at Japanese-owned textile factories in Shanghai led to the death of a Communist worker and the arrests of scores more. In response, on May 30, thousands of students and workers rallied in solidarity outside

the police station where the strikers were being held. British police shot
and killed a dozen of them. The May 30 Incident was a catalyst for action
across China. Within weeks not only Shanghai but Guangzhou and Hong
Kong were gripped by a general strike. Tens of thousands of people flocked
to the Communist Party.

The Kuomintang saw the potential to use working-class militancy
for their nationalist project, but it shared industrialists' worries about the
spread of strikes from foreign to Chinese-owned firms. Chiang Kai-shek,
the recently deceased Sun Yat-sen's successor, initially found himself allied with the KMT's left, hoping to maintain his ties to the Soviet Union.
At least outside the country, the appreciation for Chinese nationalism was
reciprocated. In Moscow, Chiang was lauded as a "red general," and the
Soviet government even established the Sun Yat-sen Communist University
of the Toilers of China.[8]

This support from the Stalin-Bukharin leadership existed despite
mounting tensions between Chiang and the Chinese Communists after he
brutally repressed strikes in Guangzhou in 1926. The main Soviet dip-
lomat in China, Mikhail Borodin, put it crassly, "The present period is
one in which the communists should do coolie service for the Kuomintang." Trotsky was among the few voices within the politburo opposing this
stance. He wrote of Chiang's courtship of the Soviet Union: "In preparing
for himself the role of an executioner, he wanted to have the cover of world
communism." Chinese Communists, Trotsky argued, should break with the
Kuomintang and create soviets that could advance working-class demands
independent of the nationalists.[9]

For others in the international communist movement, the
Kuomintang's appeal was obvious. Despite its bourgeois character, it still
used the language of anti-imperialism, and the Soviets had managed to
forge (desperately needed) fraternal relationships with regimes in Mexico
and Turkey on that basis. The CPC leadership balanced the directives
from Moscow with its own instincts, begrudgingly accepting orders from

Chiang but also unable to completely tame the radical workers in its orbit. In Shanghai a Communist-inspired general strike of over a half million and an armed insurrection took over the city in advance of Chiang's arrival there.

Some in China joined Trotsky's call for the creation of soviets and a clean break with the Kuomintang, but under Russian pressure the Communist leadership again urged caution. While wary of handing Shanghai and their mass base over to Chiang, the CPC didn't want to provoke foreign intervention, and it sought to preserve an alliance with what it saw as the KMT's progressive wing. For Stalin, the Kuomintang was "a sort of revolutionary parliament" where Communists could still exert influence. "Why make a coup d'état? Why drive away the Right when we have the majority and when the Right listens to us?" he asked the revolutionists.[10]

Almost exactly a week later, on April 12, 1927, Chiang's armed militias, dressed in blue denim uniforms and donning white armbands, targeted the headquarters of the General Labour Union and other Communist strongholds. "The policy of the Government is to have labor working in harmony with the revolutionary army and the Government," one gang member turned Kuomintang executioner reasoned, "but when labor becomes a disturbing element, when it arrogates to itself tasks which are detrimental to the movement and disturbing to law and order, labor must be disciplined."[11]

The Communists had encouraged their members to bury their arms and avoid open struggle. Now, with that struggle forced on them, they were dramatically outgunned. Thousands died, and nationalist execution squads roamed the city shooting, bayoneting, and sometimes even beheading militants. The news was slow to spread abroad. On April 16, days after the massacre, German Communist leader Ernst Thälmann published an article asserting that "the bourgeois Right wing in the Kuomintang and its leadership" had been defeated in 1926. The next week, with the scope of the disaster clear, Stalin simply claimed that events had vindicated the Comintern line.[12]

In months that followed, Chiang, who said he would rather kill a thousand innocents than let one Communist escape, was true to his word. As many as three hundred thousand died in a White Terror, including fifteen thousand of the CPC's twenty-five thousand members. Li Dazhao, the party's cofounder, was executed in 1927 after the warlord Zhang Zuolin raided the Soviet embassy in Shanghai and seized him. The severely weakened party was now pushed by Stalin (who had finally turned on the KMT) to go on a suicidal offensive. It sparked an uprising in Nanchang, but Communists only held the city for a few days. Similarly, a December 1927 rebellion in Guangzhou ended in defeat.

With its urban base in shatters, the Communist Party would have to remold itself in the countryside. None would be more significant to that effort than Mao Zedong. Mao had learned an essential lesson from 1925 to 1927: he would rhetorically claim the utmost fealty to Stalinism but maintain the freedom to tactically improvise.

IN THE AFTERMATH of the 1927 disaster, the remaining Chinese Communists argued over what had transpired. Chen Duxiu, one of the party's cofounders, knew that Moscow was to blame and was forthright about the pressure to which he had been subjected. Trotsky, he admitted, had been right about the Comintern's policy all along. Chen had wanted to oppose the Kuomintang earlier, he said, but "I, who had no decisiveness of character... respected international discipline and the opinion of the majority of the Central Committee."[13]

For these honest reflections, Chen was made 1927's scapegoat and expelled from the party. He continued to advocate an alternative course from the outside: the slow rebuilding of strength in the cities, supporting the struggle for democratic rights, and backing peasant struggles. One day, Chen thought, Chiang Kai-shek would face his February Revolution. In

Russia, it had taken twelve years for the 1905 revolutionaries' aims to be realized. Patience was necessary. Yet Chen would die of natural causes before the party he founded took power. When its official history was written, he was branded a "bourgeois democracy opportunist," a traitor not just to Communism but to China itself.[14]

Chen Duxiu's void was filled by an unlikely candidate. During the fierce debates over the events of 1927, Mao emerged as a leader with new ideas, and he would slowly bring them to life. He spent most of the revolutionary 1920s organizing peasants in his native Hunan province. Though still seeing the proletariat as "the leading force in the revolutionary movement," Mao became more excited about the peasantry's revolutionary potential.

He refused to break with the Comintern as Chen had, but Mao carried this independent streak into the Jinggang Mountains, where he and several thousand other poorly armed Communists narrowly escaped encirclement by nationalist forces. They created "revolutionary base areas" in several provinces. The largest of these remote strongholds was the Jiangxi Soviet. Through land reform, debt cancellation, and literacy campaigns, the Communists built peasant support and grew the ranks of their Red Army.

Mao's own position seesawed throughout the early 1930s. The first mention of him in the international communist press was a mistaken March 1930 obituary, mourning him as "a Bolshevik and a champion of the Chinese proletariat." But he successfully argued against those who sought to hastily return the theater of struggle to the cities.[15]

Much of intraparty debate at the time centered around military strategy. The Communists had recovered from the events of 1927 and had beaten back several nationalist offensives; they now ruled a territory of three million people that was larger in area than France. But the Kuomintang forces were still superior. They were reinforced by foreign support. American and British loans to the KMT allowed them to pay for

US-built airplanes, and they also benefited from the services of military advisors, including Charles Lindbergh and hundreds of Wehrmacht officers, who formulated a strategy to slowly strangle the CPC positions. In response, Mao continued to advocate hit-and-run attacks and guerrilla warfare, while his future deputy Zhou Enlai favored "protracted warfare" with mass formations. The Communists had their own German military advisor in Comintern agent Otto Braun. He largely agreed with Zhou and won support for a series of doomed attacks against the nationalist army.[16]

The details of the desperate struggle in Jiangxi and Fujian is beyond the scope of this book, but the fact that military and not political questions dominated during this period tells us much about what the CPC had become. In the five years after 1927, it lost 90 percent of its membership—with its urban mass base destroyed, the party was proletarian in name only. For all the frequent appeals to the "leading role" of the working class, by Zhou's estimates only two thousand of a hundred twenty thousand party members at the time were workers. Those numbers are unreliable, but there had undoubtedly been a massive shift since the 1920s, when perhaps two-thirds of the party's members were workers. Communist leaders now ruled millions of peasants through military force in the name of a working class they only had tenuous ties to. In these conditions Mao concluded that "political power grows out of the barrel of a gun."

The leader's military ideas, at least, were vindicated by the nationalist destruction of much of the Red Army in 1933–1934. The Long March from Jiangxi to the northern fringes of China cost thousands of lives but ensured Communist survival. At the end of it, Mao and his supporters were the undisputed leaders of their party.

Mao refused to meet Chen's fate: whenever the Comintern's line shifted, he changed his rhetoric accordingly. At times, the Communists waged war against the "kulaks" in their midst; at others even "confiscation of the land of the landlords" was halted. When the Japanese advanced in China, coming menacingly close to the Soviet Union, Moscow ordered the CPC to once again compromise with the "progressive national bourgeoisie." A leading party member could say in 1938 that "China needs Generalissimo Chiang Kai-shek's leadership more urgently than ever today.... No one else can lead this war except Generalissimo Chiang."[17]

Yet whatever it publicly professed, the party never repeated the errors of the 1920s. Discontent with the KMT was widespread in China, and the Communists capitalized on it. Sun Yat-sen had promised prosperity, representative government, and national glory; Chiang oversaw poverty, maintained a dictatorship, and could not unite the country. In the struggle against the Japanese—which entailed a cessation of hostilities between the CPC and KMT—and in the resumed civil war that followed, Mao proved his genius. From ten thousand survivors after the 1934–1936 Long March, the Red Army soon numbered hundreds of thousands. They chastened landlords, defeated warlords, and won genuine popular support.

But completely unbound to a working class that had a self-interest in socialist transformation, what became "Maoism" was naturally both voluntaristic and coercive. Its aim was to exhort the peasantry to build a socialism it had no reason to construct. The new revolutionary state would be created through these millions of peasants, not by them.

IT'S HARD TO overstate the misery of prerevolutionary China or the ineptitude of nationalist rule. Between 1927 and 1949, the country had been mired in foreign invasion and civil war, warlords ruled with impunity, illiteracy was the norm, life expectancy was barely forty, and women were barred from education and sold into domestic servitude. Outright slavery even persisted in some remote regions, and just 10 percent of the rural population owned 70 percent of the land. In the previous thirty years, ten million people had died in famines.

It was no surprise, then, that when they swept from the countryside back into the cities, the Communists were met with adoring crowds.

Compared to the Kuomintang's political terror and economic mismanagement, the CPC had earned a reputation for moderate, responsible leadership. Even some capitalists might have been reassured by Mao's promise
that parts of the bourgeoisie and even "enlightened gentry and other pa-
triots" were vital to freeing China from not just imperialism but economic
backwardness.[18]

Along with desperately needed capital, however, many of the nation's
trained managers had fled to Taiwan with the KMT. With the Cold War
now underway, the United States took an aggressive stance in East Asia,
moving to halt the spread of Communism in Korea. The CPC, with aid
and expertise from the Soviets, faced the daunting task of rebuilding the
country. With the outbreak of the Korean War, the party once again had to
make huge sacrifices, joining the war and forcing a stalemate in the penin-
sula at the cost of over a half million Chinese dead and wounded.

At home, the Communists faced the same dilemma the Soviet Union
had in the 1920s and '30s—how to extract surplus from the peasantry
with which to build industry in the cities. The challenge was even greater
in China, because the party had come to power on the backs of peasants
they now needed to exploit. As we have seen, even as democracy within the
Soviet Union was strangled, the 1920s New Economic Policy (NEP) presented a blueprint for development through a gradual "unequal exchange"
between town and country.

For the first few years of Communist rule, the CPC took a similar
approach. It instituted an Agrarian Reform Law in 1950, which distrib-
uted the property of rural landlords to the peasant masses. Peasants were
encouraged to pool equipment and livestock in "mutual aid teams," but
as late as 1953, the party would proclaim that "it is even necessary to
permit the continued development of the economic system of the wealthy
peasant." Under the slogan of sexual equality, other measures such as the
New Marriage Law banned child marriage and ensured that women had
to consent to their betrothal. Other Communist gains must have seemed

just as profound: the water supply and sewage systems were improved, and disease-prevention campaigns reduced the prevalence of cholera, scarlet fever, and typhoid.[19]

In the cities, the CPC faced hyperinflation—prices rose several million percent between 1937 and 1948—and the challenge of restoring production. The Kuomintang had already carried out extensive nationalizations, which the Communists promptly expanded. But even as late as 1952, 20 percent of heavy industry and 60 percent of light industry were privately owned.[20]

The most striking policy involved efforts to curb inflation through austerity and labor force discipline. Built to be a wartime military organization, the CPC could carry out harsh measures decisively. Many workers, however, were no doubt pleased to be reemployed and receiving wages again. In Russia, the civil war came after the revolution. In China, the revolutionaries had already won their civil war and generally enjoyed popular support.

At the same time, the CPC implemented some of the authoritarian measures associated with Stalinism. Trotsky's 1932 warning proved prescient: "The commanders and commissars appear in the guise of absolute masters of the situation and upon occupying cities will be rather apt to look down from above upon the workers." Citizens were encouraged to keep an eye on their neighbors, academic life came under political control, and artists and intellectuals who refused to support the CPC were thrown in jail. "Struggle sessions" and group violence and humiliation, inside and outside the party, were already widespread. Thousands were driven to suicide.[21]

The party would soon bring about an even more radical shift. Eager to push the newly stabilized economy toward socialism, the CPC inaugurated its first Five Year Plan in 1953. Explaining the policy in the state newspaper, a party official argued that "the foundation of socialism is large industrial development" and cited the Soviet Union's rise from "backward agricultural nation into a first-class industrial power." But the plan was also a nationalist measure—"only with industrialization of the state may we guarantee our economic independence and nonreliance on imperialism."[22]

By the beginning of 1956, all private industry in the country was nationalized. Soviet aid, including $300,000,000 in low-interest loans, was vital to the effort. Eleven thousand Soviet experts came to work in China, and over thirty thousand Chinese technicians were trained in the USSR. As in Stalin's Five Year Plan, the focus was on building heavy industry. Thousands of state enterprises were created, some as large as the Anshan steel complex that employed thirty-five thousand. Before the Communists took power in 1949, only fifty-seven million of China's four hundred million inhabitants lived in cities; by the plan's completion that number had risen to one hundred million. Massive infrastructure projects linked the country, allowing the flow of people and materiel. Industrial output doubled.

Though in some respects a success, Mao's industrial offensive suffered from some of the same problems as Stalin's. It neglected light industry and made little investment in agriculture. Not only that: there weren't enough trained workers to properly run the new factories. Unhappy with the pace of development, Mao debated how to boost agricultural productivity and direct that surplus into industry.

As in Russia, the Communist leadership agreed that farm collectivization would increase output but questioned how fast that shift should be made. Unlike the Bolsheviks, the CPC at first took a cautious approach, simply encouraging the creation of "mutual aid teams." In 1954, however, with the Five Year Plan underway, the pace of collectivization quickened. That year poor peasants were organized into Agricultural Producers' Cooperatives (APCs): land was pooled among groups of around forty households, but peasants retained some private ownership rights and were rewarded based on their respective contributions.

Encouraged by early success, Mao wrote about collectivization as if it was a sudden, spontaneous act brought about from below: "A high tide of socialist transformation is sweeping through the rural areas, and the masses are jubilant." Denouncing his critics, the leader asked, "Why can't 600 million 'paupers' create a prosperous and strong socialist country in several decades by their own efforts?" The party press joined in with articles such as "Who Says Chicken Feathers Can't Fly Up to Heaven?" and "A Co-operative Set Up Spontaneously by the Masses Against the Wishes of the Leadership."[23]

With 80 percent of the peasantry in cooperatives by 1956, Mao ordered them transitioned to "Higher Level Agricultural Producers' Co-operatives," composed of over two hundred households, with the land collectively owned. The peasants were now virtually state serfs, working for meager wages, though they were at least still granted some private allotments.

Overall, collectivization in China was considerably less bloody, and provoked less resistance, than in the Soviet Union. The Communist Party had genuine support among the peasantry, and as dramatic as the shifts were, they were far more gradual than the Soviet example. And though collectivization rested on the same flawed assumption that scale was the determining factor in efficiency—rather than productivity per acre through better irrigation, fertilizers, seeds, and pesticides—agricultural output in China increased steadily from 1952 to 1958.[24]

IN THE MID-1950s, despite decades of civil war, the Japanese invasion, the Korean War, and a US trade embargo, China was stable, growing, and, to some contemporary observers, even challenging the communist movement's Stalinist orthodoxy. A year after Khrushchev's "secret speech" exposed the depth of Stalin's depravity—if not the ruling bureaucracy's complicity in it—and months after the Hungarian Revolution showed popular discontent with Stalinism, Mao pursued a new, more liberal policy.

He gave a speech in February 1957 announcing a new openness to the arts, scientific inquiry, and even ("non-counterrevolutionary") criticism of the party itself. "Let a hundred flowers blossom, let a hundred schools of thought contend," Mao said, reciting a famous slogan. For the Marxist historian Isaac Deutscher, writing in the *Nation* a few months later, "Mao attempts, in effect, to redefine the whole concept of proletarian dictatorship and to restore to it the meaning which Marxists generally gave to it before the onset of the Stalin era." Whatever bloodshed it took to bring the Communist Party to power, Deutscher believed that a more pluralistic future awaited China.[25]

Yet by the time his article went to press in June, the CPC was reeling from a torrent of domestic criticism. At first Mao didn't waver, seeing protest as a safety valve for dissent and a genuine check on the bureaucracy. Mao was impressed by his own restraint, supporting Nanjing student protesters, while remarking that "if they had done the same thing in front of Stalin, heads would have rolled."[26]

In the new environment anti-authoritarian plays were written, and students circulated controversial bulletins and debated politics. Thousands of letters poured into Zhou Enlai's office, decrying abuse from state agents. A lecturer of physics and chemistry felt free enough to proclaim, "China belongs to 600,000,000 people—it does not belong to the Communist Party alone." Others spoke about a "new class" of Communist officials that "rules the people with Marxist-Leninist textbooks in its left hand, Soviet weapons in its right."[27]

Things went too far for Mao's taste, with popular democratic impulses threatening to bring about actual democratic change. The party quickly retreated, and the "Anti-Rightist Campaign" that followed saw hundreds of thousands persecuted and forced into labor camps.

WHATEVER HIS DISTRUST of the people's speech, Mao still believed that mass activity could propel China into modernity. Another Five Year Plan was considered too modest. What China needed was a project to "guide the

peasants, accelerate socialist construction, complete the building of socialism ahead of time, and carry out the gradual transition to communism."
For Mao, mass poverty didn't mean his hope for breakneck change was
impossible. Instead, he spun it as an auspicious fact: "Poverty gives rise to
the desire for change, the desire for action and the desire for revolution. On
a blank sheet of paper free from any mark, the freshest and most beautiful
characters can be written, the freshest and most beautiful pictures can be
painted."[28]

This idealism was turned into action with the transformation of Agricultural Producers' Cooperatives into massive five-thousand-household
communes. Centralized peasants offered a labor pool for infrastructure
projects, such as the mass digging of irrigation dikes and channels. Ambitious plans were designed not only to increase agricultural output but also
to build industry in rural areas and erode distinctions between town and
country, worker and peasant. Production targets were set unrealistically
high: as Zhou Enlai put it in a 1959 report, a growth of 20 percent in industrial output would be a "leap forward," an increase above 25 percent a
"Great Leap Forward," and an increase of 30 percent or more, an "exceptionally Great Leap Forward."[29]

What followed was tragedy on a massive scale. Communist cadres had
no experience managing enterprises as large as the new communes, and
could only rely on coercion and ideological exhortation to encourage peasants to work as hard as they had when managing their own plots. (Mao
rejected the material incentives favored in the Soviet bloc.) Local managers
had every reason in the frenzied environment to inflate their production
numbers. Though drought from 1959 to 1961 meant that harvests were
smaller than usual, given faulty information from their local cadres, the
party increased the percentage of grain requisitioned for the cities.

These problems were compounded by the fact that many peasants
were diverted from food production to local industrial projects, such
as the infamous "backyard furnace" policy. Driven to produce enough
steel to overtake Britain and even the United States in a matter of years,

peasants with no expertise in steel making used small blast furnaces, melting pots and pans, and even vital farm equipment. The resulting pig iron was often useless. Mao reflected on the calamity at the 1959 party conference: "I am a complete outsider when it comes to economic construction, and I understand nothing about industrial planning." He added that "Marx also made many mistakes" and argued that all of the leadership was responsible because they had listened to him in the first place. Mao's solution was that they should all study Stalin's "Economic Problems of Socialism" and do better; "otherwise we cannot develop and consolidate our cause."[30]

Mao's agricultural directives were even more destructive. Peasants were encouraged to reject their traditional farming techniques and trained in Lysenkoism, a pseudoscience imported from Stalinist Russia. A campaign against the "Four Pests" saw flies, mosquitoes, rats, and sparrows killed in the millions. As a result, their natural prey, locusts and grasshoppers, were free to devour millions of tons of grain. As Mao put it, in a different apology, "I haven't got much understanding of industry and commerce. I understand a bit about agriculture, but this is only relatively speaking—I still don't understand much." Such a frank self-criticism differentiated him from Stalin, but it hardly mattered to the 16.5 million people, by official estimates, who died during the Great Famine. (The total number of victims is undoubtedly larger than that, likely over 30 million.)[31]

Mao didn't intend to starve the peasantry or specific groups of peasants, as Stalin had in the 1930s. But the consequences were the same. The climate of fear created by the "Anti-Rightist Campaign" and the lack of a free civil society in China only furthered the problem, making it difficult for news of the devastation to spread. At the 1959 Lushan Conference, defense minister Peng Dehuai tried to inform Mao about the reality of the situation in the countryside, but his private criticisms were exposed by the leader, and he was arrested and replaced by Lin Biao. The experiment was only wound down after resistance from the peasantry, including armed rebellion, intensified.

Around the same time, a rift developed between China and the Soviet Union, culminating in the withdrawal of fourteen hundred Soviet economic advisors in 1960. The Sino-Soviet split is often described in ideological terms—the radical Mao affirming his loyalty to Stalin against Khrushchev's revisionism. The historical record, however, suggests that the Chinese Communists were receptive to criticisms of Stalin. When he met with Soviet ambassador Pavel Yudin in March 1956, Mao shared his opinion that Stalin had erred in his policy on China, leading to the CPC's near destruction, and that Stalin had overestimated the Kuomintang. Still, Mao revealed to Yudin, he regarded Stalin to be a "great Marxist, a good and honest revolutionary," while conceding that he was excessively repressive, unfair to the peasantry and certain oppressed nationalities. His mistakes were, Mao mused, a natural result of the contradictions of trying to build a new world out of the old—an excuse he would later use for himself.[32]

There is other evidence, too, supporting the idea of the CPC's openness to aspects of de-Stalinization and even peaceful coexistence with the capitalist West. The tensions between China and the Soviet Union, then, were less about socialist dogma and more about national dignity. Chinese revolutionaries had struggled for independence, and as a nation of six hundred million people, they refused to be a Soviet satellite. Mao was incensed, for instance, by the USSR's backtracking on a commitment to help China develop an atomic bomb: "In today's world, if we don't want to be bullied, we have to have this thing." Yet Chinese economic nationalism hampered growth. Concerns about national prestige, meanwhile, prevented the party from soliciting international aid during the Great Famine, the scope of which was unknown to contemporary proponents of the "Chinese model" in other countries.[33]

Unlike the micromanaging Stalin, Mao was detached from the day-to-day running of the state. He often worked all night and slept during the day. Though the CPC was modeled along Stalinist lines, it had a "two-front" leadership, divided between those who administered the country and those, like Mao, responsible for long-term decisions. Mao made frequent interventions but could safely retreat to the second, more removed tier, blaming any problems on his lieutenants. The Great Famine, however, was such a fiasco that the leadership took key powers from Mao in the early 1960s. The party admitted that a "man-made disaster" had taken place. Liu Shaoqi and Zhou Enlai pursued a more pragmatic economic direction, breaking up the communes and trying to repair some of the damage.[34]

MAO ONLY PERMITTED himself to be sidelined for so long. In 1965–1966, he reasserted his authority with a campaign for "continuous revolution" to overturn the state he himself had created. As with the Hundred Flower Campaigns, his goals might not have been completely cynical. Mao read reports of former nationalists rising within the Communist Party, inequalities cohering into a new class system, and attempts to restore relations with the Soviet Union. His was a kind of anti-Stalinist Stalinism, eager to take risks for ideological reasons, confident that he was one with the masses and that the masses demanded not peace but constant upheaval.

Mao's ally, defense minister Lin Biao, started things off by encouraging students to criticize "bourgeois liberalism and Khrushchevism" in late 1965, though the real targets appeared to be head of state Liu Shaoqi and Deng Xiaoping. Earlier that year, Mao also had his wife, Jiang Qing, and future Gang of Four member Yao Wenyuan denounce key Beijing officials. Wrestling control of press organs in early 1966, Mao established the Cultural Revolution Group. He used state media and a May politburo meeting to announce that the bourgeoisie had snuck "into the Party, the government, the army, and various spheres of culture." These clever foes would, like Khrushchev, "wave the red flag to oppose the red flag."

Lecturers and students in Beijing sprang to action. Full of revolutionary zeal, this younger generation had heard about the glories of the Long March and civil war but not witnessed its terrible cost. They looked around for "capitalist roaders" to attack. With Mao's blessing, the students organized into Red Guards, and their movement went national. Announcing his return to the fray, the elderly leader showed his vitality in a bizarre PR stunt: he took a swim in the Yangtze. According to the party press, he covered nearly fifteen kilometers in an hour, with "no sign of fatigue."[35]

The Red Guards would soon be sending dead bodies down the river after him. "Cowshed" detention centers popped up across the country, including in Peking University. "Counterrevolutionary elements" were paraded around with shaming placards, starved, and tortured. Many committed suicide after struggle sessions. One middle school published its own Cultural Revolution battle song: "We are Chairman Mao's Red Guards / We steel our red hearts in great winds and waves / We arm ourselves with Mao Zedong Thought / To sweep away all pests."[36]

Stalin's Great Terror was clinical, directed with bureaucratic precision by his secret police. Mao sparked terror from below with vague slogans like "to rebel is justified" and calls to "bombard the headquarters." The bloody summer of 1966 produced stories about children informing on their own parents, exposing them to battery, rape, or murder. Some babies were even targeted for the crime of being "counterrevolutionary offspring." Most shocking are the accounts of ceremonial cannibalism, with the livers of "rightists" consumed. Tens of millions were victimized, and a half million lost their lives to the madness.[37]

Eventually even Mao, who was trying to stage-manage chaos, realized things had gotten out of hand. Rival Red Guard units were fighting each other, the economy slowed to a halt, and workers were striking and creating alternative power structures in cities, including Shanghai. At Mao's direction, the People's Liberation Army restored order, and millions of Red Guards were sent to the countryside to "learn from the peasants," but the grassroots violence didn't come to an end until Mao's death a decade later.

His practical objective, however, was complete. Mao no longer had to apologize: he was exalted as a demigod, with "Marxism-Leninism–Mao

Zedong Thought" now constitutionally enshrined. Liu, once the second most important person in China, was arrested and subjected to public beatings and denunciations, contributing to his November 1969 death. He wouldn't be allowed to do to Mao what Khrushchev had done to Stalin.

Deng Xiaoping was a Red Guard victim, too. He was forced to re-educate himself through manual labor at a tractor factory in Jiangxi, where he once helped the party survive in the 1930s. That Deng—China's Bukharin—wasn't executed outright like the real Bukharin suggests an-other, admittedly small difference between Mao and Stalin, but he suffered for years. (Deng's son was tortured and thrown out of a four-story window, surviving as a paraplegic.) He only returned to prominence when Zhou Enlai, then dying from cancer, convinced Mao that his experience and ad-ministrative competence were needed.

During the frenzies of the Cultural Revolution, which lasted from 1966 to 1976, Maoism resonated far beyond China's borders. China became a radical alternative to the Soviet Union, which had lost its luster as it be-came perceived as just another Great Power. Its presence wasn't only felt in largely peasant countries, like Albania and Tanzania, where socialist vanguards struggled with underdevelopment, but it made inroads in the advanced capitalist world too. For New Left militants in the West, Mao-ism married the rigor of Marxism with the anti-establishment spirit of the times.

Radicals in the United States, for instance, found certain aspects of Maoist thought appealing. In the Chinese example they saw proof that new revolutionary agents (students and the poor, not peasants) could be substituted for workers and that ideological zeal could overcome objective conditions. In most cases, however, the *Little Red Book* and Mao Zedong Thought were symbols of resistance rather than guides to action.

More significant was China's role in the Third World, where its actions stood in stark contrast to its rhetoric. Mao had long criticized Khrushchev and his successors for putting the political needs of the USSR above their internationalist duties to the oppressed. But faced with its own isolation and poverty, China pursued a foreign policy far more brazenly nationalist than the Soviet Union's. It dismissed India's 1962 liberation of Goa and other Portuguese territories as a cynical ploy, joined apartheid South Africa in supporting UNITA forces in Angola, backed an anticommunist dictatorship in Sudan, jumped to recognize Pinochet's right-wing Chilean government just days after the coup against democratic socialist Salvador Allende, encouraged Pakistan's genocidal campaign in Bangladesh, and sparked a 1979 border war with Communist Vietnam. Chinese officials were even on hand for Spanish fascist general Francisco Franco's 1975 funeral.

Perhaps the most disillusioning act was the country's embrace of the United States in the early 1970s, when it gave President Richard Nixon and his national security advisor, Henry Kissinger, the royal treatment in Beijing while they were still overseeing the massacre of innocents in Southeast Asia. The CPC had begun to see its neighbor, the Soviet Union, as its primary rival and sought any advantage against it, while dressing up its new course in dogmatic Marxist language. A party dedicated to national development above all else now had a nationalist foreign policy to match.

AFTER MAO'S DEATH in 1976, the hard-line Gang of Four were his most zealous defenders and tried to carry on the "continuous revolution." Yet Deng Xiaoping eventually won a power struggle with them and challenged Maoist policies. Pro-market experiments to restore productivity were expanded, but the Great Helmsman himself could not be repudiated.

As Deng would say in 1978, "We will never do to Mao what the Soviets did to Stalin." Mao's body lies embalmed in Tiananmen Square, and his portrait is still on the Gate of Heavenly Peace and Chinese currency. The People's Republic has dropped its revolutionary pretenses, but it still needs a revered national symbol, and to properly reckon with Mao's legacy would mean hard questions for the party that empowered him.[38]

Deng provided an alternative path to development for China—still authoritarian, still rooted in exploitation, but more effective at its stated tasks. Starting in 1949, the first eight years of Communist rule, despite the heavy cost, delivered real gains. The next twenty years were an unmitigated disaster. The last forty have been rightly praised as an economic miracle. Never before have so many people been lifted out of poverty.

Yet when examining the terrible Mao years, we should consider the arguments of economists Amartya Sen and Jean Drèze, themselves staunch anti-authoritarians. There was no famine in India after it won its independence in 1947. But as Sen and Drèze showed, "comparing India's death rate of 12 per thousand with China's of 7 per thousand, and applying the difference to the Indian population of 781 million in 1986, we get an estimate of excess mortality in India of 3.9 million per year." That's a calamity on the scale of the Great Famine—every eight years since 1947. The authoritarian Communist leadership's emphasis on eliminating poverty, and its investment in education and health care, compare favorably to the neglect of Indian elites.[39]

How, then, should a socialist today assess Maoism? Certainly we cannot follow the official CPC line—70 percent good, 30 percent bad. We might respond by saying that the question is misguided in the first place. Socialism was made to be an ideology of radical democracy, of working-class self-emancipation, not a tool for state-managed development. A revolution from above, with an unelected party overseeing the creation of a social surplus and rerouting it to certain ends, even with the best of intentions, is a formula for authoritarianism.

But we cannot claim that the excesses of Maoism had nothing to do with Marxism, or even that Mao was just a nationalist who selectively invoked an ideology he barely understood to serve his ends. The teleological streak in Marxism, its belief in laws of history—that through conscious political activity humanity could be pushed toward a new, more advanced stage of civilization—surely made Stalin and Mao feel justified in their cruelties. Mao was no believer in democracy, but he did believe that mass action had "the force to topple mountains and upturn seas." He shared with his Soviet counterpart a willingness to sacrifice individual lives, even millions of them, for a collective purpose.

Any ideology built around a notion of destiny— nationalism and socialism alike—runs the risk of calamity. The solution is a banal one: valuing and protecting rights and liberties, while ensuring that ordinary people are not only consulted through mass rallies but actually have democratic avenues to make choices and hold their leaders accountable. Without this bedrock, any postcapitalist society risks creating a new caste of oppressors.

Brought to power by the sacrifices of peasant soldiers, the Communist party-state, in every instance, has stood above the people in whose interests it claimed to govern. The rhetoric and prestige of its early days, the constant calls to world revolution, made it hard to acknowledge what is now obvious: the CPC's revolution is best understood as a national, authoritarian project, capable of delivering progress at times but far removed from the classic vision of socialism. The richer socialist movements, those that followed in the footsteps of Marx, were extinguished in Russia and China in the 1920s.

THOUGH CHINA'S WAS the most significant Third World revolution, it was far from the only one. In Afghanistan, which was even less developed than China, a vanguard of military officers and academics launched a successful coup in 1978 and then tried to implement sweeping reforms. Never winning much support outside Kabul, they relied on extreme repression and finally Soviet intervention to stay in power. Ethiopia followed a similar pattern: a revolution in a backward country led by a left-wing elite, provoking civil war and leading to terror. As did South Yemen, but with less bloody consequences.[40]

In countries such as Angola, Mozambique, Vietnam, and Zimbabwe, Marxist-Leninists won victories but at grave costs. They achieved some of their national objectives by shaking off imperialist powers but were unable to build a popular socialism out of the rubble of war. Though still authoritarian, Vietnam today is pursuing Chinese-style market reforms with some success, while Angola and Zimbabwe are among the most corrupt and unequal nations in the world.

The case of Tanzania garnered considerable sympathy, especially from the socialists of Sweden and elsewhere in Western Europe. The newly independent country had been a neglected corner of the British Empire when Julius Nyerere took power in 1961 with talk of pan-Africanism, self-reliance, and socialism. Overseeing a rural, peasant country, he looked to Mao's China for inspiration, but the *ujamaa* collectivist project he pushed in the countryside had genuinely participatory dynamics. Nyerere was ultimately not able to find an alternative path to development, and most of his reforms were rolled back after 1995. Tanzania remains poor and dependent on foreign aid.

Grenada, a Caribbean island of just a hundred thousand, saw a left-wing coup led by the charismatic Maurice Bishop's New Jewel Movement in 1979. Bishop pursued development projects with Cuban help and brought about reforms, especially in health care, education, and women's rights. He was pragmatic about what could be done in such a small country. But despite his popular support and personal integrity, Bishop shared the same skepticism of civil liberties as many of his contemporaries. The United States began drawing up war plans from the early days of Bishop's rule, and when some of his ultra-leftist comrades overthrew and murdered him, the US invasion came.

Elsewhere in the Americas, democratic roads to socialism in Nicaragua and Chile, the latter supported by a powerful working-class movement, were blocked by conservative domestic elites and American meddling. The nature of this US interference was not always coups and invasions but also sanctions, trade sabotage, and election rigging. Even where Third World socialist movements had democratic impulses, the experience of those like Allende seemed to encourage authoritarian paths to change.

The most successful "revolution from above" occurred in Cuba, where Fidel Castro and his band of guerrillas arrived from the countryside in the late 1950s to overthrow the hated dictator Fulgencio Batista. Cuba had a long-standing anarchist and socialist tradition, including a powerful Communist Party and a vibrant student and workers' movement. There was mass support for Castro's early measures, including anti-illiteracy campaigns and agrarian reform, not to mention the revolutionary government's struggle against US-sponsored invasion and terrorism. Yet popular participation was always limited by what became a party-state.[41]

Fueled by Eastern Bloc subsidies, which counteracted a devastating US embargo, the transformation within Cuba after the revolution was astounding. The country was still dependent on sugar production, but for the first time ordinary Cubans had access to good schools and health care, new roads and clean drinking water, and they enjoyed a guaranteed right to basic necessities like housing. Though suffering from the inefficiencies common in command economies, the country's famous propaganda poster is not far from the truth when it reads, "200 million children in the world today sleep in the streets—none are Cuban." Cuba's international accomplishments are also worthy of mention. Cuban doctors have served millions abroad, and the country played a pivotal role defeating South African apartheid (though its record intervening in the Horn of Africa is less laudable).

At the same time, Cuba falls short of any standard of "socialist democracy." Cuba's workers don't have even basic rights to collectively bargain or protest government policies.

The 1959 Revolution served to create a new elite, though unlike the country's old elite, its legitimacy is grounded not in wealth and its relations with Washington but in its offering of free education and quality medical care and other necessities to the people. It has accomplished, in short, more than capitalism has in most of Latin America. But without the freedom to organize to defend what's good in their system and overturn what is corrupt, Cuba's future seems to be in the hands of a new generation of state bureaucrats and remerging business interests.

THE THIRD WORLD'S experience with socialism vindicates Marx. He argued that a successful socialist economy requires already developed productive forces and that a robust socialist democracy requires a self-organized working class. It would follow that encouraging capitalist growth, while mitigating its worst effects and redistributing its spoils—as the Workers' Party in Brazil and other Latin American Pink Tide governments have recently done—is the best we can hope for from states in the developing world. But we should be asking more fundamental questions.

Why do these countries need to go through the same destructive sequence as those in the Global North? Wouldn't a just world subsidize those who—through mere accidents of birth—were born in poor countries? Wouldn't we all benefit if the smokestacks that dot the Chinese landscape were replaced by a more sustainable form of progress?

There are both practical and moral cases for such a transfer of resources, or at the very least an abolition of foreign-held debt. Fortunately, some are already making this case. In advanced capitalist countries with vibrant Lefts, such as in Scandinavia, governments put more emphasis on foreign aid and internationalism. Sweden's Olof Palme felt that European social democracies had a great obligation to assist in the liberation and development of poorer countries. For Palme, advocating "full employment and social justice in industrial as well as developing countries" meant more than just devoting a generous percentage of Sweden's GDP to foreign aid—though he did that too. It also meant taking a principled stand against colonialism, which led him into confrontation with apartheid South Africa and US imperialism in Vietnam.[42]

After Palme was assassinated in 1986, Oliver Tambo, a hero of the South African liberation struggle, wrote a eulogy. For Tambo, Palme demonstrated "that leading politicians and statesmen of the Western world could overcome all constraints, both real and imagined, finally to side with the poor, the oppressed, the exploited, and the brutalized." Sweden's battle for social democracy and South Africa's struggle against apartheid were inextricably connected: "Our world will forever sing of Olof Palme as the thorn in the flesh of the forces of reaction that represented a terrible and petrified world order."[43]

A radical foreign policy animated by this spirit wouldn't be another tool of dependency but one capable of putting the future in the hands of ordinary people. We need, more than ever, a way to human uplift that doesn't require sacrificing generations in sweatshops and mines.

SEVEN

SOCIALISM AND AMERICA

WERNER SOMBART'S CLASSIC 1906 book *Why Is There No Socialism in the United States?* tried to address a crucial question. If "modern Socialism follows as a necessary reaction to capitalism," Sombart reasoned, "the country with the most advanced capitalist development, namely the United States, would at the same time be the one providing the classic case of Socialism, and its working class would be supporters of the most radical of Socialist movements."

Why hadn't it, and why hadn't they? His answer was simple: prosperity meant that workers were too full of "roast beef and apple pie" to be drawn to socialist agitation. That answer has long been seen accurate to one degree or another, as have others, including the notion of American "exceptionalism"— an attachment to individualism and a limited state that goes back to the nation's founding.

Yet socialism in fact has a long and distinguished history in the United States. In Sombart's day, socialism might not have been a mass force in American politics, but it seemed to be gathering momentum. In 1912, the Socialist Party won almost a million votes in the presidential election, had a membership of a hundred twenty thousand, and elected more than a thousand people to office. Mayors of cities including Berkeley, Flint, Milwaukee, and Schenectady were all socialists. So was a congressman, Victor

Berger, and dozens of state officials. Oklahoma alone was home to eleven socialist weeklies. And in clusters of the country—from the Jewish enclaves of the Lower East Side to the mining towns of the West—the "cooperative commonwealth" was the American dream that workers actually subscribed to.[1]

Nor were these sentiments new to America. In the late 1820s, the United States gave birth to the first workers' parties in the world, in Boston, New York, Philadelphia, and elsewhere. These movements largely represented the interests of artisans, as factory production was just being introduced and was concentrated in New England, employing mostly women and children. In New York, more straightforward demands to limit the working day coexisted for a brief while with the radical agrarianism of the party's leader, Thomas Skidmore, who called for the equal distribution of all land. Drawing on the republicanism of the American revolution, Skidmore had a language for his criticism of wage labor: "thousands of our people of the present day in deep distress and poverty, dependent for their daily subsistence upon a few among us whom the unnatural operation of our own free and republican institutions, as we are pleased to call them, has thus arbitrarily and barbarously made enormously rich."[2]

For the more fanciful parts of his program and his authoritarian personality, Skidmore was booted from the organization before its first electoral campaign, which was a relative success. Within two years, however, the New York "Workies" would be subsumed into the Democratic Party, in what would become a pattern for independent labor efforts.

In the same period, the United States proved itself fertile ground for utopian socialism. Robert Owen, a Welsh former industrialist, founded a community he called New Harmony in southwest Indiana in 1827. He even described his ideals of communal living to a session of Congress attended by outgoing president James Monroe and the newly elected John Quincy Adams. The "terrestrial paradise" Owen sought to build was continually reorganized over the following years, and he soon had to admit defeat and return to the United Kingdom. Followers of Charles Fourier—Nathaniel

Hawthorne and Ralph Waldo Emerson among them—made their own attempts at communes a decade later, with similar results.

After the 1848 Revolutions in Europe, "scientific socialism" was introduced to the United States by German refugees. Joseph Weydemeyer was one notable example. A former Prussian artillery officer turned committed Marxist, he fled to America in 1851. He worked as a journalist for the German-language press and wrote perceptive analyses of American capitalism. In 1853, he was involved in the formation of the American Workers League, which aspired to be an independent party for workers "without respect to occupation, language, color or sex." The League put forth a modern socialist program that combined support for trade unions with immediate demands, such as a ten-hour workday, naturalization of immigrants, and an end to child labor.

Though it persuasively combined economic and political struggles, the organization never reached beyond German American workers. Still, Weydemeyer and many of those involved in the League did go on to play important roles supporting the Union in the Civil War. Weydemeyer died soon after the war, but many of the former members who survived the conflict became radical Republicans.

Marx and Engels frequently turned their gaze to the United States. As they saw it, since the country didn't have a legacy of feudalism, class divisions appeared more permeable. But new immigrants and future generations of proletarians wouldn't have expanses of land to live off of, and would eventually come to develop class consciousness similar to their European peers.

They had hopes that such a shift was imminent. A bitter opponent of slavery, Marx famously wrote to Lincoln, whom he called "the single-minded son of the working class," to say that the First International supported the Union in the Civil War and hoped that the conflict might be followed by a wave of working-class struggle.[3]

The Civil War was the true American Revolution. The Republican Party expropriated $3.5 trillion in "private property" in emancipating the

South's four million slaves. The Reconstruction that followed saw the country's most oppressed people attempt to construct a new world free of their former masters' whips.

The fight against black slavery inspired battles against what was denounced as "wage slavery." Such a spirit motivated the Knights of Labor, which started off with just nine members in 1869 but organized hundreds of thousands by the 1880s. It rallied workers in all trades and brought tens of thousands of black workers into what had been an overwhelmingly white movement.[4] Just as many women joined up, as the Knights spanned from Pennsylvania mines to New York garment factories to Denver railroads and Alabama foundries.[5]

The 1870s and 1880s were a time of labor unrest. The Panic of 1873 led to a squeeze on workers, which fueled a wave of strikes, most notably the 1877 Great Railroad Strike. One hundred thousand workers were routed by state and private militias, as well as federal troops. A similar fate befell the Homestead and Pullman Strikes in the 1890s, the latter of which saw the radicalization of American Railway Union leader Eugene V. Debs.

The Workingmen's Party of the United States was founded in 1876. It was split from the beginning between Marxists and Lassalleans, and much like in the Old World, their theoretical disputes had real-world implications. The Lassalleans wanted to form a socialist political party and win reforms through the ballot box. In particular, they advocated for state funding for a network of cooperatives. Since they believed in an "iron law of wages," they didn't think there was a point in trade union activity. The Marxists took the opposite tack, believing that years of trade union organizing were needed before the ground would be ready for a socialist party. The Lassalleans managed to wrestle control of the Workingmen's Party, with its leaders denouncing the 1877 strikes as futile.

Many party activists, however, were actively engaged in the Great Railroad Strike. One was Albert Parsons. Perceiving both the power of direct action and the class nature of a repressive state drew him to anarchism. He dedicated himself to the struggle for an eight-hour day and was a part of the much broader movement of socialists and trade unionists that rallied in Haymarket Square on May 1, 1886. Late that night, with the event already over, a bomb was thrown in the square, killing a policeman. Parsons was among six Chicago radicals baselessly arrested for the act. He was executed by hanging a year later.

The armories built in American cities after the Civil War weren't intended to fend off foreign invasion but to guard against working-class revolt along the lines of the 1871 Paris Commune. "Load Your Guns, They Will Be Needed Tomorrow to Shoot Communists" blared the *Chicago Times* in 1875. These concerns seem outsized with hindsight, but they were very real in an era when striking workers were often armed and when anarchists assassinated world leaders (an anarchist would murder President William McKinley in 1901).[6]

Though the media stoked fears about anarchistic and communist violence, it was private employer militias and state terror that made America's nineteenth-century labor history more violent than Europe's. This violence undid the loosely organized Knights of Labor and encouraged craft unionists such as American Federation of Labor (AFL) founder Samuel Gompers to endorse "class harmony" and incremental reforms. (Gompers had been a socialist, but put off by the Lassallean influence, he shifted to "bread-and-butter" trade unionism.) At a time when American capitalism was pushing forward, deskilling workers and incorporating more and more people into the factory system, attempts to organize unskilled labor were in retreat.

But ferment was still growing in rural America. The Populist Movement sprang from the 1870s struggles of indebted farmers in central Texas but soon spread throughout the country. As the price of cotton collapsed and the economy entered a depression in the 1890s, the Populists fervently supported Debs during the Pullman Strike, backed many demands made by labor, and were leading tenant and sharecropper efforts against the crop-lien system. Populist leader Tom Watson challenged white and black farmers to organize across racial lines, telling a crowd, "You are deceived and blinded that you may not see how this race antagonism perpetuates a monetary system which beggars both."[7]

In 1892, the movement formed a national political party around a progressive platform that called for a graduated income tax, nationalized railways, debt relief, and public works to combat unemployment. Planter elites responded with a campaign of electoral fraud and violence, including the lynching of hundreds of organizers, while the Democratic Party came to co-opt much of the movement's platform in 1896. After the pro-Populist Democrat William Jennings Bryan's election loss that year, the movement fell apart. Legislative efforts to disenfranchise blacks through poll taxes and biased "literacy tests" were expanded, helping prevent another multiracial movement from emerging for decades.

BY 1890, THE Workingmen's Party, now known as the Socialist Labor Party (SLP), came under the sway of Daniel De Leon. An immigrant from Curaçao, De Leon was a lecturer at Columbia School of Law when he became active in the 1886 mayoral candidacy of Henry George. George was backed by the Central Labor Union, a New York–area union broadly Marxist in orientation. George's own politics, however, were eclectic. He was the best-selling author of *Progress and Poverty*, which advocated an egalitarian land value tax. The idea was that people should control the fruits of their own labor, but land and other natural resources belonged to society as a whole.

George finished second in the election (beating out future president Theodore Roosevelt), and De Leon was denied a full-time job at Columbia for his political activity. De Leon wasn't put off from politics, however. Like hundreds of thousands of other Americans, he read utopian socialist Edward Bellamy's *Looking Backward*, which depicts a socialist society in the year 2000. It is a world without unnecessary hardship, one that had worked out the problems of industrial capitalism. De Leon went on to read Marx and Engels, and he soon joined the SLP.

Engels was a persistent critic of the sectarian and "foreign garbed" SLP (the party's communiqués were often issued in German), accusing it of reducing Marxism to "a rigid orthodoxy" inaccessible to ordinary workers except as "an article of faith" to "gulp down." To his credit, De Leon solved the "un-American" problem by creating new English-language publications to supplement the party's main paper, *Vorwärts (Forward)*. Within eight years the SLP would reach ten thousand members and win ninety-seven thousand votes for president.[8]

The sectarianism remained, however. Lenin echoed Engels's grumblings, accusing rancorous American socialists of being "incapable of adapting themselves to the theoretically helpless but living and powerful mass labor movement that is marching alongside them." Under De Leon, the increasingly sectarian SLP pursued a dual union strategy, advocating that socialists withdraw from broad working-class organizations such as the American Federation of Labor and organize themselves into parallel union federations composed entirely of socialists.[9]

While this approach did manage to attract a fair number of principled socialists to the SLP, it ultimately isolated the party from the labor movement. De Leon himself seemed untroubled by the relative smallness of his Socialist Trade and Labor Alliance (STLA), characterizing the efforts of other socialists to win more general support as "nothing short of idiocy."

But history did not vindicate De Leon: the STLA ignominiously dissolved, and his intransigence later got him ejected from the newly formed Industrial Workers of the World (IWW). Today he is remembered as a contradictory figure. De Leon showed himself to be a prescient theorist, capable of creative thought, but the organization he led didn't often reflect his personal sophistication.

His debates with future Irish martyr James Connolly were illustrative. Connolly first traveled to the United States in 1902 at the Socialist Labor Party's invitation for a speaking tour aimed at Irish immigrant workers, who were being discouraged from joining the movement by the Catholic Church. So successful was his message that the SLP brought him over as a full-time organizer. But Connolly, ever the internationalist, didn't consider himself a guest and challenged De Leon about the SLP's program. The most important limitation, as Connolly saw it, was the party's stance on wages.

De Leon was the son of a surgeon and a colonial official; he never really understood the realities of working life as Connolly did, as the latter had been born in the Cowgate ghetto of Edinburgh and started working at age nine. In their distance from the day-to-day realities of the working class, the De Leonists clung to an abstract theory of wages that claimed any wage increase would automatically be offset by price increases. Therefore, fighting for higher wages was a waste of time and resources. This, Connolly said, might "sound very revolutionary" but was in fact making it hard for working people to see in the socialist movement the means to improve their lives. It was an important debate, and it offers insight into how American radicals failed to take full advantage of labor unrest in the 1890s.[10]

In other words, one answer to Werner Sombart's famous question might be "Daniel De Leon." Would the SLP under different leadership have been able to unite American trade unionists, left-wing populists, and socialists into a more powerful force? Such an effort would have encountered fierce resistance. What made the United States exceptional at the start of the nineteenth century was its abundance of land (allowing small producers to be more self-sufficient) and the relative egalitarianism that prevailed among white men. But by the end of it, industrial capitalism had created conditions similar to those in other capitalist countries. The nation remained exceptional, however, in the extreme level of state and private violence directed at the workers' movement. Sectarianism, failed unionization strategies, ethnic and racial divisions—all played a role in the disorganization of the country's working class, but the threat of violent repression seems paramount.

STILL, THE TURMOIL of the 1890s had revealed the power of US workers. With the founding of the Socialist Party of America (SP) in 1901, the movement finally had its big tent.

The most famous of the party's founders, Eugene V. Debs, was a leading labor organizer who had been radicalized while serving a six-month term in prison after the Pullman Strike. Like many socialists of his era, he was inspired by German social democracy. As he put it, "the writings of Kautsky were so clear and conclusive that I readily grasped, not merely his argument, but also caught the spirit of his socialist utterance." Victor Berger—an Austrian who knew Kautsky personally and had been organizing in Milwaukee—visited Debs in jail, left him a copy of Marx's *Capital*, and "delivered the first impassioned message of Socialism [Debs] had ever heard." Together they created an organization they called Social Democracy of America in 1897, which a year later became the Social Democratic Party of America (SDP). Only a few years after that, they were joined by dissidents from the SLP, including Morris Hillquit, a Jewish immigrant who settled in New York, in forming the Socialist Party.[11]

The party was small, but it had a national leader in Debs, a few bastions of union support, and the backing of a vibrant socialist press. No publication was more significant than *Appeal to Reason*, which was founded by J. A. Wayland, who would boast that he was "of American Revolutionary stock" and knew how to speak in the popular vernacular. The publisher and real estate speculator was politicized by reading Edward Bellamy's *Looking Backward* (like De Leon) and by the turmoil of the 1890s. The tagline of his first radical newspaper, *The Coming Nation*, proclaimed it to be "for a government of, by, and for the People as outlined in Bellamy's *Looking Backward*, abolishing the Possibility of Poverty." It offered an eclectic mix of republicanism, Bellamy's "nationalism," and radical populism.[12]

After a failed effort at creating a utopian commune in Tennessee, Wayland launched *Appeal to Reason* in 1897, which also used the language of populism and democracy in its attempts to root socialism in American soil. As the Socialist Party took off, and with Debs as a supporter and contributor, circulation grew to the hundreds of thousands. At its peak, *Appeal to Reason* was the fourth-most-read publication in the country and spawned a broader publishing empire, popularizing authors including Jack London and Upton Sinclair.

ALL WAS NOT well in the socialist camp, however, with the party riven along ideological lines similar to those that fractured the Social Democrats in Germany. On the right, Victor Berger proved himself to be an American Eduard Bernstein in his advocacy for evolutionary change within the system as the path to socialism. Members of Berger's Milwaukee wing were called "sewer socialists" for their emphasis on local government, particularly public health efforts. They focused on winning elections and showing themselves capable of honest and competent administration once in office. The reforms they supported would prefigure many of the demands of the Progressive movement, but their "realistic" approach to the middle class also meant turning away from core socialist commitments. William A. Arnold, the Socialist candidate for Milwaukee mayor in 1904, claimed that the city's business interests "will be safer in the hands of an administration made up of Social Democrats than they have been under the Republican and Democratic administrations." Berger himself bragged that the socialist presence in the city was keeping strikes down and business humming.[13] These moderate Socialists occupied Milwaukee's mayoralty for much of a half century, starting with Emil Seidel's 1910 election.[14]

Their socialism, such as it was, couldn't have sounded more different from Debs's revolutionary politics. Debs traveled across the country giving speeches and raising the profile of the party. An Indiana native, like Wayland, Debs connected with ordinary workers through simple and direct rhetoric, sharing with them his hope that the twentieth century would be, as Victor Hugo prophesied, "the century of humanity." Though sympathetic to the left of the party—then dominated by radical Western syndicalist workers and poor farmers in states like Oklahoma—Debs avoided intraparty disputes and conventions and attempted to be a unifying figurehead.[15]

One question that he joined other socialists in grappling with was how to relate to the labor movement and move its ranks toward socialism.

Debs joined the IWW, with seemingly all of the era's famed radicals—
Dorothy Day, Mother Jones, Elizabeth Gurley Flynn, Bill Haywood, Helen
Keller, Jack Reed, James Connolly, and future Communist leader William
Z. Foster. The organization was founded as an alternative to the "business unionist" American Federation of Labor. The AFL had two million
members, but it organized along narrow craft lines, which caused interun-
ion squabbling and locked out unskilled workers. It also had produced a
privileged layer of bureaucrats unchecked by rank-and-file democracy who
sought partnership at all costs with business interests.

The IWW was the polar opposite of the AFL. It practiced industrial
unionism, meaning it organized all workers in an industry—regardless of
skill—in the same union. It also adopted such a radical stance toward
management that the union refused to institutionalize any gain won
through struggle. "No contracts, no agreement, no compacts. These are
unholy alliances, and must be damned as treason when entered into with
the capitalist class," Bill Haywood, an early leader, said in a speech.
Their fierce independence and distrust of centralization were very much
part of the American ethos, especially among the frontier miners and
loggers initially drawn to their ranks. But without the ability to win practical reforms, or provide necessities like insurance and death benefits to
members, even many left-wing workers felt better off in the meeker AFL
unions. Unwilling to make demands on the state, the IWW even opposed the women's suffrage movement, labor regulations, and other social
protections.[16]

The IWW also drew radicals away from existing AFL locals, depriving
anti-Gompers reform movements within the larger federation of their most
competent organizers. William Z. Foster, who joined the IWW in 1909 and
left soon after, went down a more promising path. The future Communist
created the Syndicalist League of North America (SLNA). The organization
was to the left of the Socialist Party and even the IWW, but it fought to
create a "militant minority" within the AFL rather than outside of it. In a
different guise, his strategy would bear fruit in the 1920s and '30s.[17]

For its part, the IWW did make an impact. Actions such as the 1912 textile workers' strike in Lawrence and the 1913 Paterson silk strike galvanized tens of thousands. But tellingly the organization didn't institutionalize those gains or create a functioning bureaucracy, refusing to even set up permanent strike funds. In 1912, the IWW had fourteen thousand members in Lawrence—a year later, it had less than a thousand. Unions, after all, need to deliver steady economic gains for their members through transactional bargaining, and their political activity can complement, but not replace, the more visionary political work of a political party. There was a reason successful left movements were all patterned on a version of this "sword" and "shield" division.[18]

The IWW's sectarian attitude toward even other left-wing unions and the Socialist Party caused Debs to leave in 1908. He complained that "the IWW for which Haywood stands and speaks is an anarchist organization in all except in name, and this is the cause of all the trouble. Anarchism and Socialism have never mixed and never will."[19]

Haywood, in turn, famously did battle with Morris Hillquit on the trade union question in early 1912. Haywood expressed his opinion that not only the AFL but the capitalist system as a whole could not be slowly reformed. Hillquit, though otherwise tempered in his tone, offered his rather fanciful opinion that "within five years and no longer the American Federation of Labor and its rank and file will be socialistic."[20]

Besieged by the leadership, Haywood left the SP when the organization denounced lawbreaking and sabotage—hallmarks of any worthwhile labor militancy. In a letter to the *New York Call*, Helen Keller expressed the sentiment of many party activists: "While countless women and children are breaking their hearts and ruining their bodies in long days of toil, we are fighting one another. Shame upon us!"

WHATEVER DEBATES AROSE, Debs remained the heart of the party. In his speeches, he somehow managed to synthesize populism, the messianic rhetoric of Christianity, Western syndicalism, and Marxist socialism into a coherent whole. Like Wayland, his moral case for socialism found a wide audience. But Debs never presented a clear political strategy to go along with this shared rhetoric.

American socialism spoke in a variety of idioms, and even in different languages, and was more of a coalition than a unified force. It helped that it was operating in a country as geographically large, and as regionally divided, as the United States. Berger could run an electoral machine in Wisconsin at the same time other party members could use Socialist locals to build the IWW, which he despised. Rival factions traded polemics in the socialist press and clashed at conventions, but didn't—indeed, couldn't— interfere with each other.

For his 1908 presidential campaign, Debs toured the country on a train called the Red Special, and repeated the effort in 1912, when he spoke to more than five hundred thousand people. The Socialists revived the encampments of the Populist days, which resembled Protestant revival meetings. They often lasted for an entire week, as thousands rolled in on covered wagons, picked up socialist literature, and listened to the gospel of the Cooperative Commonwealth.

Debs ended up with 901,551 votes in 1912, almost a half million more than his showing in 1908. The party polled in the double-digits in more than a half-dozen states. Today, we view these results as the high point of the Socialist movement. But to Wayland the 1912 election was a bitter disappointment. Depressed by the death of his wife and harassed by the capitalist press and federal authorities, he took his own life after the election. "The struggle under the competitive system is not worth the effort; let it pass," was his parting note.[21]

Many others still saw a movement on the rise. The 1912 election was just one indicator. Another was that in the nine years between 1903 and 1912, the SP's membership grew sevenfold, despite all the internal battles. The party now had twelve hundred elected officials across the country. The Socialists drew strength from the same broad current of reform that powered the growing Progressive movement and also informed Theodore

Roosevelt's Bull Moose party and Woodrow Wilson's Democrats. The Socialist Party appealed to voters not by articulating a clear vision of socialism or how to achieve it, but by expressing anger at the status quo and calling for improvements in public health, taxation, and education and an end to corruption. Yet with its message co-opted by other reformers, no doubt thousands who were inspired by Debs or SP local efforts voted for more viable candidates for national office instead of Socialists.[22]

Between Wilson's 1912 election and the entry of the United States into the First World War in 1917, the Socialist Party didn't meet the expectations of those like Hillquit who thought the party would reach two hundred thousand members. Membership actually dipped in this period, but there was no dramatic collapse. In short, socialism seemed to be a stable, if not dominant, factor in American political life. But the war changed everything.[23]

When the United States entered the war on April 6, 1917, millions had already pointlessly died in Europe, and the February Revolution in Russia had inspired American socialists to imagine a worker-led end to the madness. Hillquit presented the majority resolution at the party's emergency conference on the conflict. It claimed that "the declaration of war by our government" was "a crime against the peoples of the United States and against the nations of the world," and proposed "active and public opposition to the war, through demonstrations, mass petitions and all other means within our power." John Spargo, an English-born biographer of Marx, countered that "having failed to prevent the war, we can only recognize it as a fact and try to force upon the government through pressure of public opinion a constructive policy." But the Hillquit resolution won resounding support.[24]

The SP was almost entirely united against the war, but some prominent right-wing members including Walter Lippmann and William English Walling supported US intervention, and believed that their patriotism would help the socialist cause in America. Spargo left the SP in June, complaining that "the Socialist Party is probably the greatest single obstacle to the progress of Socialism in America."[25]

Though the war was popular among much of the country, the Socialists benefited from their opposition. The party was a rare voice of dissent
and distinguished itself from a disingenuous "progressivism" that retreated
from its previous antiwar stance.

In Dayton, Ohio, the SP swept nine of the city's twelve wards in nonpar-
tisan 1917 primaries, despite being outspent by their opponents $28,058 to
$395. With the American death toll in Europe mounting, antiwar sentiment
was spreading. The next month, Buffalo socialists came just a few hundred
votes short of winning the mayor's office. Soon after, Hillquit's campaign
for New York City mayor drew a raucous crowd of twenty thousand to Madison Square Garden. With business interests united against him and President Wilson paying special attention to the race, Hillquit ended up with
21.7 percent of the vote, five times the party's previous result. In Dayton
and New York alike, Socialists performed best in working-class districts.
The party, more so than even in 1912, was tied to a mass base.[26]

But internal dissension brought new challenges. The SP's Left was
emboldened by outrage at the party's pro-war minority, the gains of the
previous few years, an uptick in trade union militancy, and the success of
the Russian Revolution. This growing current seemed to be an existential
threat to the leadership.

That wasn't immediately apparent to outsiders. Hillquit and even
Berger were not like the pro-war right of social democracy in Germany and
elsewhere in Europe. Unlike the Germans, they greeted the October Revolution with enthusiasm. Debs's response—"From the crown of my head to
the soles of my feet I am Bolshevik, and proud of it"—is well known. But
Hillquit also saluted the Russian revolutionaries, and even Berger could
say at the end of 1918, "Here is a government of the people and for the
people in actual fact. Here is a political and industrial democracy."[27]

When the US government cracked down on the party for its antiwar activities, starting with the 1918 Espionage and Sedition Acts and the barring
of socialist papers from the postal service, the party's right was certainly
not spared. Berger became the United States' first Socialist congressman

in 1910, but even his moderate socialism was too much for the government. In March 1918, he was indicted under the Espionage Act and charged with twenty-six "disloyalty acts." The House voted 309 to 1 to deny him his democratically won seat.

Many more elected officials met a similar fate, and thousands of SP members were arrested or deported. Such was the scale and success of the repression that few today remember that the Oklahoma Socialist Party was among the most important political organizations in the state. For his part, Debs once again found himself in prison, delivering his most famous address at his sentencing: "Your Honor, years ago I recognized my kinship with all living beings, and I made up my mind that I was not one bit better than the meanest on earth. I said then, and I say now, that while there is a lower class, I am in it, and while there is a criminal element, I am of it, and while there is a soul in prison, I am not free."

Debs ran for president from a Georgia prison in 1920, winning 3.41 percent of the vote. But by that time the party he represented had already split. Its revolutionary wing had grown, fueled by the arrival of Russian and Finnish workers, among others. With the Left on pace to win commanding majorities at the 1919 conference, the party's right began sweeping purges. As many as two-thirds of the membership were banned from the party, with many of them going on to form the nucleus of American communism. Berger and his like-minded colleagues might have admired the Bolshevik Revolution from afar, but they feared radicalization would undo their own party. They chose to burn much of it down rather than make principled, democratic arguments within the organization.[28]

The obvious question is whether things might have turned out differently had the SP acted as ignobly as their counterparts in Europe and supported the national war effort in 1917–1918. But it's hard to imagine that a party awash in idealism and millenarian rhetoric could have chosen that route. The better question is, What could the SP have done to maintain itself despite its resolute opposition to the state? After all, socialists elsewhere had survived repression. The Bolshevik Party thrived underground for many years, in far worse conditions, and Germany's Social Democratic Party grew by leaps and bounds under Bismarck's antisocialist laws. The key in each case was a centralized organization, a unity not necessarily of sentiment but of action. The multilingual, geographically dispersed, and ideologically divided Socialist Party of America lacked just that, and no new leadership came about to change things.

It's also worth reflecting on the fact that the Americans tried to create a socialist political party along German lines, rather than mirror British efforts to first create a labor party. The latter might have been possible in the 1890s if not for the combination of elite violence, Socialist Labor Party sectarianism, and the conservatism of Gompers's AFL. There were no guarantees of success, of course. By the early 1900s, most American workers were already partisans of one party or another, and unlike the Germans the socialists didn't have great universal male suffrage battles to galvanize political support around. Institutionally, as well, the two-party system encouraged progressive reformers to co-opt socialist demands. This inheritance gave socialists little room for error.

The Socialist Party would persist for decades after 1919. Socialists and former socialists would go on to become forefathers of Cold War liberalism, democratic socialism, and even neoconservatism. But aside from a resurgence in the 1930s, the party was no longer a serious force in national politics.

COMMUNISM BRIEFLY TOOK its place, though in fits and starts. The first few years of American communism were hardly glorious. It was an alien tradition besieged by the US government, clustered in ethnic enclaves, and shot through with division. Thousands in the United States responded to Lenin's call for a clean break from the opportunism of the Second International and for the creation of a new Communist International. Foreign-born left-wingers expelled from the SP formed the Communist Party of America in 1919, and the mostly native-born radicals led by John Reed and Benjamin Gitlow created the rival Communist Labor Party the same year.

The Comintern forced the two organizations to merge together, but only a handful of the combined twelve thousand members were native English speakers—this despite much of the SP's historic left coming from American-born Western radicals. The Communists were so far to the left that in 1919, amid the most important strike wave in US history, they denounced left-wing trade unionists like their future leader William Z. Foster. Without a base in the labor movement the Communists made pronouncements such as, "The revolution is the real issue in the steel strike," and called for "the destruction of existing trade union organizations."[29]

The Comintern fought against these isolating tendencies and tried to forge a multiracial movement that could win over non-Communist workers. It pushed radicals to work above ground, as well as within the AFL. At the Comintern's Second Congress, international Communist leader Karl Radek noted that the massive postwar uptick in unionism had benefited reformist, not revolutionary, unions and that "there is no tactical advantage in our stubbornly refusing to join the A.F. of L." Reed bitterly replied that the "only friends the Communist International have in America are the Industrial Workers of the World," but the foreigners were right about the American worker, and the American delegation was wrong.[30]

A Comintern agent, however, might have blown one of the US left's biggest opportunities. The Hungarian-born József Pogány, known here as John Pepper, arrived in the United States in 1922 and joined in making useful appeals to the Americans—learn English, create a legal party, emphasize black liberation. But his most decisive intervention was derailing a promising effort to build a national labor party.[31]

Chicago Federation of Labor head and Gompers critic John Fitzpatrick was leading such an effort in 1923, which he invited Communists to join. However, rather than be a good-faith partner in a growing coalition, patiently reaping the benefits, Pogány encouraged the party to take over the infant organization. It was successful, but the action drove non-Communist unions and activists away for good and scuttled the initiative.[32]

The leadership in Moscow would have opposed Pogány had it known his plans, but it was responsible for the party's next rounds of discord. Leading US organizers fell afoul of the Soviet regime: Stalin expelled James Cannon for his Trotskyism and then the Cannon denouncer Jay Lovestone for his Bukharinism. And then during the crazed Third Period—when the Stalinist international leadership declared social democrats the primary barrier to an impending revolution—the American Communists pursued a sectarian course.

In the years prior, the party embraced William Z. Foster and his Trade Union Educational League (TUEL), which made progress supporting radical rank-and-file caucuses within the AFL. It was now suddenly dismantled and turned into the Trade Union Unity League (TUUL), which like many Communist fronts through the years meant the opposite of its name. TUUL created small "red" unions that adopted the entire Communist program and battled with the AFL from the outside. Not surprisingly, few actual workers agreed that the American Federation of Labor was "an instrument of the capitalists for the exploitation of the workers." Between 1928 and 1932, those great years of capitalist crisis, the party's membership dropped from twenty-four thousand to six thousand.

IN THE 1930S, with the rise of Hitler and the abject failure of its Third Period policy internationally, the Comintern returned again to the "united front" policies that seemed to be working in the mid-1920s. Starting in 1934, the party played a crucial role in the struggles that gave birth to the Congress of Industrial Organizations (CIO).[33]

CIO founder John L. Lewis was a United Mine Workers (UMW) leader and former business unionist. Having seen that approach go nowhere during the Depression, he chose a more militant one, pushing for organizing mass-production workers along industrial lines. Losing a battle to win the AFL leadership over to this strategy, the UMW and nine other unions were cast out of the federation in 1936. Together they formed the CIO, which had a mobilized rank and file but needed more trained organizers. Lewis found these in his former Socialist and Communist foes: perhaps a third of the CIO's staff were CPUSA members. When questioned about this, Lewis replied: "Who gets the bird? The hunter or the dog?"[34]

But the Communists feasted as well. The Comintern inaugurated a Popular Front across the West, composed not just of working-class parties but also middle-class reformers. No party adopted the concept more eagerly than the Communist Party USA under leader Earl Browder. The party named its educational efforts after Thomas Jefferson—more appropriately, Abraham Lincoln, Frederick Douglass, and Thomas Paine were other touchstones. It proclaimed that "Communism Is 20th Century Americanism." When a Daughters of the American Revolution chapter neglected to do its annual commemoration of Paul Revere's famous ride, the Young Communist League hired a rider, dressed him up like a Minuteman, and had him gallop down Broadway with a sign reading "The DAR forgets, but the YCL remembers."[35]

Less ridiculously, beyond its key role in trade union organizing, the party engaged with New Deal sentiments and shaped a broader left-liberal movement through its front groups such as the National Negro Congress and the American Student Union. The CPUSA amassed not just eighty-five thousand members but also a much larger network of fellow travelers. Communists came to play a prominent role in American cinema, music, and the arts. From the domestic fights against racism and for union rights to their support for the Spanish republican cause abroad, Communists were seen as defenders of democracy, even as news of Soviet purges trickled in.

If the CPUSA went too far in dissolving its identity, the Socialist Party offers an example of how badly the opposite approach could go. The SP recaptured some of its former prominence under Norman Thomas, a former Presbyterian minister cut in the figure of Debs; Thomas was able to win close to nine hundred thousand votes in his 1932 presidential run. The party attracted not just young leftists navigating between social-democratic

reformism and revolutionary Leninism, but extremely talented union organizers such as Walter and Victor Reuther.

But Thomas and most of the Socialist Party clung to its Debsian-era
strategy of opposition to bourgeois reformers—class independence was
paramount. Thomas saw the New Deal as a "program that makes concessions to workers in order to keep them quiet a while longer and so stabilize
the power of private owners." No doubt this was true, but these reforms
didn't placate workers; they led them to demand more.[36]

Whatever President Franklin D. Roosevelt's intentions, millions believed that he wanted them to join a union and thought they deserved a
decent paying job and social protections. These American workers began
to demand things of the state for the first time, and the Socialist Party
told them they were going about it the wrong way. As a result of the gap
between the SP's stance and the beliefs of the workers they organized, socialist labor leaders like the United Automobile Workers' Reuther brothers,
the Amalgamated Clothing Workers Union's Leo Krzycki, and the Hosiery
Workers Union's Emil Rieve resigned from the party.

In the 1936 presidential election, workers around the country were
making a rational decision to support the Democratic Party, hungry to continue Roosevelt's reforms and recognizing the institutional barriers to independent politics. Thomas's cohort couldn't offer a strategy to overcome any
of those barriers or even a way to not counterpoise themselves to the best
New Deal reforms. They just had slogans about opposing capitalist parties.
Ironically, the more fringe Communist Party was better able to relate to
Roosevelt supporters.

Of course, in aligning with Democrats, the Popular Front CPUSA hid
its socialist identity. When forced to reveal it, the party pointed to an authoritarian Soviet Union as its model. A month before the infamous 1939
Hitler-Stalin nonaggression pact, Browder said, "There is as much chance
of Russo-German agreement as of Earl Browder being elected President
of the Chamber of Commerce." But when word of the accord came, the

CPUSA adopted the new line without debate. The party's key allies were permanently alienated and its moral authority tarnished.[37]

When Nazi Germany invaded the Soviet Union in June 1941, the party evolved the Popular Front into an even more extreme "democratic front" policy. The Communist leadership advocated cooperation in the prosecution of the war at all costs, abandoning militant workers by pledging to oppose strike actions. Desperate to avoid isolation and to find institutional partners in trade union leaderships and the Democratic Party, the Communists gambled that the shift would help them stay relevant.

The party's devotion to the US state—it supported the 1940 Smith Act being used against antiwar socialists and Trotskyists—was not reciprocated. The same act would be turned against them at the end of the decade. The Communist Party was pushed from key CIO leadership positions after the war. Among other consequences of this, CIO plans to unionize the disproportionately black South (Operation Dixie) were scuttled. A labor party might not have been possible in the 1940s, but at the very least a different strategy could have prevented the CIO from taking a conservative turn and empowered rank-and-file radicals.

The Popular Front put the CPUSA in a position that prevented them from winning hegemony within the US working-class movement from liberal forces. But the era was also the last time socialism had a mass presence in the United States. The CPUSA pushed Roosevelt's New Deal to be more inclusive and supported the mass unionization drives of the time. Communists, bound together by membership in an organization most ordinary Americans came to fear and despise, played an outsized and largely positive role in American politics and culture.

American communism wasn't gray, bureaucratic, and rigid, as it had become in the Soviet Union, but rather creative and dynamic. *Dissent* founder Irving Howe thought the CPUSA was a put-on, a "brilliant masquerade" that fought for some of the right causes but in a deceptive, opportunistic way. But there was a less monolithic side to the Communist Party. It was an organization that hosted youth dances and socials, in addition to

militant rallies. Despite the machinations of their leaders, and their apol-
ogetics for the crimes of Stalinism, Communists were the underdogs in
America, fighting the establishment for justice. They were the victims of
censorship and police repression, not its perpetrators.[38]

The question today is whether we can bring the Left into the mainstream—
modulating our rhetoric, rooting ourselves in everyday life—while building
a project of independent working-class politics that can be more than liberalism's loyal opposition. In other words, can we make *socialism* twenty-first-
century Americanism, without losing our soul in the process (or dressing
up like Paul Revere)?

THE IMMEDIATE POSTWAR period seemed promising for Communists. In 1946,
a massive strike wave convulsed the nation, including general strikes in
Rochester, New York, and Oakland, California. President Truman's crush-
ing of a railroad strike, and rejection of the most ambitious parts of Roosevelt's 1944 platform, created murmurs of a new labor campaign against
him, maybe even a labor party. But whereas connections to the Soviet
Union used to give the CPUSA prestige, they now made it a pariah. The
Cold War was beginning, and fewer liberals wanted to be involved in Communist front groups or believed the *New Masses* when it said that "the Soviet Union is the highest form of democracy."[39]

Overcorrecting for their Browder days and misreading signals from
Moscow, the CPUSA, now led by William Z. Foster, supported former vice
president Henry A. Wallace's 1948 presidential campaign as the nominee
of the Progressive Party. In doing so it might have heeded a Soviet official,
who noted that given the CPUSA's limited influence and the labor movement's disunity, "it is perfectly obvious that if such a party were created,
it would not receive broad support among workers' and progressive organizations and would not be successful in its struggle against the powerful
political parties."[40]

The party's endorsement of Wallace, much like Socialist support
for Norman Thomas in 1936, cost them key union supporters, including

Transport Workers Union founder Mike Quill, and made it easier for the remaining Communists to be pushed from the CIO. The endorsement also devastated Communist-influenced state parties, such as New York's American Labor Party, which saw the Amalgamated Clothing Workers and other unions withdraw from it that year.

The CPUSA at least expected to revive links with progressive liberals and for the Progressive Party to win as many as eight to fifteen million votes. Wallace ended up with just over a million votes, less than segregationist Strom Thurmond. Truman's surprise victory over Republican Thomas Dewey led UAW leaders to shelve plans to create a labor party. Never again would American socialists mount a serious third-party challenge to the Democratic Party.[41]

The Communists' predicament was compounded by the rise of McCarthyism. By the time Khrushchev's 1956 "secret speech" revealed some of the crimes of Stalinism, the party was already a shell of itself.

Still, by the late 1950s, as the old parties of the Left disintegrated, a new wave of activism took shape. From the 1870s through the 1940s, an overriding concern of socialists was how to organize the working class into industrial trade unions. That goal was largely accomplished by the end of World War II, but radicals were locked out of the resulting movement. Now the goal was to forge a new marriage of radical activists and intellectuals on the one hand, and the labor movement on the other. Leftists would once again encourage the best parts of American liberalism—its "social democrats" in a political culture that didn't use that language—to actually deliver gains for working people.[42]

Many leftists, such as Democratic Socialists of America founder Michael Harrington, argued that labor had created a social-democratic party *within* the Democratic Party. This force advocated for expansions of the welfare state and sought to make the world's "second most enthusiastic capitalist party" play a political role similar to that of Europe's workers' parties.

In the 1960s, labor and other progressive movements were able to push important legislation through Democratic-controlled Congresses. The most significant concerned civil rights. Radicals played vital roles in the Second Reconstruction of mid-decade, which married demands for political equality for black Americans with calls for economic justice. Socialists including Ella Baker, Bayard Rustin, and A. Philip Randolph joined Martin Luther King Jr. in trying to replace Jim Crow with an egalitarian social democracy. Randolph was the elder statesman of the group; he had been a socialist since the 1910s and at the forefront of both labor and civil rights struggles. King himself would embrace democratic socialism as he radicalized over the course of the 1960s. But none of them marched for change under the socialist banner or worked through the socialist organizations that sustained previous generations of left activism.

The Democratic Party was never realigned into a force that would deliver social democracy. Nevertheless, the end of Jim Crow transformed the United States and may be the most important and enduring legacy of the American left.

As they pushed to make radical equality a reality, Bayard Rustin and other socialists compromised some of their most deeply held principles. By the late 1960s, many felt they had to mute their criticisms of the Vietnam War and reconcile themselves to conservative union leaders. They found themselves at odds with the young people of the rising New Left. When Stokely Carmichael met Bayard Rustin for the first time, he was in awe: "This man was a radical activist, an intellectual, and a strategist. That's what I want to be when I grow up." But rifts would soon appear between younger militants unhappy with the pace of change and an older mentor who cautioned that "the ability to go to jail should not be substituted for an overall social reform program."[43]

Many of the groups that fell under the rubric of the New Left, including Students for a Democratic Society (SDS), sprang from the institutions of the old labor-oriented left. But amid the turmoil of the 1960s—with Cold War liberalism committing mass murder in Vietnam and trade unions seemingly acting as a narrow interest group—young leftists wanted a radical break with the present. The Communist Party had little luster left, unlike Maoism and Third Worldism. Much of the New Left activism was generated by students, who struggled to build a base through antiracist and community organizing, but eventually devolved into sectarianism. At the 1968 SDS convention, two rival "Marxist-Leninist" sides began chanting at each other, "Ho, Ho, Ho Chi Minh!" and the other, "Mao, Mao, Mao Zedong!" (A third camp tried to get a "Let's go Mets" chant going.)[44]

But the radical flowering left a real impact. With groups like the Socialist Workers Party playing a role, a massive movement helped end the war in Vietnam. Black power, feminism, and gay liberation changed the United States for the better. Nevertheless, while individual socialists were at the helm of many of these efforts, socialism's presence was no longer felt institutionally.

The 1960s certainly did not witness the comeback of the Socialist Party of America. It split into three in 1972. The Right formed the Social Democrats, USA, with Rustin as its first chair. The organization became associated with hawkish anticommunism and acted as a minor pressure group within the trade union establishment. The Left became the Socialist Party USA, which attempted to continue the Debsian focus on independent electoral efforts with meager results (in 1912, Debs polled nearly a million votes; in 2012 his inheritors won just 4,430).

The center, led by Michael Harrington, formed the Democratic Socialist Organizing Committee (DSOC), a precursor to the Democratic Socialists of America. DSOC tried to tie together progressive trade union leaders, Democratic Party officials, and new social movements in a broad, effective coalition. Though his political goals and style were far different, Harrington essentially pursued the strategy of Browderism. But there was little to show for all the effort.

One of Harrington's most prominent allies, Senator Ted Kennedy, said at his 1989 funeral that "Michael Harrington never believed that we could not do better and never stopped urging us to try harder." He may have been talking about American society or humanity as a whole. But it's an apt description of Harrington's relationship to the Democratic Party. He tried to rally its progressive wing to rebuild the New Deal coalition and usher in a new program of reform. But even though many Democratic voters were with him, the party was in the midst of a slow lurch rightward. By the turn of the century, not just socialism but even welfare liberalism were almost wiped off the American political map.

WHY WAS THE United States different from other advanced capitalist countries? Why didn't it have an independent working-class party to build, if not socialism, then at least a social-democratic welfare state? As Sombart had put it, why is there no socialism in the United States?

These questions still plague us today. Though the socialist tradition in America has been more influential than commonly thought, we haven't stormed the barricades and taken power. Socialists have managed to play important roles in struggles to make the United States more democratic and humane, but the inequalities that mark American society today are stark reminders of our failures.

Michael Harrington used to say that radicals had to "walk a perilous tightrope." We had to "be true to the socialist vision of a new society" and also "bring that vision into contact with the actual movements fighting not to transform the system, but to gain some little increment of dignity or even just a piece of bread." At various moments, American socialists have either isolated ourselves in sectarian irrelevance or subsumed our identities within the Democratic Party and the broader nexus of liberalism in pursuit of relevance. Finally walking that tightrope would mean creating an electoral strategy that can represent the distinct interests of working people, but without demanding that voters start immediately supporting unviable third-party candidacies. Similarly, we need to grow and radically democratize the labor movement, but without asking workers to take a leap of faith and support fledgling "red unions."[45]

The question now is whether, with a vicious ruling class trying everything it can to widen the divide between the haves and the have nots, we can create a more durable socialist politics in America. The popularity of the democratic socialist Bernie Sanders and the inspiring activism of the last several years make even this pessimist think the answer is yes.

PART II

EIGHT

RETURN OF THE MACK

THE BEST WE can say about socialism in the twentieth century is that it was a false start. But that was far from clear in the moment. American journalist Lincoln Steffens thought "the future was bright" when he visited Stalin's Soviet Union. Nikita Khrushchev was sincere when he said that communism would be built "in the main" by 1980. At the very least, socialism of other stripes seemed to offer the only way out of underdevelopment for the formerly colonized world and welfare-state prosperity for the former colonizers.

Socialist confidence was destroyed over the course of the 1980s. By the early '90s, the Marxist theory of history was stood on its head: proponents of capitalism were confident that their own "end of history" had been reached. If you could even find Marx outside of university classrooms (where he was increasingly presented as a humanist philosopher instead of a revolutionary firebrand), it was on Wall Street, where cheeky traders put down Sun Tzu and heralded the long-dead German as a prophet of globalization.

Capitalism had certainly yielded immense progress in countries such as China and India. In 1991, when Indian finance minister Manmohan Singh announced plans to liberalize India's economy, he quoted Victor

Hugo: "No power on Earth can stop an idea whose time has come." Over the next twenty-five years, India's GDP grew by almost 1,000 percent. An even more impressive process unfolded in China, where Deng Xiaoping upturned Mao-era policies to deliver what he called "socialism with Chinese characteristics" and what the rest of the world recognized as state-managed liberalization. China is now as radically unequal as Latin America, but over five hundred million Chinese have been lifted out of extreme poverty during the past thirty years.[1]

One doesn't have to be optimistic to say that now is the best time in human history to be alive. However, when we look more closely at India and China, we see that workers have engaged in massive strike waves to defend their dignity and rights and to win back a portion of the wealth they've helped create. And in the developed world—where real wages have stagnated for a generation and millions have been left behind—the appeal of capitalism is in large part that there appears to be no viable alternative to it.

It's easy to forget that in the mid-twentieth century, capitalism and socialism were contending for the future. At the 1939 World's Fair in New York, corporations showcased new technologies—nylon, air conditioning, fluorescent lamps, the ever impressive View-Master. But more than just products, an ideal of middle-class leisure and abundance was offered to those weary from economic depression and scarcity. The "Futurama ride" at the World's Fair took attendees through miniature versions of transformed landscapes, depicting new highways and development projects—in short, the world to come.

In the wake of World War II, some of this vision became a reality. But when the battles of the 1970s came and went, with social democracy and its lite American equivalent beaten back, dreams of widely shared prosperity began to fade. An emergent neoliberalism curbed inflation and restored growth, but only through a vicious offensive against the working class. Since then real wages have stagnated, debt has soared, and the prospects for a new generation, still hoping to live better lives than their parents, are bleak.

The 1990s technological boom brought about talk of an adaptive "new economy," something to replace the old Fordist workplace. But it was a far cry from the future promised at the 1939 World's Fair. With few avenues for collective action available, people behaved as rationally as any Marxist would expect: they kept their heads down and tried to fix what they could. Can't find a job? Reformat your CV, and work on that handshake. Your factory is being outsourced? Stop whining, and take a coding class. As one popular libertarian title puts it, *You're Broke Because You Want to Be.*

Today, the masters of Silicon Valley are presenting a new vision of the future—space travel, 3-D printing, artificial intelligence, self-driving cars. But without the promise of mass employment to go along with all that disruption, they summon more concern that robots are coming to steal our jobs than awe. We all can't just go to an "innovation clinic" and launch our own app. This hasn't stopped the new captains of industry from trying to expand their appeal into the political realm. Mark Zuckerberg and other tech leaders and philanthropists aim to disrupt the public sector with their advocacy and donations, while keeping it underfunded by shielding their fortunes from taxation. Many moonlight as self-help gurus imploring people to "do what they love," even as millions struggle to get by in a nightmarish "task rabbit" economy.

The 2008 recession, spurred by speculative capital free of threats from below, at least temporarily broke the triumphalism. Plainly enough, the ideological underpinnings of capitalism have gone wobbly. Even many college-educated people are finding themselves unemployed and indebted. Free of both Cold War memories and loyalty to the existing system, Americans between the ages of eighteen and twenty-nine have a more favorable opinion of socialism than of capitalism. What young people understand as socialism is not clear, but when even basic welfare programs are denounced as "creeping socialism" by the Right, it's no wonder that many are supportive of the idea.

The pain is not limited to one generation. It's widely felt. In the United States, hourly wages have grown by a paltry 0.2 percent since 1979. Things are actually worse in the United Kingdom, where wages fell by about 10 percent between 2007 and 2014, even as economic productivity grew by about the same amount. And in both countries, as in other "postindustrial" economies across Europe, increased flexibility for employers has meant increased uncertainty for workers. In the United Kingdom, about 9 percent of part-time workers reported being unable to find a full-time job in 2008, and that percentage more than doubled by 2013. The "involuntary part-timer" or "1099-er"—unseen in the postwar era—is now a feature of our economic landscape.[2]

You might think that a socialist movement would be inevitable in times like these. You'd be right.

THE 2007–2008 FINANCIAL crisis provoked no great protests, but it did provide plenty of villains. Advances in information technology and the loosening up of financial industry regulations since the 1980s had set bankers free to take enormous risks. By the late 1990s, with home prices climbing higher and higher every year, private mortgage lenders saw an opportunity to reap tremendous profits while passing the risks on to the public.

A shadowy industry developed in the cubicles and corner offices of investment banks across the country. Home lenders originated exorbitantly priced mortgages as fast as they could print the paperwork and then sold that debt off to third parties, converting the promise of future income into liquid assets that could be used to immediately originate even more loans. Mortgages became what researcher Kathe Newman has called "postindustrial widgets": since loans were generated just to be resold, mortgages were soon packaged together, spliced apart, combined into big pools, and marketed to investors many thousands of miles removed from the actual, physical homes they represented—and the real families housed inside them.[3]

So it shouldn't have come as a surprise when, in 2007, a periodic downturn turned into something far graver. Home prices started to fall for the first time in decades, and the flows of fictional money that buoyed the market evaporated overnight. This led to the worst financial crisis since the Great Depression and to the largest bank failure in US history. Seattle's Washington Mutual, worth more than $300 billion at the time, collapsed entirely, just two years after executives had kicked off a morale exercise by rapping, "I like big bucks and I cannot lie," at a luxurious company retreat in Hawaii. Washington Mutual ended up getting absorbed by JPMorgan, and its president got an $11 million payout. Big bucks indeed! This pattern was repeated across the financial sector, as banks deemed "too big to fail" received life-saving injections of public dollars from the federal government.[4]

Ordinary Americans, including those who had fallen victim to predatory lenders, got no such bailout. Soon the banks went about rebuilding their portfolios by ejecting indebted homeowners from their houses— foreclosure rates spiked by more than 81 percent in 2008, with 3.2 million foreclosure notices served that year. There were some rumblings of discontent, as people in hard-hit cities organized campaigns appealing to political leaders for help. The revelation, in summer 2009, that the banks used part of their bailout money to pay year-end bonuses of more than $1 million to about five thousand executives led to a brief public outcry. Still, despite simmering anger, Americans were more scared than anything else.[5]

To the extent people found inspiration in politics, they did so in Barack Obama's 2008 presidential campaign. In contrast to eight years of the George W. Bush administration, Obama had a message of "hope" and "change" that proved malleable enough to sustain a coalition. As Obama

himself put it, "I serve as a blank screen on which people of vastly different political stripes project their own views." But the support for him was
real all the same—the election of the first black president was a watershed
for a nation built off the exploitation of black slaves and marked by discrimination against African Americans.[6]

The rise of Obama and the recession coincided with talk of a "New
New Deal." Commentators including Paul Krugman and Joseph Stiglitz
demanded a historic federal stimulus to revive the economy, and people
across the political spectrum welcomed the return of Keynesian economics to the national stage. *Time* featured a picture of the new president
dressed like FDR on its cover and updated its 1965 article "We Are All
Keynesians Now" with a celebration of "The Comeback Keynes." Even
the far left *Socialist Worker* took a moment to appreciate the novelty: business elites, the Democratic Party, and a popular groundswell had come
together to support Obama's proposed stimulus package, signaling "a final
end to the conservative dominance that goes back more than a generation." It was a far cry from the gleeful market liberalism of the 1990s and
the attempts of Third Way Democrats like Bill Clinton to privatize even
social security. The occupation by workers of Chicago's Republic Win-
dows and Doors factory in late 2008 seemed to portend labor militancy
unseen in decades.[7]

In the end, that hope and many others were not realized. The Obama
administration, unlike many European ones, was smart enough to avoid
extreme austerity measures, and recovery came. Unemployment, which
had reached a high of 10 percent in 2009, fell to its 2007 rate by the
end of Obama's second term, and GDP returned to its precrisis level as
early as 2011. If you were a banker looking down from a high-rise office
tower, you probably would have believed all the talk about the economy's
miraculous turnaround. But from the perspective of an ordinary person—
maybe looking down at the local classified ads, or at a meager paycheck,
or at a stack of mortgage bills—this rosy picture did not correspond to
reality.

Obama might have stabilized a volatile economy, but he did little to confront powerful business interests. Even Obama's signature achievement—the Affordable Care Act (ACA), which expanded health insurance to millions of Americans through Medicaid and protected those with preexisting conditions—was conceived not as an offensive against the for-profit health care system but as a great compromise with it.

The most prominent political revolt during this period came in response to the ACA, but it did not come from the Left. Rather, it came from the Right, in the form of the anti-government Tea Party. The Tea Party was mainly composed of embittered, middle-class whites who were already firmly within the Republican tent but whose rage helped push the party to the right. For the broader public, Obama's policies were enough to justify a second term in office.

Yet the trend of stagnating wages and declining opportunity continued. Not only that, but the Democratic Party was eroded from within by mismanagement and neglect. During the Obama administration, the Democrats lost control of thirteen governors' mansions, leaving the party with its lowest number since 1920—a paltry sixteen. Democrats also saw their control over state legislatures slip dramatically, from 59 percent at the beginning of Obama's presidency to 31 percent at its end.[8]

Rollbacks began in earnest in many Republican-dominated states. The most significant flashpoint was Governor Scott Walker's attempt to annihilate a century of labor victories in Wisconsin, all in one fell swoop. In 2011, Walker introduced the Budget Repair Bill, which would have hobbled unions by outlawing collective bargaining for public sector workers. It proposed cutting into vital social programs, including Medicare, environmental protections, even public education. The measures provoked resistance—more than a hundred thousand people marched on the state capital, teachers across the state organized "sick outs" to get around rules banning strikes, and protesters occupied the Wisconsin capitol building for two and a half weeks, demanding that Walker step down.

What began as the most radical popular upsurge in recent memory, however, quickly became a variable in the Democratic Party's political calculus. A statewide referendum turned into a redo of the most recent gubernatorial election, and soon the groundswell of energy that had led thousands of public sector workers and their allies to swarm the capitol had been redirected into an awkward campaign for a candidate who had already lost once. The results were predictable: after a rough-and-tumble race, Scott Walker won again, by an even larger margin than before. His assault on workers continued. In 2015, he succeeded in doing what he had failed to do in 2011: among the devastating reforms passed that year was a $300 million cut to public education and the introduction of "right to work" laws that gutted Wisconsin unions.

The battles in Wisconsin were of real interest to citizens of the state and to those who sought a revival of the labor movement, but they had limited national resonance. By contrast, the Occupy Movement, a rebellion against inequality and financial power, captured the media spotlight. It was an idea that by all rights should have failed. Occupy sprung out of the same tradition of the antiglobalization movement of the late 1990s and 2000s—more specifically, out of North America's tiny anarchist movement. While socialists waited for another Wisconsin, fronted small single-issue organizations, or simply argued among themselves, anarchists took action. It was a moment when the Left had nothing to lose.

The movement, kicked off in September 2011 by an email blast from the anticonsumerist magazine *Adbusters*, grew into a national spectacle. Occupy encampments cropped up in every major city throughout the country. Clashes with police, especially in cities like New York and Oakland, were polarizing events that attracted even more public sympathy for the protesters, whose PR savvy and appeals to international counterparts—including Spain's Indignados movement and those who

participated in Egypt's Tahrir Square uprising—expanded the movement's profile. Soon, income inequality became a national political issue.
Less than a month after the protests began, a poll showed that Occupy
Wall Street enjoyed 54 percent approval nationwide—more than double
the Tea Party's rating.[9]

The spirit of the young Occupiers resonated with millions who would
never join an urban encampment because it was married to an easily com-
prehensible populist appeal. Even some of Occupy's most radical-sounding
sound bites had mainstream, even genteel, roots. The slogan "We are the
99 percent, they are the 1 percent" might have found its wings in Zuccotti
Park in downtown Manhattan, but its origins actually lie in a May 2011
Vanity Fair article by retired World Bank economist Joseph Stiglitz. The
call captured popular discontent, and even the Congressional Budget Office seized on the phrase in a report issued about a month after Occupy
began.[10]

"We are the 99 percent" resonated for a reason. Between 1979 and
2007, income for the wealthiest 1 percent of Americans increased by 275
percent, or a total of $700,000 in new annual income, on average. Mean-
while, wages for the rest of us grew slower than inflation, and the bottom 90
percent of Americans actually experienced a loss of about $900 a year. Not
since 1928 had the top 1 percent of Americans captured such a large slice
of the national pie.[11]

The openness and undefined nature of Occupy owed much to the hori-
zontalist tendencies of the anarchist movement, but some of these features
eventually became liabilities. For one, as Jo Freeman pointed out in the
1970s, abandoning structure to promote spontaneity can not only make political action harder but often make it less democratic. Without coherent organization or links to a social base, the movement fizzled out more quickly
than it would have otherwise.[12]

But it's a bit unrealistic to expect that young people getting politicized for the first time would be able to build an organization and realize

far-reaching reforms. The real legacy of Occupy Wall Street was in its revival of a form of mass protest and its foregrounding of the issue of austerity and inequality in an accessible way. It was a glimmer, more obvious
than the Wisconsin uprising, that a simple message based on fairness and
democracy could garner widespread support.

A FEW YEARS AFTER Occupy, another movement made it impossible to ignore
the failures of American democracy. On August 9, 2014, in the St. Louis
suburb of Ferguson, Missouri, a white police officer named Darren Wilson
gunned down a black teenager, Michael Brown. Only two years earlier,
Trayvon Martin, a black seventeen-year-old from Florida, had been shot to
death by a white vigilante while walking in his own neighborhood, elicit-
ing outrage around the country. The man who killed him, a self-appointed
neighborhood watchman named George Zimmerman, said he was terrified
of the skinny teenager, and avoided punishment by claiming he acted in
self-defense.

Now history seemed to be repeating itself in Ferguson: Wilson ab-
surdly maintained he felt like a "five-year-old" next to Brown's "Hulk Ho-
gan" and said he fired to protect his life. Less than a day later, Ferguson
was gripped by massive protests that turned into violent confrontations at
night as police tried to disperse the demonstrations. The actions lasted for
weeks and inspired solidarity protests in cities around the country.

This was the inaugural moment of the nationwide Movement for
Black Lives (MBL), which called for an end to racist law enforcement.
MBL challenged accepted realities about state violence and harassment
faced by black Americans. After Ferguson, as unarmed people continued
to die at the hands of US police—with some of it caught on cell phone
cameras—similar protests rocked cities like Baltimore, Baton Rouge, Chicago, and New York. The demands advanced by the protesters in Ferguson and their counterparts around the country—including an end to
police impunity and the creation of poverty-alleviation programs in black

neighborhoods—were broadly social-democratic and garnered widespread sympathy.

Protesters were grappling with the tension between the undeniable progress since the Civil Rights Movement—there were now black mayors, police chiefs, even a black president—and the fact that the social and economic conditions of black Americans were still deplorable. MBL was a challenge, then, to local Democratic machines and a national party that took black voters for granted. But, like Occupy, the diffuse organizational nature of the Movement for Black Lives went from strength to weakness. Looking for avenues to actually change policy, segments of the movement were drawn toward the world of elite NGOs and the Democratic Party. Many of its leading figures came to represent the rhetoric and interests of a professional managerial class far removed from those who rallied in Ferguson and Baltimore.[13]

Today, demands for social equality and an end to state violence clash with branding exercises and the more individualistic prerogatives of the professional class—for representation, not material redistribution. It's no surprise that liberal foundations helped elevate the movement's most banal voices, while radical ones were marginalized. In the end, the Movement for Black Lives' trajectory is another reminder that any serious struggle against oppression has to demand the massive redistribution of power and wealth from the elite to the poor and working classes.

BERNIE SANDERS'S 2016 presidential campaign started with some haphazard remarks delivered to an empty National Mall. Bernie stood calmly behind a podium, said a few words about inequality, and then walked off the stage as if nothing had happened.

Sanders's political life started in obscurity, amid the dying remnants of the Socialist Party of America. As a college student in its youth branch, he came to an understanding of the world that he never left behind: the rich

were not morally confused but rather had a vested interest in the exploitation of others. Power would have to be taken from them by force, or nothing
would change. Sanders threw himself into civil rights and labor struggles
through the 1960s, but by the end of the decade the native New Yorker
retreated to rural life in Vermont.

His trajectory was like that of many leftists of his generation. He
lived in Stannard, a town of fewer than two hundred tucked away in
Vermont's Northeast Kingdom. There were no schools, post offices, or
paved roads. But he embraced small community life, learning how to
survive and cooperate with others. The moral and life lessons of Stannard
certainly weren't a substitute for a broader politics. Fortunately, Sanders
returned to the fold within a few years. He connected with the Liberty
Union Party, a local left-wing group committed to remaining free of the
Democratic Party. His first foray into electoral politics yielded results
familiar to the American left—2.2 percent of the vote, in a 1972 Senate
special election.[14]

But Sanders was persistent, and his message was simple: he denounced
"the world of Richard Nixon, and the millionaires and billionaires whom
he represents." Even back then he was reminding audiences, "This is the
world of the 2 percent of the population that owns more than one-third of
the personally held wealth in America."[15]

His message was too clear and important not to resonate. Though
his electoral record was dotted with noble failures throughout the 1970s,
he triumphed in his campaign as an independent socialist running for
Burlington mayor at the height of Reaganism in 1981. In the almost forty
years since, Sanders's message hasn't changed: inequality in America is
a yawning chasm, and only a coalition of working people can close it. In
the 2016 presidential campaign, when he tied this message to a concrete
program of Medicare for All, tuition-free college, and a $15 national min-
imum wage, it won the support of millions. Most of them had never heard
much about socialism but were ready for a politics oriented around their
needs.

Almost all of the US left embraced the Bernie Sanders movement, but there were questions over just what he meant when he called himself a democratic socialist. The senator would invoke Eugene V. Debs and the Danish welfare state in the same breath. But far from being "just" a modern social democrat, Sanders believed the path to reform was through confrontation with elites. Rather than saying we were all going to work together to make a better America, Sanders declared that we were going to seize power from the same "millionaires" (and now even some "billionaires") that he'd denounced a half century ago. In this way, he is more closely aligned with socialists throughout history than with the liberal reformers he's had to ally with to pass laws. Sanders gave American socialism a lifeline by returning it to its roots: class struggle and a class base.

The 2016 campaign set Sanders up against an almost perfect foil. As an establishment figure, Hillary Clinton seemed to tailor her entire message and delivery around focus group feedback. As Sanders puts it, "The Clinton approach was to try to merge the interests of Wall Street and corporate America with the needs of the American middle class an impossible task." Sanders's arena of battle, however, was within the Democratic primary; he could not have gotten very far advancing his positions as an independent socialist candidate (consider the dismal showings of the Green Party's Jill Stein and Libertarian candidate Gary Johnson).[16]

Even at its height the Democratic Party was always less coherent than the labor and social-democratic parties in Europe. Though deprived of independent politics of its own, working-class interests were brought into its tent, but much of the party's agenda was always set—even during the height of the 1930s New Deal and 1960s Great Society programs—by allied business interests. One result was that the United States never had a welfare state comparable to other industrial nations even during the early postwar years.

In the neoliberal age, the Democratic Party had to reinvent itself: it could now only deliver limited material goods to workers, so instead it presented itself as a less vicious option than Republicans, and as a force for helping oppressed groups—blacks, women, LGBT people, and others. (Though the substantive victories in civil rights for LGBT people, for one, came from grassroots mobilization, not Democratic initiatives.) Clinton's campaign employed this strategy; she scoffed at $15 minimum wage proposals and at the same time embraced the academic rhetoric of "intersectionality."

Yet Sanders offered a true alternative. In the beginning, his campaign seemed little more than a protest candidacy. But it quickly attracted mass support, drawing tens of thousands to rallies and winning almost thirteen million votes in the Democratic primaries.

It also attracted the ire of the party establishment, which was firmly behind Clinton. For Clinton, Sanders seemed like a demagogue. In her 2017 book about the campaign, *What Happened*, she created a mock conversation with Bernie and his backers:

> BERNIE: I think America should get a pony.
>
> HILLARY: How will you pay for this pony? Where will the pony come from? How will you get Congress to agree to the pony?
>
> BERNIE: Hillary thinks America doesn't deserve a pony.
>
> BERNIE SUPPORTERS: Hillary hates ponies![17]

But for voters, health care, good jobs, and affordable education weren't metaphorical ponies; they carried life and death stakes. Like Trump, and decidedly unlike Clinton, Sanders was able to speak to the anger simmering among many Americans, including white workers who had seen their living standards decline without even the limited social gains other groups in the Democratic coalition could point to. Though Sanders was further to the left than any major Democratic candidate, he won over independent and self-described "moderate" voters turned off by the party. To be a "moderate" in the United States, after all, doesn't mean you're a fan of Michael Bloomberg and other centrist politicians. Rather, it often means that someone is fed up with "liberalism" (the Democratic Party) and "conservatism" (the Republican Party), and looking for something different.

Sanders attacked greedy elites, highlighted the ways in which they controlled policymakers, and spoke of the suffering of the American working class. But the Sanders platform was still fairly moderate. It called for the universal provision of some basic social goods and a reevaluation of trade deals as part of a call to return to the shared prosperity of the postwar period.

It was telling that this modest dream saw Sanders portrayed as a wild-eyed radical by Democratic elites. Every segment of the party's nomenklatura—from the remnants of the Democratic Leadership Council to even the labor bureaucracy and the Congressional Black Caucus—opposed Sanders. They didn't need direct orders from the Democratic National Committee (DNC) to know not to run afoul of the donor class and the corporate interests that kept them in business.

That's not to say that Clinton's primary victory was merely the product of Democratic National Committee manipulation or that she didn't genuinely enjoy more support than Sanders among the party's rank and file. The DNC might have put a thumb on the scale for their preferred candidate, but they didn't have the power to do much more than that. It didn't stop them from trying. During the primary season, a trove of leaked emails revealed that members of the Democratic National Committee had coordinated with media personalities to paint Sanders in a bad light. Most of these efforts were more laughable than sinister: the DNC's chief financial officer apparently thought Bernie's chances in West Virginia would evaporate if only a reporter could be convinced to ask the candidate if he believed in God. Still, the leak led to the resignation of DNC chair and longtime Clinton ally

Debbie Wasserman Schultz. A new chairperson, Donna Brazile, rushed to calm voters' concerns about backroom deals and secret back channels, but apparently even she couldn't resist the urge to tip the ball to Clinton. A few months later, a new round of email leaks revealed that Brazile invited the Clinton campaign to preview debate questions before a much-publicized town hall with Sanders.

Still, the challenges that Sanders faced were more structural than conspiratorial: many Democratic stalwarts simply made a rational calculation. Take black voters in the South. By an overwhelming margin they backed Clinton in early primaries, yet the determining factor was less policy preferences than the fact that Sanders had little name recognition at the time and seemingly less chance of winning in the general election. For those who had the most to lose from a Republican presidency, going with the surer bet makes all the sense in the world. The mechanisms for getting people to the polls in low-turnout primary elections also favored Clinton: she had long-standing connections with important black churches, professional associations, and other organizations.

As the race went on, Sanders improved his popularity among black voters, particularly young people, such that by the end of the primary season, Sanders enjoyed a 73 percent favorability rate among black Americans, according to a Harvard-Harris poll. But he ran short of time and was forced to concede to a relieved Clinton.[18]

With Sanders defeated, the party had a strategy to beat Trump in the general election: it would win over moderate Republican voters in suburbs and convince capital to back Clinton over the erratic Trump. New York Democratic senator Chuck Schumer captured the supposedly foolproof plan in the months before the vote: "For every blue-collar Democrat we lose in western Pennsylvania, we will pick up two moderate Republicans in the suburbs in Philadelphia, and you can repeat that in Ohio and Illinois and Wisconsin." The overtures to business were well received, as well, especially in the finance, entertainment, and tech sectors—DreamWorks Pictures contributed a whopping $2 million to

Clinton campaign activities, while Time Warner, JPMorgan Chase, Alphabet (Google's parent company), and Morgan Stanley each contributed upward of a quarter million. The second most enthusiastic party of capital in the world (after the GOP) was perceived by many elites as the most responsible choice.[19]

Clinton's messaging was molded along these lines. Whereas Donald Trump spoke confidently about his plans to "Make America Great Again," Clinton focused on running defensively, against Trump, not for a vision of a better deal for ordinary people. Clinton was the target of countless sexist attacks (not to mention many elaborate conspiracy theories). But beyond that she had to grapple with the fact that for enough Americans who hate politicians and haven't thought highly of the past thirty years of neoliberal austerity, voting for someone whose pitch was that they had been in politics for thirty years was a hard sell. Clinton won about three million more votes than Trump but lost narrowly in former Democratic strongholds in Michigan, Pennsylvania, and Wisconsin.

"Berniecrats" were vindicated by Clinton's surprise defeat, and even the most torpid of Democrats took notice. They may have opposed Sanders's vision, but they sensed its electoral potency after the fact. The same Senator Schumer who weeks before was looking forward to losing proles and replacing them with professionals now could say, "If you want to appeal to the manufacturing worker in Scranton, the college student in Los Angeles and the single mom making minimum wage in Harlem, one economic message will work."[20]

Schumer might have not been committed to that course, but the fact that it was entertained shows how adrift Democrats were after the election. Bernie went from outsider and liability to potential savior for a party he wasn't even a member of. Yet new scapegoats quickly emerged. The racism and sexism of American voters was cited. But then so was the role of Russia, fake news, and the FBI. These factors—even the blame put on Clinton's personal abilities as a campaigner—distracted from the overarching need for a new direction. Some were as hyperbolic as liberal commentator

Keith Olbermann, who announced that the mighty United States was the "victim of a Russian coup."[21]

The facts of inequality, indebtedness, and poverty are not going away, however. Sanders identified and helped create what could be an enduring constituency in American politics. Sanders is running again, and others will follow in his wake, with possibly even more radical proposals. The success of Congresswoman Alexandria Ocasio-Cortez, a self-professed democratic socialist, is just one example.

If it's possible that Bernie Sanders can win a national election, that means that the capital of capitalism may be months away from having a socialist in the White House. But as we will see, winning power, as opposed to just an election, is a much more difficult proposition.

"OF POLITICAL PARTIES claiming socialism to be their aim, the Labour Party has always been one of the most dogmatic—not about socialism, but about the parliamentary system." That's how Marxist academic Ralph Miliband opened his classic 1961 text *Parliamentary Socialism*, a critical analysis of the party that most of the British left wanted to take over.

Miliband was skeptical of that plan. But a socialist left had long survived, if not exactly thrived, within the Labour Party. Allied with radical unions and sometimes even Communists, they were voices of conscience within Labour governments. Nye Bevan, a socialist minister, was the driving force behind the National Health Service in the 1940s, the greatest endeavor of any postwar social-democratic government. The baton was passed to Tony Benn, who served as a minister in the Harold Wilson and James Callaghan governments and as a member of Parliament for nearly a half century. An elite background and all the accolades that came with public service did nothing to moderate Benn's politics, who led a tireless battle for democracy inside and outside the party.

By the 1970s the crisis of British capitalism—and the welfare state dependent on it—was already apparent. Labor's militant wage demands combined with the 1973 OPEC embargo, which quadrupled the price of crude oil, to prompt skyrocketing inflation. Weak growth should have meant low, not high, inflation, but this was the era of "stagflation"—and Keynesian countercyclical policies weren't working.[22]

The miners went on strike in 1972 and 1974, and public sector unions flexed their muscle, but by 1975 it was clear to Harold Wilson's minister Anthony Crosland that "the crisis that faces us is infinitely more serious than any of the crises we have faced over the past 20 years.... For the time being at least, the party is over." What's often not remembered in that oft-quoted speech is what he said next: "We are not calling for a headlong retreat. But we are calling for a standstill." However, by the next year—when Labour's James Callaghan replaced Wilson and had to borrow $3.9 billion from the International Monetary Fund—the standstill had become a rout. Within the cabinet, Benn put forward an Alternative Economic Strategy, characterized by capital controls and protectionism, but like elsewhere in Europe, there didn't appear to be either the technical or the political means to avoid the monetarist call for a restoration of profit rates through tightening the money supply, diminishing the power of unions, and deregulation.[23]

The lead-up to the 1979 election saw a polarized response from the Left. For Tony Benn, who had moved radically to the left during his years in government, Labour had to do more than oversee austerity. It had to once again deliver the goods: "You can't go on forever and ever saying you're a socialist party when you're not, saying you'll do something when you won't, confining yourselves to attacks on the Tories when it's simply not enough. People want to know what the Labour Party will do." Others were more subdued. Eric Hobsbawm's 1978 Marx Memorial Lecture was appropriately titled "The Forward March of Labour Halted?" In it, the famed Marxist historian discussed the changing composition of British capitalism and asked whether the organized working class could be the lynchpin of a left movement. Even as Labour's political coalition had fractured since the 1951 general election, its trade unions had grown mil-itant, but this was "an almost entirely economist militancy" in workplaces, and "straightforward economist trade union consciousness may at times actually set workers against each other rather than establish wider pat-terns of solidarity."[24]

The "landslide" May 1979 victory of Margaret Thatcher (she won only 43.9 percent of the vote) turned Hobsbawm's cautious reexamination into something more urgent. The continental theorist Andre Gorz said "farewell to the working class" entirely, preferring "new social movements" based on race, gender, peace, or ecology over the narrow "economism" of organized labor. He and others confused a recomposition of the working class (the shift away from industrial and toward service sectors, for example) with its decline and underestimated, as Ralph Miliband put it, how "the exploita-tion, discrimination and oppression to which women, blacks and gays are subjected is also crucially shaped by the fact that they are workers located at a particular point of the production process and the social structure." The dire situation was compounded by Thatcher's 1983 reelection, which caused the cultural theorist Stuart Hall and others of like mind to overstate neoliberalism's popular appeal and the extent of working-class conserva-tism. What should have been cause to reexamine the Left's strategy in a changing era became an excuse to jettison Marxist theory and socialist politics.[25]

This turn against class politics had practical effects. A decade earlier, few would've guessed that the New Left and the old Communist intelligent-sia would see Trotskyists and "Bennites" as more the source of Labour's problems than a staid leadership or the defection of the party's right wing to the Liberals. They didn't use the same language, but they might have agreed with moderates that 1983 Labour candidate Michael Foot's center-left election manifesto was "the longest suicide note in history." While Benn and the Labour Left fought campaigns to win the leadership and democratize the party, and while Arthur Scargill led a last great miners' strike in 1984–1985, the intellectual cover was provided for Foot's replacement, Neil Kinnock, and an emerging New Labour current to challenge these movements.

Kinnock gave way to Tony Blair, who doubled down on centrist politics and constructed a public relations machine to rebrand Labour as fresh-faced modernizers. This approach won a massive victory in 1997—a rare one for a party that's been called the least successful major party in the world. Labour had also been the most scarcely socialist of the Second International generation of parties to begin with, but it clung to the old working-class "production politics" longer than others. The next ten years in power would witness a radical transformation, with Blair trying to turn an old workers' party into a catch-all social liberal one.

For some commentators, the rise of New Labour was the final vindication of the mid-century reformer Anthony Crosland. Blair's ally and successor Gordon Brown even wrote a foreword for a new edition of *The Future of Socialism*, to mark the fiftieth anniversary of its publication in 2006. Brown argued that the party's new orientation would be both "radical and credible." But New Labour turned out to be neither. If Eduard Bernstein presented a reformist path to socialism and Crosland a reformist path to social equality, Brown advocated for a not-even-reformist path to pro-capitalist policies.

The Japanese have a word for looking worse after a haircut: *age-otori*. Its synonym in English should be Blairism. Despite initial electoral success and some attempts on the margins to solve social issues such as child poverty, Blair and Brown pursued policies that undermined their own social base. When Blair became prime minister in 1997, Labour had four hundred thousand party members. By 2004, it had half that. That year Labour lost 464 seats in local elections. With anger over the party's privatization agenda and oversight of the financial crisis, as well as its support for the disastrous Iraq War, Labour was out of power and completely discredited by 2010.[26]

The failure of New Labour did not immediately benefit the Left. When Tony Benn passed away at the age of eighty-eight in 2014, it seemed that the project to which he devoted his life had no future. Ed Miliband was Brown's first successor in 2010, a surprise choice from the party's center-left, though hardly a radical. Ed Miliband competed for the leadership against his brother, David. Both were offspring of Ralph Miliband. The joke at the time was that Ralph thought that Labour would never be a vehicle for socialist transformation, and he made two sons to prove it.

Ed Miliband did unwittingly open the floodgates for a shift leftward, however. He challenged what he saw as "predatory capitalism" and drew the ire of the *Economist* before the 2015 election for wanting to "remake British capitalism in favor of a fairer society." He lost that election, but his lasting legacy was in the institutional reform of the party. Traditionally, the Labour leader had been elected by an electoral college of members, public representatives, and trade unions, with each of the three categories getting one third of the vote. However, under pressure from the party right to limit trade union influence, Miliband introduced a one member, one vote system that allowed even party "supporters" to participate in the election process.[27]

Such a system had long been a goal of Tony Blair's followers, who believed that Labour's membership and voters were to the right of the union leadership and a broadened franchise would make it almost impossible for a left-winger to be elected leader. As it turned out, exactly the opposite was the case. With Miliband standing down after his 2015 defeat, the new system paved the way to the election (on 59.5 percent to his nearest competitor's 19 percent) of longtime Labour MP Jeremy Corbyn. To even get on the ballot, Corbyn had needed the nomination of thirty-five other MPs. He got the necessary votes at the last minute, with many coming from right-wing Labour MPs who wanted a leftist on the ballot to give the perception of balance. They would later rue that decision.

A protégé of the late Tony Benn, Corbyn is a genuine radical and by far the most left-wing leader in Labour's history. Like Bernie Sanders in the United States, he is an unreconstructed survivor of a different era of socialist politics. Unlike Sanders, he had the benefit of a close connection to progressive trade unions, social movements, and a wider milieu of left politicians to draw on for support, including such figures as John McDonnell and Diane Abbott.

Despite constant media attacks—smearing him as an anti-Semite and KGB agent, or simply as someone who eats cold beans for dinner and didn't properly romance his ex-wife—and despite facing attempted coups from within his own party, Corbyn's tenure as leader has been a remarkable success so far. He has helped rebuild the party's base, turning Labour into Europe's largest party, with more than a half million members. Momentum, the grassroots formation created to support the effort, organizes tens of thousands in communities across Britain.[28]

The first eighteen months of his leadership didn't look so promising, however. The majority of Labour's parliamentarians bitterly opposed Corbyn, and so did much of the party's full-time staff. Labour's historic allies in the media—from the *Guardian* to the *Daily Mirror* and *The New Statesman*—abandoned their role of fighting back against Tory attacks and contributed to the pile-on against the party leader. The small team around Corbyn was bombarded with hostile internal leaks and misinformation, and understandably struggled to forge a socialist direction for a party so thoroughly bogged down by neoliberal ideas. Despite the failure of an attempted coup against Corbyn's leadership in the wake of the Brexit vote in 2016, the calls for him to go as party leader continued well into the following year.

But Corbyn and his supporters persevered. And when Theresa May called a snap election for June 2017 to capitalize on Labour's perceived weakness, the movement around him sprang to life. A campaign powered by unprecedented grassroots mobilization turned the election into something of a defeat for the Tories. It was the first election Labour had won seats in since 1997. The party got its largest share of the vote in over a decade—all while closing a 24-point deficit in the polls to deny the

Conservatives a majority and force them to govern with Northern Ireland's fringe Democratic Unionist Party.

Corbyn salvaged the election by bucking Labour's conservative slide and sticking to his left-wing guns. His strategy provides a blueprint for what democratic socialists worldwide need to do in the years to come. It also confirms what the Left had argued since Tony Benn: people like an honest defense of public goods. Labour's manifesto was sweeping, its most socialist in decades. It is a straightforward document, calling for national-ization of key utilities; access to education, housing, and health services for all; and measures to redistribute income from corporations and the rich to ordinary people. With promises of £6.3 billion to primary schools, the protection of pensions, free tuition, and public housing construction, there was no longer any doubt what Labour would do for Britain's workers. The plan was attacked in the press for its old-fashioned simplicity—summed up by its tagline "for the many, not the few"—but it resonated with the public.

If the economic program put forward by Corbyn's Labour Party was inspiring, the leadership also revived a vision of social-democratic politics that looks beyond capitalism. The most striking thing about Corbynism is that its protagonists see the inherent limits of reforms under capitalism and aim to expand the scope of democracy and challenge capital's own-ership and control, not just its wealth. Significantly, Labour is now the only traditional center-left party in the world drafting plans to expand the cooperative sector, create community-owned enterprises, give employees shares in the companies they work in, and restore the state's control of key sectors of the economy. These strategies aren't in themselves radical, but they are necessary prerequisites for any deeper socialist transforma-tion in the future. It's a lofty dream, one that will take decades to come to fruition, but it now seems plausible for the first time in a long while because of a Labour Party that looks far beyond the horizon of traditional Labourism.

Like Bernie Sanders's presidential campaign, Corbyn's breakthrough has shown that socialists can garner popular support by building a credible opposition rooted in an unapologetically left vision—that is, by offering hopes and dreams, not just fear and diminished expectations. There are still roadblocks to a Corbyn election as prime minister. However, if he does triumph, with a mobilized social base, trade union support, and a politically committed leadership, Labour offers the best chance for the Left since the 1980s to break with neoliberalism.

IN BOTH THE United States and Britain there is a surprising opportunity for socialist politics today. But though socialism has been resuscitated, its pulse is weak. The populist right still appears better suited than the socialist left to speak to the inequality, anger, and resentment that neoliberal policies inevitably produce. To succeed, the Left needs not only to construct a narrative of opposition to economic elites but to deliver real victories that can also help build a network of institutions to challenge capital.

NINE

HOW WE WIN

Leftists haven't just been daydreaming utopians. For both good and ill, socialists won power, at various points, across much of the world. But nowhere have we been able to decisively break with capitalism and build a democratic alternative. Even with the more modest ambition of just humanizing capitalism, no national left government in Europe has been able to carry out its program in at least forty years. In the United States, the socialist movement hasn't been relevant for decades longer than that.

Yet a better future still seems in reach. For all its resilience, capitalism remains prone to crisis, as people today know well. Its inequalities provoke resistance. Billions resent the unfair choices offered to them. But most people don't have any reason to believe that politics can improve their lives. Collective action—either in the workplace or outside it—is often riskier than accepting the status quo. The dilemma for socialists today is figuring out how to take anger at the unjust outcomes of capitalism and turn it into a challenge to the system itself.

The task is made even more daunting by the fact that we in the United States lack the three ingredients necessary for almost every socialist advance of the past hundred fifty years: mass parties, an activist base, and a mobilized working class. We're not starting from scratch, though. The Bernie Sanders campaign encouraged millions to believe that things can be different. New mass actions, such as 2018's teacher strikes, have also revealed in our own age the power of working people. What we need now are organizations: working-class parties and unions that can unite scattered resistance into a socialist movement.[1]

Easier said than done. But this chapter offers a road map based on the long, complex, variously inspiring and dismal history of left politics—for challenging capitalism and creating a democratic socialist alternative to it.

1. Class-struggle social democracy does not close avenues for radicals; it opens them.

On the face of it, Corbyn and Sanders advocate a set of demands that are essentially social democratic. But they represent something far different from modern social democracy. Whereas social democracy morphed in the postwar period into a tool to suppress class conflict in favor of tripartite arrangements among business, labor, and the state, both of these leaders encourage a renewal of class antagonism and movements from below.

To Sanders, the path to reform is through confrontation with elites. Rather than talking about an entire nation struggling together to restore the US economy and shared prosperity, and rather than seeking to negotiate a better settlement with business leaders (if only they saw that progressive change was in their interests!), Sanders's movement is about creating a "political revolution" to get what is rightfully ours from "millionaires and billionaires." His program leads to polarization along class lines; indeed, it calls for it.

Sanders's vision is conflated so often with that of progressives that commentators frequently talk about the Democratic Party's "Sanders-Warren wing." But there is a vital difference between the class struggle approach of Sanders and the more wonkish approach of someone like Elizabeth Warren, who seeks to construct better policy but not an alternative politics. Not surprisingly, Warren is quick to assure business interests that she believes that "strong, healthy markets are the key to a strong, healthy America" and that she "is a capitalist."[2]

Sanders was trained as a student in the Young People's Socialist League and through trade union and civil rights organizing. His worldview was formed by this unusual background. For his part, Corbyn has been a long-standing member of the Labour left, a socialist committed to social movement and union struggles and the battle against Blairism.

Sanders and Corbyn don't represent a social-democratic politics that will serve as a moderate alternative to more militant socialist demands. Rather, they offer a radical alternative to a decrepit center-left. They have introduced a language of class struggle and redistribution to audiences that haven't ever heard demands like these. Class-struggle social democracy, then, is generating working-class strength through electoral campaigns rather than subordinating existing struggles to the goal of getting a few people elected. The difference between this political current and the social democracy of Tony Blair or even Olof Palme is striking.

2. Class-struggle social democracy has the potential to win a major national election today.

This is more imminently likely in the United Kingdom, where Corbyn leads a working-class party, but consider where popular mood is in the United States. There's widespread anti-establishment sentiment, but despite the rise of Donald Trump, the Left's policies are favored on key issues, including immigration.

The president may want to build a big beautiful wall, but 60 percent of Americans oppose the idea. In a 1994 Pew survey, 63 percent thought that immigrants were a burden, and only 31 percent said they were strengthening the country. When asked the same question in 2016, just 27 percent saw immigrants as a burden, and 63 percent thought immigration was a good thing.[3]

Even after being subjected to three years of attacks from both the Right and corporate Democrats, Bernie Sanders is among the most popular politicians in the United States. His central demands—a universal jobs program and single-payer health insurance—both enjoy substantial support among voters. Polls show that 52 percent want a jobs guarantee nationwide, with even higher favorability in poor states like Mississippi (72 percent). Medicare for All could be just as popular a platform plank: in April 2018 support for the measure crept above 50 percent.[4]

The challenge is to take these individual "policy preferences" and bundle them into a coherent politics, but this has been precisely the Sanders campaign's breakthrough. If not by Sanders, it seems a presidential election can be won by a left-populist candidate who shares his straightforward message and working class–oriented demands.

3. Winning an election isn't the same thing as winning power.

There's been something of an overcorrection on the Left, from the "change the world without taking power" drum circle days of the postsocialist 1990s to an overemphasis on electoral mobilization today.

Elections are indeed important. In many countries, voting and paying attention to campaigns are the only political acts that most people engage in. Electoral races not only help advance our political vision, including among those who might otherwise not be listening to us, but also involve the construction of organizations and networks that can galvanize energy beyond the campaign trail.

But what's the point of winning an election unless we can actually do the things we promise? In certain contexts, we could justify merely "occupying power"—like French socialist Léon Blum did in the 1930s—to keep out the Right for an election cycle or two or to dull the impact of austerity on workers, but that's a surefire way to disillusion your base and lose in the medium- and long-term. Ever since the 1980s—with the impasse of François Mitterrand's government and the retreat of Nordic welfare states—social democracy has just been the more humane face of neoliberalism. What appears at first to be a victory can soon enough be revealed as a defeat.

Working-class voters today are generally disillusioned with the ruling-class political consensus. But they and other voters don't have faith in the potential of politics to change their lives; they don't turn out to vote, and they're less active in parties, unions, and civic organizations than they once were. This "crisis of politics" is principally a crisis of the Left. The European center-right doesn't need a conscious, active base of supporters to carry out their program; they can manage capitalism in the interests of capitalists with the help of just a dozen EU technocrats. In the United States, the Right is very effective at seizing and wielding power as a minority, through its institutions, gerrymandering, and the court system. Yet the Left has always depended on mass mobilization, not only to win elections, but to enact change.

So how do we make elections work for us? Class-struggle social democracy through the ballot box is exceedingly difficult, because candidates face both incentives to compromise and structural pressure: administering a capitalist state requires maintaining business confidence and corporate profits. This was the dilemma that Mitterrand's government ran into. The solution is through creating some pressure of our own. Street protests and strike actions can discipline wayward candidates for not going along with a redistributive agenda and can force businesses to make concessions to reformers once they are elected.

Still, one dilemma is unresolved: we need a mass base to win reforms but struggle to rally that base without giving people proof that politics can change their lives for the better.

4. They'll do everything to stop us.

Donald Trump's early days in office were a good lesson in Marxist state theory. He brought with him a contradictory set of politics: a right-populist challenge to both NATO and the network of US-led free trade deals, on the one hand, and more traditional pro-business Republican pledges, on the other. The parts that got through, not surprisingly, were those that capital found more acceptable. Paul Ryan–backed tax cuts have been passed, but Trump's more extreme protectionist plans have gotten stymied, and gone is Steve Bannon, along with his dreams of a massive jobs program built around deficit-financed infrastructure construction.

If these are the pressures that rabidly pro-capitalist Trump was under, we can only imagine the forces that could be brought to bear on a President Sanders in 2021. For one thing, he would have to contend with a vicious media offensive—each new policy or proposal would be systematically smeared, with eager help from corporate Democrats.

The example of Jeremy Corbyn's first years as Labour leader might offer an instructive preview. By the end of his first term, Corbyn had faced smear attempts from both Conservative and establishment Labour voices, a move from inside his own party to purge many of his supporters from the voting rolls, and many other challenges. From claims of anti-Semitism and sexism, to criticism of his opposition to a second Brexit vote, the internal opposition to Corbyn has taken on a progressive guise to undermine his leadership.

More significant will be the role of capital strikes—businesses choosing to withhold investment until more "favorable conditions" prevail, blackmailing left-voting workers in the process.[5] Some of these threats will be less dramatic than others. Labour parliamentarian Tony Benn highlighted the mundane coercion that came with power: do what we want, and we'll make you look good; try pursuing your own agenda, and we'll make your life impossible.

5. Our immediate demands are very much achievable.

Social democracy's dilemma is impossible to resolve: even when nominally anticapitalist, it is reliant on the continued profitability of private capitalist firms. Aspirations to usher in an alternative political economy haven't been pursued since the interwar nationalization commissions. Similarly, attempts to imagine a more gradual socialization from the starting point of an existing welfare state have been dropped since the late 1970s neutering of the Meidner Plan in Sweden.

But that's not to say that there isn't space for us to win reforms in the here and now. Consider the United States, a country not even close to bumping up against the limits of social democracy. Medicare for All, or the decommodification of a sixth of the most important economy in the world, does not seem beyond reach. We can also guarantee access to nutritious food, safe and secure housing, free child care, and public education at all levels. Other demands should center around allowing people to freely organize unions and collectively bargain, helping to rebuild the political agency necessary to sustain and deepen reforms.

Luckily, the United States doesn't have to contend with antidemocratic supranational organizations like the eurozone, and it has immense resources to work with. We ultimately have larger ambitions than "socialism in one country," but if it's possible anywhere, it's possible here.

Cobbling together the legislative power to achieve these reforms will not be easy. But it is possible to achieve certain socialist goals within capitalism. As we've seen in the history of social democracy, any achievements will be vulnerable to crises and resisted at every step, but they are morally and politically necessary nonetheless.

6. We must move quickly from social democracy to democratic socialism.

Any social democrat, no matter their intentions, will always find it easier to move to the right than to the left. On one side lie guarantees of stability from powerful interests, on the other capital strikes and stubborn resistance. Today, even more so than in the twentieth century, democratic socialists face not only the problem of how to win power but the problem of how to fend off capital's attempt to undermine their program.

In other words, the social-democratic compromise is inherently unstable, and we thus need to figure a way to advance rather than retreat in the face of that instability. Social democracy faces challenges in two directions. Capital seeks to control it from the outset, but if initial reforms are successful, workers have more leverage to strike, and the increased bargaining power of labor can make unsustainable inroads into firm profitability. The welfare state of the '60s and '70s didn't placate workers; it made them bolder. "Transitional demands" such as a jobs guarantee could do the same in our own time. We need to understand, though, that when the crisis comes, the next step isn't retreat but to press on further.

In many other ways, we face a much different environment than did the social democrats of the postwar era. Capital has been internationalized, growth rates have slowed in the advanced capitalist world, and automation threatens core areas of working-class strength. All this means that we probably don't have thirty years to make reforms the way social democrats did in the postwar period.

In this shorter cycle, we have to imagine that the limits of reform will be reached much sooner, but that the route to a more radical socialism will come from the crisis of social democracy our very success initiates. Class-struggle social democracy, then, isn't a foe of democratic socialism—the road to the latter runs through the former.

The question is, How do we make sure that any left government can actually stick around long enough to win some victories (and not just immediately retreat like Greece's Syriza did)? In particular, how do we win the "nonreformist reforms" that not only benefit workers in the short term but can empower them to win the battles that enacting them will provoke?

Our task is formidable. Democratic socialists must secure decisive majorities in legislatures while winning hegemony in the unions. Then our organizations must be willing to flex their social power in the form of mass mobilizations and political strikes to counter the structural power of capital and ensure that our leaders choose confrontation over accommodation with elites. This is the sole way we'll not only make our reforms durable but break with capitalism entirely and bring about a world that values people over profit.

7. We need socialists.

Clusters of ideological socialists by themselves can't usher in socialism—and even if we could, we certainly don't want to repeat the last century's attempts, whether in Russia or in China, to impose "socialism from above." But we do play an irreplaceable role in the battles to win reforms and make those reforms durable and cumulative.

Better than others, we can perceive class relations and how they offer common avenues of struggle. However, we can't isolate ourselves from broader currents of progressive change that may not yet be socialist. These movements have the potential to win material improvements for workers. Without constant engagement with them, we will slide into sectarian irrelevance much like the Socialist Labor Party of Daniel De Leon's day.

The challenge is to do this while building our organizational strength and ability to operate as an independent political force. We must be ca pable of resisting the transactional approach to politics often practiced by trade union leaders and the professional middle-class stewards of advocacy groups.

Even a relatively small organization like the Democratic Socialists of America (DSA), something far short of a mass party with working-class roots, shows the disruptive role we can play if we embed our efforts within the class. DSA today has over fifty thousand members—that's forty-five thousand more than it did a few years ago. Buoyed by the rise of Sanders, youth disillusionment with the politics of the Democratic center, and outrage over Trump's actions, DSA has quickly garnered widespread attention and its share of local victories.

It's fifty thousand people in a country of three hundred thirty million. But the mobilization capacities of political parties, of trade unions, and of civic organizations have been hollowed out. Tens of thousands of people, if organized in common campaigns, if trained to speak and connect with people and assist them in their struggles, can indeed have a national impact. Many fewer than that can swing local races and bring new ideas and demands into popular consciousness.

That's why training a new generation of nonsectarian socialist organizers is so important. We need democratic socialists who are skilled speakers, effective writers, and sharp thinkers—who are humble enough to learn but bold enough to inspire confidence. Our organizations depend on a disciplined core of such people if we hope to rebuild working-class power that can exert an alternative pressure to that of capital. Even though their efforts won't be enough in and of themselves, we can't achieve socialism without them.

8. The working class has changed over the past hundred fifty years—but not as much as we think.

Socialists won't be effective if we exist solely on college campuses or spend our time attacking one another on social media. For the last century and a half, the working class has been at the center of socialist politics for a reason. Marxists didn't romanticize workers because they were oppressed, ripped from their land, and suffering in crowded factories and squalid slums. They paid attention to the working class because workers were more powerful than any other dominated group: capitalists depend on their labor for profits, and, when organized, workers can withhold that labor to win reforms.[6]

Some things have changed since Marx published *Capital* a hundred fifty years ago, or even since powerful parties of the Left ruled from Kingston, Jamaica, to Stockholm, Sweden, in the 1960s and 1970s. There was a time when one could immediately identify a working-class neighborhood in a place like Turin, Italy. A few industries would have been the key source of employment for the area. People lived densely packed together, forced by capitalism into, if not solidarity, then at least commonality. True to this shared condition, workers voted in the main for parties of the broad Left. The job of the revolutionary was to convince workers committed to a politics of reform to embrace a politics of rupture.

Today you might find pockets of organized, class-conscious working-class people across the advanced capitalist world, but these are the exception, not the rule. The twenty-first-century working class is fragmented. William Morris wrote in 1885 that while workers are a class, socialists must convince them "they ought to be Society." Now we have to convince them about the class part, too.

Though the working class has changed, the shifts are overstated by those who proclaim this to be the era of the "precariat." There's nothing new about workers suffering through precarious, low-wage employment. After all, Karl Kautsky confronted the question of working-class heterogeneity in the 1880s, the "golden age" of the industrial proletariat, as did Engels when he studied 1840s Manchester. Whatever semblance of security existed in the past was not due to the inherent nature of "pre-neoliberal" capitalism but the result of successful class struggle and organization. Auto workers, for example, weren't inherently militant trade unionists. Up until the 1930s Renault and Ford and other big manufacturers were just as union hostile as Walmart is today.[7]

While the percentage of workers employed in industrial manufacturing has declined in recent decades, the trend lines go back to the late nineteenth century. The workers still left in those sectors (who, in raw numbers, are actually more numerous than ever) can still exert significant economic power. However, to build a majoritarian coalition, socialists need to think more broadly.

Our conception of a working class today goes beyond formally employed workers to the labor and political agency found in households and neighborhoods. But the traditional workplace should still be central to our vision. That means putting special emphasis on workers in growing sectors, such as education and health care, as well as those working in supply and logistics. It also means developing connections between the unemployed and the employed and pursuing a broad practice of social justice unionism—union organizing that goes beyond typical workplace demands—capable of marshaling broader popular support for strikes and left-wing policy initiatives.

How many people are we talking about in all? In most developed societies around 60 percent of the population still has to rely on wages to survive and possesses little to no net wealth. Those working people are as different and divided as ever, yet they still have the potential to rattle the system and win real gains. We simply cannot have an emancipatory politics within capitalism that doesn't revolve around the class whose labor makes the system run. Socialists need to arise from, try to create a political culture around, and organize within this class, not find substitutes for it.

9. Socialists must embed themselves in working-class struggles.

In 2018, the United States witnessed a wave of public sector strikes, the most significant labor upsurge in the country since the 1970s. These weren't spontaneous outbursts—they were sparked by both intolerable conditions and the efforts of small groups of organizers.[8]

Consider the dynamics in the teacher strike in 2018 West Virginia: Bernie Sanders campaigned extensively in the state, and his supporters built up enough of an infrastructure to win every county in the 2016 Democratic primary. Some young recruits eager to continue the "political revolution" after Sanders's loss to Hillary Clinton flocked to the Democratic Socialists of America. They went from being isolated progressives in a red state to an organized network of like-minded socialists capable of helping initiate and lead the historic nine-day strike. Those who were teachers were able to connect and organize with coworkers from across the political spectrum, all with the goal of improving working conditions and ultimately transforming the state's politics.[9]

Similar actions by underpaid teachers in Arizona, Kentucky, and Oklahoma mobilized tens of thousands of people. Like West Virginia, these were relatively conservative states with weak union bureaucracies. The strike wave caught the media and politicians off guard. Only those who understood that a "militant minority" could foster mass mobilization—and how once in motion those workers could have their consciousness and sense of political possibility transformed—could have anticipated the size and fervor of the strikes.

These strikes won national attention and public sympathy. After Arizona teachers joined the strike wave in April 2018, a national poll conducted by the Associated Press showed that a vast majority sided with the teachers: 78 percent of the country thought teacher salaries were too low (only 6 percent thought they were too high). This sentiment cuts across party lines: sizable majorities of Democratic (90 percent), independent (78 percent), and Republican (66 percent) voters believe teachers should make more money. And 52 percent of Americans support teachers' right to strike for better pay—despite union-busting laws that make such actions illegal in many states.[10]

By going on strike, educators not only demonstrated their own strength as political actors but developed a political consciousness and a grassroots infrastructure. It's a sign of what needs to happen, though on a much larger scale, in the years to come.

Further organizing efforts by committed and effective socialists will be key to building on the gains of the 2018 teacher strikes. But young socialists should not see themselves solely as outside organizers: we should also encourage one another to take rank-and-file jobs in a range of growing sectors. Socialists once consciously avoided middle-class jobs in order to "industrialize" in strategic sectors, and for good reason. Our last major attempt in the United States—the effort to organize heavy industry in the 1970s—required immense sacrifice among those who pursued it and suffered from bad timing, as those sectors were entering a period of brutal neoliberal restructuring. But that doesn't mean we should abandon the strategy of joining the fight on the shop floor.

This is not only good organizing advice; it's good career advice! In today's economy, young socialists, despite their relatively high levels of education, can't get the kind of professional jobs afforded to their 1970s counterparts. They might actually have better economic prospects if they were to enter strategic sectors such as nursing and education rather than stitching together part-time or temporary work in the professional world.

10. It is not enough to work with unions for progressive change. We must wage democratic battles within them.

Unions are important. They might not be revolutionary organizations, but they are labor's primary vehicle in the battle with capital over the spoils of production. Today, despite organizing just 11 percent of the US workforce, unions are still the only institutions capable of exerting political pressure at the scale required to push back against national elites. Importantly, they also look less like the industrial workforce of the nineteenth century and more like the diverse working class of the twenty-first. Though their image in the popular mind hasn't caught up, unions today disproportionately represent black, Latino, and women workers.

Unions serve a purpose beyond collective bargaining: namely, that they can prompt workers to become more class-conscious and learn political skills. A nurse active in her union can become an educator and an organizer.

But unions can only be effective at fighting for member interests and developing these capacities if the rank and file are allowed to play an active role within them. Beyond obvious cases of corruption, US unions are often extremely hierarchical and bureaucratic. They're dominated by full-time staff and salaried officials. Members are trained to see their unions as service organizations. Workers' interactions with their unions are often limited to automatic dues deductions and brief consultations over wage bargaining or political endorsements. They have little reason to go to a union meeting.[11]

Union staff occupy an intermediary position between company management and regular workers. The stability they offer sometimes works to everyone's benefit, but while workers can make progress through strikes, the labor bureaucracy usually prefers stability. An analogy could be drawn to the structure of political parties, in which the leadership often prefers caution to bold action.

Some degree of specialization is no doubt necessary, and ordinary workers don't want to be subjected to endless meetings, but without avenues to membership participation and oversight, the gap between union "professionals" and the rank and file will continue to grow, and workers will feel less and less tied to their unions.

In short: we need to do more than defend existing unions from attacks from the Right. Our goal must be to transform them into vehicles of a more expansive, democratic unionism through facilitating membership engagement and creating structures that make leaderships more accountable. Yet we can't just be content to democratize a dwindling movement—a key task today is also finding ways to organize in the twenty-first-century economy to restore union density.

11. A loose network of leftists and rank-and-file workers isn't enough. We need a political party.

When we talk about a Left political party today, some recall the drab, monolithic parties of the old Stalinist and social-democratic lefts. But we should also recall that these parties coordinated the work of disparate activists and deepened the analysis and vision of generations of working-class militants.

Because of the peculiar structure of the British political system, Labour's long-standing left wing was able to win control of the party in 2015. In general, we shouldn't try to capture discredited social-democratic parties but rather work within the left-wing ones that have appeared in recent years. Parties like Die Linke in Germany, the Left Bloc in Portugal, and Podemos in Spain bring together forces from across the Left, radical and reformist alike. They face a litany of challenges but represent a real opening to build a politics that's left of social democracy.

For democratic socialists, it makes sense to organize within these formations. Not as infiltrators seeking to opportunistically capture their membership and resources, but as members genuinely trying to both build these parties and maintain an independent profile—challenging leaderships as necessary. There is much to learn on this count from the history of social democracy: parties that were forces for working-class reform became capital's junior partners. The presence of organized socialists is a necessary brake on the inevitable move away from class-struggle politics and toward bureaucratization and political moderation.

Developing new parties involves challenges, too. Though we have seen recent successes in Europe and elsewhere, not all of the examples are positive. Many of the new parties in Europe are built on the shaky ground of social movements, on the premise that we can build a "movement of movements" in which the workers' movement is one element but not necessarily the decisive one. Moreover, an overemphasis on ideological heterogeneity—in an attempt to reunite a divided and fractured Left—has weakened those parties' ability to articulate a clear political program and unified strategy.

The experience of the last two decades, starting with Portugal's Left Bloc in 1999, shows the hopelessness of an approach that doesn't foreground the disruptive capacity of labor but instead tries to haphazardly build a defensive electoral coalition, while rallying people into the streets for what amounts to little more than political theater. Instead, a political party should be the decisive link between explicitly socialist currents and a wider workers' movement. If things go right one day, we'll be able to speak of the two as one and the same—a socialist workers' movement.

12. We need to take into account American particularities.

Building a socialist movement in the United States will require a distinct approach—not for cultural reasons but for structural ones.

As *Jacobin* editor Seth Ackerman has explained, the United States has not only "winner-take-all" elections but a uniquely antidemocratic election law. The two-party system in American politics didn't arise naturally. Rather, it was constructed piecemeal as the Democratic and Republican parties consolidated power around the turn of the twentieth century. Politicians on both sides used their positions inside state legislatures to enact laws designed to prevent third-party challenges. The restrictive system of election laws that developed in the United States is unique among advanced capitalist democracies.[12]

Both Democratic and Republican elites have an interest in maintaining the two-party system—and it requires a lot of maintenance. The political scientist Theodore Lowi compared it to a patient on life support that would "collapse in an instant if the tubes were pulled." But the two ruling parties continue to keep those tubes firmly in place—for example, by passing laws like the 1971 Federal Elections Campaign Act, which grants large amounts of "public" campaign financing to the major parties while leaving smaller parties to fend for themselves.[13]

Things were difficult during the era of Eugene V. Debs's Socialist Party, where despite having a presence in much of the country, socialists never cracked 6 percent of the national popular vote. Today, every state requires third parties to collect thousands of signatures just to appear on the ballot in a single race, a practice unheard of in democratic countries. The GOP and the Democrats are even governed differently from most political parties: individual members don't vote on party platforms, nor are they held to political lines. These are not democratic institutions but antidemocratic machines that provide well-oiled pathways to political power while stymieing challenges from below.

As Ackerman puts it, we're facing a set of challenges more similar to those facing opposition parties in "soft-authoritarian" countries like Russia or Singapore than those in Britain or Canada.

It will come as no surprise that I've been a registered Democrat since my eighteenth birthday—the same day I joined the Democratic Socialists of America. I joined the latter because the DSA reflected my actual political beliefs, the former because I lived in New York and wanted to participate in the only meaningful elections in my area, which were closed Democratic Party primaries.

As a registered Democrat, I don't have the power to influence the party's politics in any meaningful way: like most registered voters in this country, I don't get a vote when it comes to my own party's political platform. But on the flip side, there's no way for the Democrats to expel me or hold me to a political program. I can spend most of my waking hours attacking the Clintons and other corporate Democrats, and I can't be disciplined in any way. I can only lose my ability to vote in Democratic primaries in New York if I change my registration or commit a felony and am incarcerated or on parole. Precisely because it is so undemocratic, the Democratic Party may actually be vulnerable to what Ackerman calls "the electoral equivalent of a guerilla insurgency."

Which is not to say that the Democratic Party is just a ballot line that can be taken over by socialists. The fragmentation of the party—the fact that it's more like a thousand parties at local, state, and national levels than a single, coherent organization—means that it's not clear which barricades we should be storming. This diffusion is a source of strength for the business interests that shape the Democratic Party.

What we need is to create the first traditional mass-membership party in the United States, an organization based on the delegate model of representation. Imagine a workers' party created outside the Democratic Party that runs hundreds if not thousands of candidates and that is composed of various factions that debate one another and put together a democratically decided-on program. In the short term, it might run some candidates as independents, others as Democrats. But all these candidates would subscribe to the basic principles of the program and have to draw their funding from the party membership and its allied unions and organizations. They would also be accountable to the party rank and file. The immediate goal would be to create an independent ideological and political profile for democratic socialism.

Such a party would need to be a flexible organization merging electoral campaigns with shop floor mobilization. In time, the party could make the leap to a completely independent, democratic socialist ballot line.

13. We need to democratize our political institutions.

Consider a few facts: Donald Trump is in the White House, despite winning almost three million fewer votes than Hillary Clinton. The Senate, the country's most powerful legislative chamber, grants the same representation to Wyoming's 579,315 residents as it does to 39,536,653 Californians. Key voting rights are denied to citizens in the District of Columbia, Puerto Rico, and other US territories. The American government is structured by an eighteenth-century text that is almost impossible to change.

These ills didn't come about by accident; the subversion of democracy was the explicit intent of the Constitution's framers. For James Madison, writing in *Federalist No. 10*, "Democracies have ever been spectacles of turbulence and contention" incompatible with the rights of property owners. The byzantine Constitution he helped create serves as the foundation for a system of government that rules over people, rather than an evolving tool for popular self-government.[14]

While preserving and expanding the Bill of Rights' incomplete safeguards of individual freedoms, we need to start working toward the establishment of a new political system that truly represents Americans. Our ideal should be a strong federal government powered by a proportionally elected unicameral legislature. But intermediary steps toward that vision can be taken by abolishing the filibuster, establishing federal control over elections, and developing a simpler way to amend the Constitution through national referendum.

More generally, these changes could challenge a federalism that fragments power and allows for antidemocratic regional and local control. As the late labor journalist Robert Fitch put it, "The aim of the Right is always to restrict the scope of class conflict—to bring it down to as low a level as possible. The smaller and more local the political unit, the easier it is to run it oligarchically."[15]

Abolishing the Electoral College and pushing toward more proportional voting systems that encourage participation must be immediate demands. Other reforms such as Bernie Sanders's Workplace Democracy Act could help encourage working-class militancy by making it easier to form unions, protect workers from employer retaliation, roll back "right to work" measures, and expand the scope of legal workplace actions. (Not that labor activists should refrain from breaking these laws in the meantime—often, that's exactly what it takes for the labor movement to be successful.) In other countries, the battle for democracy will center on civil service reforms, eliminating undemocratic upper houses of parliament, or eroding the power of corporate media interests.

14. Our politics must be universalist.

Racism has existed for centuries, sexual oppression for even longer. Both were present at the beginning of the modern working class, and we shouldn't count on interpersonal bigotry simply disappearing through socialist revolution, much less through socialist reforms.

The socialist record on oppression is uneven but still better than that of any other political tradition. Most of history's Marxists have actually been people of color: one need only recall the proliferation of Marxist-led national liberation movements in the twentieth century to appreciate this fact. Socialists have also long been at the forefront of the struggle against women's oppression and for sexual liberation. They've been animated by the idea that any struggle for justice needs to address basic questions about the distribution of power and resources.

However, since the broader defeat of class-based movements in the 1970s and '80s, narrower, identity-based struggles to address injustice have filled the void. These movements have won some significant gains in the realm of culture and representation, improving millions of lives. (I'm glad I grew up in 1990s America, not the 1950s version.) But many of those advances have succeeded mainly in diversifying our elites, not in bettering the lives of the most oppressed. A world where half the Fortune 500 CEOs are women and fewer of them are white would be better than our world today, but still doesn't mean much if there are just as many poor kids experiencing the same oppression they are now. Without the bedrock of a class politics, identity politics has become an agenda of inclusionary neoliberalism in which individual qualms can be addressed but structural inequalities cannot.

Of course, we still have a long way to go before we even equalize opportunity within the current neoliberal system. Socialists shouldn't reject people's experiences, but if we want to tackle oppression at its root, we need to ask questions about the redistribution of power and wealth—that is, questions rooted in class. As Martin Luther King Jr. put it in 1967, "We aren't merely struggling to integrate a lunch counter now. We're struggling to get some money to be able to buy a hamburger or a steak when we get to the counter."[16]

Socialists also need to argue against the idea that racism and sexism are innate and that people's consciousness won't change through struggle. Racism has taken on an almost metaphysical role in liberal politics—it is somehow the cause of, explanation for, and consequence of most social phenomena. The reality is people can overcome their prejudices in the process of mass struggle over shared interests, but that requires getting people involved in those common struggles to begin with.

Socialists don't reject fights against oppression but instead try to bring them into a broader workers' movement. We should strive for the elimination of bigotry, chauvinism, and any form of prejudice within our organizations. That means taking equality seriously, not as a goal for the distant future but as a practice in the here and now. But it also entails avoiding a narrow "call-out culture" along with the kind of identity politics that, taken to its extreme, will lead us down the path to a hyper-individualized and anti-solidaristic politics. Hyperbole and the politics of personal shaming are a recipe for demoralization, paranoia, and defeat.

The socialist premise is clear: at their core people want dignity, respect, and a fair shot at a good life. A democratic class politics is the best way to unite people against our common opponent and win the type of change that will help the most marginalized, all while engaging in a far longer campaign against oppression rooted in race, gender, sexuality, and more.

15. History matters.

If nothing else, that's what this book has aimed to show. While the excitement around socialism today feels new and fresh to many people outside the movement (and many within it, too), we have little hope of realizing our aims if we don't learn from those who marched and organized and dreamed before us.

The lessons and analysis that socialists offer—along with the Marxist framework—are vital for plotting a way out of today's extreme inequality and into a just society. It's also vital that we have a tradition that people can refer to. In this era of atomization and alienation, that tradition can provide us with a sense of our place in history and a meaning to our work. That's not to say that a popular class movement for redistributive policies needs to be explicitly socialist to win reforms, but socialists are needed within such a movement to provide vision and push things forward.

Naturally, there are also lessons from the Communist movements' time in power: the difficulties of central planning, the importance of civil rights and freedoms, what happens when socialism is transformed from a democratic movement from below into an authoritarian collectivism. But pluralism and democracy are ingrained not only in civil societies in the advanced capitalist world but within the socialist movement itself. What seems most relevant are the lessons of social democracy, namely that the antidemocratic power of capital will overwhelm democratically backed pro-worker reforms.

But what about the end goal of socialism—extending democracy radically into our communities and workplaces, ending the exploitation of humans by other humans? Fundamentally, political strategy for the Left has to put these more radical questions, one by one, on the table, all the while struggling to stay mobilized. And while we defend newly won gains, we must fight to avoid the crippling bureaucratization that pushed the great social-democratic movements of the early twentieth century into a self-defeating accommodation with the system. It won't be easy, but we still have a world to win.

TEN

STAY FLY

I N RECENT DECADES, socialism has been challenged from all directions. The influential German sociologist Ralf Dahrendorf was right when he wrote that Francis Fukuyama's proclamation of "liberal democracy as the final form of human government" was "a caricature of a serious argument," but he agreed with its core premise: "socialism is dead, and none of its variants can be revived for a world awakening from the double nightmare of Stalinism and Brezhnevism." From the Left, Andre Gorz echoed that sentiment: "As a system, socialism is dead. As a movement and an organized political force, it is on its last legs. All the goals it once proclaimed are out of date."[1]

Gorz's frustrations were directed at the workers' movement as a whole. It hadn't fulfilled its revolutionary destiny, though socialists were still wedded to it and its failures. Capitalism has proved remarkably durable. But from a different perspective, the history of working-class politics since the days of Marx and Engels has been a stunning success. God rested on the seventh day; the labor movement gave us the sixth off. We went from an era when capital ruled unchallenged to one with powerful limits on its conduct—the forty-hour week, labor and environmental regulations, and more. These reforms, and the broader progress toward women's liberation and racial equality, are under constant siege, but they happened.

We do not live in the worst of all possible worlds. The world we live in, as brutal and unequal as it is, has been made more humane by class movements. That consolation seems like a small one, however, given how lofty our ambitions once were. Many would agree that socialists have always understood how capitalism works and even proved capable of reforming some of its ugliest features. But why, they ask, would we repeat the disasters of the twentieth century by once again trying to create a socialist system?

This book has offered a few answers to that question. The first is that the tremendous suffering in the world today demands a response. Capitalist development has created mass abundance, but it hasn't met the basic needs of the most vulnerable. Millions still die every year of preventable diseases. Many more spend their lives mired in poverty. The second answer is ideological: capitalism is built off wage labor, which rests on the exploitation and domination of humans by other humans. Democratic workplaces embedded in an economy committed to the moral worth and flourishing of all could make this subordination no longer necessary. A third answer: even if we're content to simply reform capitalism, those reforms will be continually undermined by capital's structural power. Addressing that dilemma will mean pressing on to democratic socialism.

Yet another answer, which I have only alluded to, is the climate crisis and the real possibility that capitalism could destroy civilization as we know it. We're on pace for over 3 degrees Celsius of warming above preindustrial levels, even if existing international climate pledges are upheld. We likely need to keep that number below 1.5 degrees to prevent deep economic recession, massive crop failure, and the irreversible decline of ice sheets. That suggests we are fated to undergo the catastrophe so many now predict.[2]

The intensification of the climate crisis will be the test by which future generations judge us, much as we look back to the action (or lack thereof) taken against fascism in the 1920s and '30s. As global warming intensifies, we'll likely see massive refugee flows, economic destabilization, and the elevation of vicious new right-wing movements. Far from trying to push beyond capitalism to a new stage of civilization, we might find ourselves looking back with nostalgia at our far from ideal present.

Fighting climate change can't wait until "after the revolution," and we'll have to find a way to shape capitalist investment priorities and win sweeping reforms in the here and now. Yet it would be politically counterproductive and morally unconscionable if the "greening" of capitalism is merely used as a tool for austerity in the North or to deny those in the Global South much needed development. Still, socialists need to understand the complexity of nature and the unintended consequences of certain attempts to "master" it. Capital seeks to infinitely expand, but the material world—both human labor and the physical environment—has finite limits. Marx hailed reforms such as the Ten Hours' Bill as a triumph of "the political economy of the working class," because it limited the scope of capitalist exploitation over workers. We need to radically impose new limits on the ability of capital to exploit the planet.[3]

The Soviet Union and China under Mao were hardly paragons of environmentalism. In their rush to catch up with capitalist rivals, industrialization poisoned landscapes for generations. There was little environmental oversight by state planners and managers as they tried to expand production.

There are reasons to believe that a democratic socialism would do far better at keeping humanity flourishing along with the wider ecology in which we're enmeshed. Worker-controlled firms don't have the same "grow or die" imperative as capitalist ones. A more empowered citizenry, too, would be better able to weigh the costs and benefits of new development. At the very least, more democracy means a better chance to argue for a politics that defends the interests of our children and grandchildren.

The final answer to "Why socialism?" is simple: it would be the best guarantor of peace. If you were alive a few hundred years ago, a lord might have summoned you and other peasants, given you pikes, and told you that you had to go to war with people in a neighboring village. You rallied under a blue banner with a griffin or some such creature on it; they rallied under a green banner with a dragon on it. In battle, you piked some poor soul or got piked yourself. One day, people will look upon the division of this tiny world into rival nations and armies with the same dismay that characterizes our reactions to premodern history. The flags of countries might not be replaced by red ones overnight, and we might not all one day sing "The Internationale" in Esperanto, but the internationalist appeal of socialism will be a far more potent challenge to nationalism than liberal cosmopolitanism.

SOCIALISM HAS SURVIVED a lot over the past century. It's survived persecution from tyrants and the tyrants that it itself gave birth to. It survived the radical reshaping of capitalism and that of its great protagonist, the working class.

But does socialism really have a future? I have the utmost moral confidence that a world in which some thrive by depriving others of freedom, billions needlessly suffer amid plenty, and we move ever closer to ecological catastrophe is unacceptable. I also believe that as long as we live in a society divided into classes, there will be natural opposition to inequality and exploitation. Technical and political barriers to progress can't be underestimated, but if we are to make something better of our shared world, socialist politics, broadly conceived, offer us the best tools we have for getting there.

In *The Tailor of Ulm*, Lucio Magri recounted a debate from the Italian Communist Party's last days. It was 1991, and most members wanted to shed their pasts and pursue a more moderate course. The old hopes had proven to be illusions. The leader of the minority that opposed the majority's decision, Pietro Ingrao, responded by reciting a Bertolt Brecht parable, set in 1592:

> *Said the Tailor to the Bishop:*
> *Believe me, I can fly.*
> *Watch me while I try.*

And he stood with things
That looked like wings
On the great church roof—
That is quite absurd
A wicked, foolish lie,
For man will never fly,
A man is not a bird,
Said the Bishop to the Tailor.
Said the People to the Bishop:
The Tailor is quite dead,
He was a stupid head.
His wings are rumpled
And he lies all crumpled
On the hard church square.
The bells ring out in praise
That man is not a bird
It was a wicked, foolish lie,
Mankind will never fly,
Said the Bishop to the People.

The dream of flight, Ingrao meant, was an example of humanity's hubris for three hundred years, before it became a premonition. For the sake of our species and the planet, let's hope the same will one day be said of socialism.

ACKNOWLEDGMENTS

Any good publisher needs to be surrounded by people smarter than they are. I'm grateful for the tireless work of my colleagues at *Jacobin*—particularly our creative director, Remeike Forbes—which allowed me to find the time to write this book.

I'm indebted to everyone who read portions of this manuscript or had discussions with me about it: Seth Ackerman, Marcus Barnett, Mike Beggs, Eric Blanc, David Broder, Ronan Burtenshaw, Asher Dupuy-Spencer, Dan Finn, Dustin Guastella, Connor Kilpatrick, Sean Larson, Cyrus Lewis, Ella Mahony, Neal Meyer, Emily Morrow, and David Schweickart.

Special thanks to all those around *Socialist Register* for their support. The same goes to my comrades at Verso, especially Rosie Warren.

This book wouldn't have been made without Melissa Flashman's encouragement and the skilled work of Dan Gerstle at Basic Books. It might have been possible but wouldn't have been any good without the efforts of Jonah Birch and Jonah Walters.

I'd be remiss if I failed to mention how much I've learned from New York University professor Vivek Chibber over the years. If he's a great chef, I'm doing to his recipes what Chef Boyardee did to pasta. I happen to like SpaghettiOs. I hope you do too.

NOTES

Chapter One: A Day in the Life of a Socialist Citizen

1. My title is borrowed from a May 1968 *Dissent* essay, "A Day in the Life of a Socialist Citizen," by Michael Walzer.

2. Ellen Meiksins Wood, "The Question of Market Dependence," *Journal of Agrarian Change* 2 (2002): 50–87.

3. G. A. Cohen, "The Structure of Proletarian Unfreedom," *Philosophy & Public Affairs* 12, no. 1 (1983): 3–33.

4. Charles Ziegler, *Environmental Policy in the USSR* (Amherst: University of Massachusetts Press, 1987), 132.

5. Seth Ackerman, "The Red and the Black," *Jacobin* (Winter 2013).

6. See Leigh Phillips and Michal Rozworski, *People's Republic of Wal-Mart: How the World's Biggest Corporations Are Laying the Foundation for Socialism* (London: Verso, 2019) for a good alternative perspective on planning.

7. Michael Albert, *Parecon: Life After Capitalism* (London: Verso, 2003).

8. Jan Vanek, *Economics of Workers' Management: A Yugoslav Case Study* (Routledge Library Editions: Employee Ownership and Economic Democracy), vol. 3 (London: Routledge, 1972).

9. For an elaborated version of the model upon which this is based, see David Schweickart, *Against Capitalism* (Boulder: Westview, 1996).

10. David Schweickart, *After Capitalism*, 2nd ed. (Lanham, MD: Rowman & Littlefield, 2011), 48.

11. Ibid., 50.

12. Based on a Yugoslav work-point assignment system, as cited in Richard L. Carson, *Comparative Economic Systems*, vol. 2. (Armonk, NY: M. E. Sharpe, 1990).

13. Problems are also resolved as the system evolves through deliberations. To give one example: It turns out that a pure profit-sharing model had its drawbacks. Some people had only limited income security. There was also the risk of inefficient techniques hanging around too long due to self-exploitation at those firms. Workers were making up for inefficiencies by accepting lower incomes—competing with more efficient enterprises when everyone was better off if they either bowed out or adopted better labor techniques or technology. Setting minimum wages solved most of these issues.

14. Peter Frase, *Four Futures* (London: Verso, 2016).

15. Schweickart, *After Capitalism*, 72.

16. David Schweickart, "Is Sustainable Capitalism Possible?" Beijing Forum, 2008.

17. Backstreet Boys, "As Long As You Love Me," *Backstreet's Back* (Jive Records, 1997).

18. Irving Howe, "From Sweden to Socialism: A Small Symposium on Big Questions," *Dissent* (Winter 1991).

19. Erik Olin Wright, *Approaches to Class Analysis* (Cambridge: Cambridge University Press, 2005).

20. Corey Robin, "Socialism: Converting Hysterical Misery into Ordinary Unhappiness," *Jacobin*, December 10, 2013, https://www.jacobinmag.com/2013/12/socialism-converting-hysterical-misery-into-ordinary-unhappiness/.

21. Karl Marx, "Afterword to the Second German Edition," *Capital*, vol. 1 (1873).

Chapter Two: Gravediggers

1. Ellen Meiksins Wood, *The Origins of Capitalism: A Longer View* (London: Verso, 2003), 11.

2. Robert Brenner, "Agrarian Class Structure and Economic Development in Pre-Industrial Europe," *Past & Present* 70 (1976): 30–75.

3. Wood, *The Origins of Capitalism*, 96.

4. Ole L. Benedictow, *The Black Death 1346–1353: The Complete History* (Woodbridge: Boydell, 2008).

5. Wood, *The Origins of Capitalism*, 103.

6. Paul Heideman and Jonah Birch, "In Defense of Political Marxism," *International Socialist Review* 90 (July 2013).

7. David McNally, *Monsters of the Market: Zombies, Vampires and Global Capitalism* (Leiden: Brill, 2011), 51.

8. Michael Andrew Zmolek, *Rethinking the Industrial Revolution: Five Centuries of Transition from Agrarian to Industrial Capitalism in England* (Leiden: Brill, 2013).

9. E. J. Hobsbawm, *The Age of Revolution: Europe 1789–1848* (London: Phoenix, 2000), 43.

10. Ibid., 50.

11. Friedrich Engels, *Condition of the Working Class in England* (1845).

12. Friedrich Engels, Letter to Marx, 17 March 1845, in *Letters of the Young Engels 1838–1845* (Moscow, 1976), 231.

13. David Riazanov, *Karl Marx and Friedrich Engels: An Introduction to Their Lives and Work*, translated by Joshua Kunitz (1927; reprint, New York: Monthly Review, 1974), 38.

14. Engels, *Condition of the Working Class in England*.

15. Ibid.

16. *Economist*, January 18, 1851.

17. Francis Wheen, *Karl Marx: A Life* (New York: Norton, 2000), 179.

18. See G. A. Cohen, *Karl Marx's Theory of History: A Defence* (Oxford: Oxford University Press, 1978); Karl Marx, *The Eighteenth Brumaire of Louis Bonaparte* (1852); Michael Harrington, *Socialism* (New York: Saturday Review, 1972), 40.

19. Marshall Berman, *Adventures in Marxism* (London: Verso, 1999), 34.

20. Karl Marx, "The General Formula for Capital," Chapter 4 in *Capital*, vol. 1.

21. Karl Marx, "The Working Day," Chapter 10 in *Capital*, vol. 1.

22. Harrington, *Socialism*, 60.

23. Karl Marx, *The German Ideology* (1846).

24. Karl Marx, *Critique of the Gotha Programme* (1875).

25. Karl Marx, *The Civil War in France* (1871).

26. Harrington, *Socialism*, 20.

27. Ralph Miliband, *Socialism for a Sceptical Age* (London: Verso, 1995), 13.

28. Karl Marx, "Theses on Feuerbach," in *Karl Marx and Frederick Engels: Selected Works*, vol. 1 (Moscow: Progress Publishers, 1969), 15; Frederick Engels, Speech at the Grave of Karl Marx, Highgate Cemetery, London, March 17, 1883.

Chapter Three: The Future We Lost

1. Michael Harrington, *Socialism: Past and Future* (New York: Arcade, 1989), 50.

2. Marx to Ferdinand Lassalle in Berlin, London, 6 November 1859, marxists.catbull.com/archive/marx/works/1859/letters/59_11_06.htm.

3. Karl Marx, *Critique of the Gotha Programme* (1875).

4. Donald Sassoon, *One Hundred Years of Socialism: The West European Left in the Twentieth Century* (New York: New Press, 1996), 5–6.

5. Carl E. Schorske, *German Social Democracy 1905–1917: The Development of the Great Schism* (Cambridge, MA: Harvard University Press, 1955), 168.

6. Gary P. Steenson, *Karl Kautsky, 1854–1938: Marxism in the Classical Years* (Pittsburgh: University of Pittsburgh Press, 1991), 21.

7. Marx to [daughter] Jenny Longuet in Argenteuil, London, April 11, 1881, marxists.org/archive/marx/works/1881/letters/81_04_11.htm.

8. See Vernon L. Lidtke, *The Alternative Culture: Socialist Labor in Imperial Germany* (Oxford: Oxford University Press, 1985).

9. Joseph Hansen, "Bernstein's Challenge to Marx," *Fourth International* 13, no. 4 (Fall 1954): 139–143.

10. Schorske, *German Social Democracy 1905–1917*, 170.

11. Sebastian Haffner, *Failure of a Revolution: Germany 1918–19*, translated by Georg Rapp (Chicago: Banner, 1986).

12. Nicholas Stargardt, *The German Idea of Militarism: Radical and Socialist Critics, 1866–1914* (Cambridge: Cambridge University Press, 1994), 47.

13. Schorske, *German Social Democracy 1905–1917*, 77.

14. "Resolution Adopted at the Seventh International Socialist Congress at Stuttgart," *International Socialist Congress at Stuttgart*, August 18–24, 1907 (Berlin: Vorwärts, 1907), 64–66, marxists.org/history/international/social-democracy/1907/militarism.htm.

15. Jens-Uwe Guettel, "The Myth of the Pro-Colonialist SPD: German Social Democracy and Imperialism Before World War I," *Central European History* 45, no. 3 (2012): 452–484.

16. Stargardt, *The German Idea of Militarism*, 133.

17. "To Prevent War: Manifesto of the International Congress at Basel," *British Socialist* 25 (December 1912): 556–560, marxists.org/history/international/social-democracy/social -democrat/1912/12/manifesto.htm.

18. Stargardt, *The German Idea of Militarism*, 142.

19. Friedrich Engels, Letter to Paul Lafargue, 25 March 1889, in *Correspondence, Volume 2: 1887–1890* (Moscow: Foreign Languages Publishing House, 1960), 210.

20. Stargardt, *The German Idea of Militarism*, 147.

Chapter Four: The Few Who Won

1. Felix Dzerzhinsky, *Prison Diary and Letters* (Moscow: Foreign Publishing House, 1959), 86.

2. See Lars Lih, *Lenin Rediscovered* (Chicago: Haymarket, 2008).

3. Vladimir Lenin, *Lenin Collected Works*, vol. 4 (Moscow: Progress, 1964), 230.

4. Leon Trotsky, "Karl Kautsky," *New International* 5, no. 2 (February 1939): 51.

5. See Massimo Salvadori, *Karl Kautsky and the Socialist Revolution 1880–1938* (London: Verso, 1978).

6. Alec Nove, *An Economic History of the U.S.S.R.* (London: Penguin, 1992), 11.

7. Yurii Colombo, "From the Finland Station," *Jacobin*, April 16, 2017, jacobinmag .com/2017/04/april-days-lenin-russia-world-war-one.

8. Vladimir Lenin, *Lenin Collected Works*, vol. 24 (Moscow: Progress, 1964), 24.

9. Daniel Gaido, "The July Days," *Jacobin*, July 27, 2017.

10. V. I. Lenin, *State and Revolution* (Chicago: Haymarket, 2011), 86.

11. Irving Howe, *Trotsky* (New York: Viking, 1978), 52.

12. Nove, *An Economic History of the U.S.S.R.*, 34.

13. John Reed, *Ten Days That Shook the World* (New York: Boni and Liveright, 1919), 129.

14. Nove, *An Economic History of the U.S.S.R.*, 80.

15. China Miéville, *October: The Story of the Russian Revolution* (London: Verso, 2017), 321.

16. Samuel Farber, *Before Stalinism* (London: Verso, 1990), 45.

17. Nove, *An Economic History of the U.S.S.R.*, 124.

18. Ibid., 136.

19. Alec Nove, *Stalinism and After* (London: Routledge, 1988), 50.

Chapter Five: The God That Failed

1. Adam Przeworski, *Capitalism and Social Democracy* (Cambridge: Cambridge University Press, 1985), 46; Kjell Östberg, "The Great Reformer," *Jacobin*, September 10, 2015.

2. Karl Kautsky, "Revolution and Counter-Revolution in Germany," *Socialist Review* 23, no. 127 (April 1924).

3. Mitchell Abidor, "Assessing Léon Blum," *Jacobin*, September 26, 2016, https://www.jacobinmag.com/2016/09/leon-blum-popular-front-france-socialists-ps-fascism.

4. Karl Kautsky, *The Labour Revolution* (London: Ruskin House, 1924), 163.

5. Chris Wrigley, "The Fall of the Second MacDonald Government, 1931," in *How Labour Governments Fall: From Ramsay MacDonald to Gordon Brown*, edited by T. Heppell and K. Theakston (London: Palgrave Macmillan, 2013), 54.

6. "The Great Fiasco: Contemptible 'Labour' Government," *Socialist Standard*, no. 325 (September 1931).

7. Donald Sassoon, *One Hundred Years of Socialism: The West European Left in the Twentieth Century* (New York: New Press, 1996), 55.

8. Pelle Neroth, *The Life and Death of Olof Palme: A Biography* (independently published, 2017), 19.

9. Tim Tilton, *The Political Theory of Swedish Social Democracy: Through the Welfare State to Socialism* (Oxford: Oxford University Press, 1992), 31.

10. Ibid., 194; David Zachariah and Petter Nilsson, "Waiting in the Wings," in *Europe in Revolt*, edited by Catarina Principe and Bhaskar Sunkara (Chicago: Haymarket, 2016).

11. See Jonas Pontusson, *The Limits of Social Democracy. Investment Politics in Sweden* (Ithaca, NY: Cornell University Press, 1992).

12. Rudolf Meidner, "Why Did the Swedish Model Fail?," *Socialist Register* (1993): 222.

13. Catherine Ellis, "'The New Messiah of My Life': Anthony Crosland's Reading of Lucien Laurat's *Marxism and Democracy* (1940)," *Journal of Political Ideologies* 17, Issue 2 (2012): 189.

14. Anthony Crosland, *The Future of Socialism* (New York: Macmillan, 1957), 20.

15. Neroth, *The Life and Death of Olof Palme*, 17.

16. Ibid., 35.

17. Ibid., 40.

18. Ibid., 42.

19. Jonas Pontusson, "Radicalization and Retreat in Swedish Social Democracy," *New Left Review* 165 (September–October 1987): 11.

20. Peter Gowan and Mio Tastas Viktorsson, "Revisiting the Meidner Plan," *Jacobin*, August 22, 2017, jacobinmag.com/2017/08/sweden-social-democracy-meidner-plan-capital.

21. Rudolf Meidner, "Why Did the Swedish Model Fail?," *Socialist Register* (1993): 224; Jonas Pontusson, "Radicalization and Retreat in Swedish Social Democracy," *New Left Review* 165 (September–October 1987): 14.

22. Neroth, *The Life and Death of Olof Palme*, 92.

23. Alexandra Kollontai, *Selected Writings of Alexandra Kollontai* (Westport, CT: Lawrence Hill, 1978), 51.

24. Eva Mobert, *Kvinnor och människor (Women and people)* (Stockholm: Bonnier, 1962).

25. Joyce Gelb, "Sweden: Feminism Without Feminists?," chapter 5 in *Feminism and Politics: A Comparative Perspective* (Berkeley: University of California Press, 1989).

26. Adam Przeworski, "Social Democracy as a Historical Phenomenon," *New Left Review* 1, no. 122 (July–August 1980).

27. Jonah Birch, "The Many Lives of François Mitterrand," *Jacobin*, August 19, 2015, https://www.jacobinmag.com/2015/08/francois-mitterrand-socialist-party-common -program-communist-pcf-1981-elections-austerity/.

28. Ibid.

29. Curtis Atkins, "The Third Way International," *Jacobin* (Winter 2016).

Chapter Six: The Third World Revolution

1. John Riddel, ed., *Workers of the World and Oppressed Peoples, Unite!: Proceedings and Documents of the Second Congress, 1920, Volume 1* (New York: Pathfinder, 1991), 39.

2. Robert C. North and Xenia J. Eudin, *M. N. Roy's Mission to China: The Communist-Kuomintang Split of 1927* (Berkeley: University of California Press, 1963).

3. Rosa Luxemburg, *The National Question: Selected Writings by Rosa Luxemburg* (New York: Monthly Review Press, 1976), 110.

4. Leon Trotsky, "Manifesto of the Second World Congress—The Proletarian Revolution and the Communist International," in *The First Five Years of the Communist International*, 2nd ed. (New York: Pathfinder, 2009).

5. Michael Harrington, *Socialism* (New York: Saturday Review, 1972), 222.

6. Isaac Deutscher, *Marxism, Wars & Revolutions: Essays from Four Decades* (New York: Verso, 1985), 183.

7. Perry Anderson, "The Antinomies of Antonio Gramsci," *New Left Review* 1, no. 100 (November–December 1976).

8. Elizabeth McGuire, *Red at Heart: How Chinese Communists Fell in Love with the Russian Revolution* (Oxford: Oxford University Press, 2017), 98–99.

9. Duncan Hallas, *The Comintern* (Chicago: Haymarket, 2008), 123.

10. Harold R. Isaacs, *The Tragedy of the Chinese Revolution* (Stanford: Stanford University Press, 1961), 162.

11. Harold R. Isaacs, "X. The Coup of April 12, 1927," in ibid.

12. Ibid.

13. Isaac Deutscher, *Marxism, Wars & Revolutions: Essays from Four Decades* (New York: Verso, 1985), 183; Gregor Benton, ed., *Prophets Unarmed: Chinese Trotskyists in Revolution, War, Jail, and the Return from Limbo* (New York: Brill, 2015), 402.

14. Qiaomu Hu, *Thirty Years of the Communist Party of China: An Outline History* (New York: Hyperion Press, 1951).

15. Edward Hallett Carr, *Twilight of the Comintern, 1930–1935* (New York: Pantheon, 1982), 324.

16. Ibid., 359.

17. Harrington, *Socialism*, 226; Li Fu-jen, "After the Fall of Wuhan," *New International* (January 1939): 22–25.

18. Mao Tse-Tung, "On Coalition Government (April 24, 1945)," in *Selected Works of Mao Tse-Tung*, vol. 3 (1965; reprint, New York: Pergamon, 2014).

19. Harrington, *Socialism*, 227.

20. Jonathan Holslag, *China's Coming War with Asia* (New York: John Wiley & Sons, 2015), 29.

21. Leon Trotsky, "Peasant War in China and the Proletariat (September 22, 1932)," *Militant*, October 15 and 22, 1932, marxists.org/archive/trotsky/1932/09/china.htm.

22. Ji Yun, "How China Proceeds with the Task of Industrialization," *People's Daily*, 1953, http://afe.easia.columbia.edu/ps/cup/jiyun_industrialization.pdf.

23. Mao Tse-Tung, "A 'Backward' Village Is Not Necessarily Backward in Every Respect," in *Selected Works of Mao Tse-Tung*, vol. 1 (1965; reprint, New York: Pergamon, 2014); Mao Tse-Tung, "The Party Secretary Pitches In and All Party Members Help Run the Co-ops," in *Selected Works of Mao Tse-Tung*, vol. 1 (1965; reprint, New York: Pergamon, 2014).

24. Justin Yifu Lin, "Collectivization and China's Agricultural Crisis in 1959–1961," *Journal of Political Economy* 98, no. 6 (December 1990): 1228–1252; Kalyani Bandyopadhyaya, "Collectivization of Chinese Agriculture, Triumphs and Tragedies (1953–57)," *China Report* (January 1, 1971).

25. Isaac Deutscher, "The Doctrine of a Hundred Flowers," *The Nation*, June 29, 1957.

26. Lucien Bianco, "Comparing Mao to Stalin," *China Journal* 75 (2017): 88.

27. Tony Cliff, "China: The Hundred Flowers Wilt," *Socialist Review* 9 (May 1959).

28. Mao Tse-Tung, "Introducing A Co-operative (April 15, 1958)" in *Selected Works of Mao Tse-Tung*.

29. Werner Draguhn and David S. G. Goodman, eds., *China's Communist Revolutions: Fifty Years of the People's Republic of China* (New York: Routledge, 2002), 93.

30. Mao Tse-Tung, "Speech at the Lushan Conference (July 23, 1959)," in *Selected Works of Mao Tse-Tung*, vol. 1.

31. Mikhail A. Klochko, *Soviet Scientist in China* (London: Hollis & Carter, 1965); Mao Tse-Tung, "Talk at an Enlarged Working Conference Convened by the Central Committee of the Communist Party of China (January 30, 1962)," in *Selected Works of Mao Tse-Tung*, vol. 1.

32. "From the Journal of Ambassador P. F. Yudin, Record of Conversation with Mao Zedong, 31 March 1956," Wilson Center History and Public Policy Program Digital Archive.

33. "Talk by Mao Zedong at an Enlarged Meeting of the Chinese Communist Party Central Committee Politburo (Excerpts), April 25, 1956," in *Selected Writings of Mao Zedong*, vol. 7 (Beijing: Renmin chubanshe, 1999), 27; "Mikihail Zimyanin's Background

Report for Khrushchev on China (Excerpt), 15 September 1959," Wilson Center History and Public Policy Program Digital Archive.

34. Lucien Bianco, "Comparing Mao to Stalin," *China Journal* 75 (2017): 92.

35. Renmin Ribao, "Chairman Mao Swims in the Yangtse," *Peking Review* (July 29, 1966): 5.

36. Ji Xianlin, *The Cowshed: Memories of the Chinese Cultural Revolution*, translated by Chenxin Jiang (New York: New York Review Books, 2016); "Battle Song of the Red Guards (1967)," (Alpha History: *Chinese Revolution*), alphahistory.com /chineserevolution/battle-song-red-guards-1967.

37. See Tan Hecheng, *The Killing Wind: A Chinese County's Descent into Madness During the Cultural Revolution* (Oxford: Oxford University Press, 2017); Donald S. Sutton, "Consuming Counterrevolution: The Ritual and Culture of Cannibalism in Wuxuan, Guangxi, China, May to July 1968," *Comparative Studies in Society and History* 37, no. 1 (1995): 136–172.

38. Nicholas D. Kristof, "Legacy of Mao Called 'Great Disaster,'" *New York Times*, February 7, 1989, nytimes.com/1989/02/07/world/legacy-of-mao-called-great-disaster.html.

39. Jean Drèze and Amartya Sen, *Hunger and Public Action* (Oxford: Oxford University Press, 1991), 210–215.

40. See Raja Anwar, *The Tragedy of Afghanistan: A First-Hand Account* (New York: Verso, 1990); Fred Halliday and Maxine Molyneux, *The Ethiopian Revolution* (New York: Verso, 1981); and Fred Halliday, *Revolution and Foreign Policy: The Case of South Yemen, 1967–1987* (Cambridge: Cambridge University Press, 2002).

41. See Richard Gott, *Cuba: A New History* (New Haven, CT: Yale University Press, 2005).

42. B. Vivekanandan, *Global Visions of Olof Palme, Bruno Kreisky and Willy Brandt: International Peace and Security, Co-operation, and Development* (London: Palgrave Macmillan, 2016), 28–32.

43. Oliver Tambo, "Olof Palme and the Liberation of Southern Africa," in *New Perspectives in North-South Dialogue: Essays in Honour of Olof Palme*, edited by Kofi Buenor Hadjor (London: I. B. Tauris, 1988), 258.

Chapter Seven: Socialism and America

1. Irving Howe, *Socialism and America* (San Diego: Harvest Books, 1986), 3.

2. Alex Gourevitch, "Wage-Slavery and Republican Liberty," *Jacobin*, February 28, 2013, jacobinmag.com/2013/02/wage-slavery-and-republican-liberty.

3. Andrew Hartman, "Marx's America," *Jacobin*, May 5, 2018, jacobinmag .com/2018/05/marx-america-lincoln-slavery-civil-war.

4. Its record on Chinese immigration, however, was poor—a discrimination that would plague left and labor movements for years.

5. Alex Gourveitch, *From Slavery to the Cooperative Commonwealth: Labor and Republican Liberty in the Nineteenth Century* (New York: Cambridge University Press, 2014); Alex Gourevitch, "Our Forgotten Labor Revolution," *Jacobin* (Summer 2015).

6. Ibid.

7. Lawrence Goodwyn, *The Populist Moment: A Short History of the Agrarian Revolt in America* (Oxford: Oxford University Press, 1978); Nancy Maclean, "The Promise and Failure of Populism," *Socialist Worker* (April 1985).

8. Gary Marks and Seymour Martin Lipset, *It Didn't Happen Here: Why Socialism Failed in the United States* (New York: Norton, 2001), 33.

9. Ibid., 34.

10. Ronan Burtenshaw, "Connolly at 150," *Jacobin*, June 5, 2018, jacobinmag .com/2018/06/james-connolly-ireland-socialism-iww-labor.

11. Eugene V. Debs, "How I Became a Socialist," *New York Comrade* (April 1902); Paul Heideman, "The Rise and Fall of the Socialist Party of America," *Jacobin* (Fall 2016).

12. Elliott Shore, *Talkin' Socialism: J. A. Wayland and the Role of the Press in American Radicalism, 1890–1912* (Lawrence: University Press of Kansas, 1988), 40.

13. Unlike the antiracist Debs, Berger also thought "negroes and mullatoes constitute a lower race." William P. Jones, "'Nothing Special to Offer the Negro': Revisiting the 'Debsian View' of the Negro Question," *International Labor and Working-Class History* 74 (2008): 212–224.

14. Ira Kipnis, *The American Socialist Movement 1897–1912* (Chicago: Haymarket, 2005), 168–169.

15. Eugene V. Debs, "Eugene V. Debs Predicts a Social Revolution," *St. Louis Chronicle*, September 3, 1900.

16. Joe Richard, "The Legacy of the IWW," *International Socialist Review* (November 2012): 86.

17. James Weinstein, *The Decline of Socialism in America: 1912–1925* (New York: Monthly Review Press, 1967), 13.

18. Ibid., 14.

19. Eugene V. Debs, "A Letter to William English Walling from Eugene V. Debs in Terre Haute, Indiana, March 5, 1913," in *Letters of Eugene V. Debs*, vol. 2: 1913–1919, edited by J. Robert Constantine (Champaign: University of Illinois Press, 1990), 11.

20. Kipnis, *The American Socialist Movement*, 388.

21. Shore, *Talkin' Socialism*, 218.

22. Kipnis, *The American Socialist Movement*, 347; Theodore Draper, *The Roots of American Communism* (New York: Viking, 1957), 42.

23. Weinstein, *The Decline of Socialism in America*, 27.

24. William Z. Foster, *History of the Communist Party of the United States* (New York: International Publishers, 1952).

25. John Spargo, "Spargo Resigns: Letter to Adolph Germer in Chicago from John Spargo," *Milwaukee Leader*, June 9, 1917, 6.

26. Weinstein, *The Decline of Socialism in America*, 147–150.

27. Eugene V. Debs, "The Day of the People," *Class Struggle* 3, no. 1 (February 1919).

28. Paul Heideman, "The Rise and Fall of the Socialist Party of America," *Jacobin* (Fall 2016).

29. Draper, *The Roots of American Communism*, 199.

30. Jacob Zumoff, *The Communist International and U.S. Communism, 1919–1929* (Chicago: Haymarket, 2015); Branko M. Lazić and Milorad M. Drachkovitch, *Lenin and the Comintern*, vol. 1 (Stanford: Stanford University Press, 1972), 345.

31. Thomas Sakmyster, *A Communist Odyssey: The Life of József Pogány* (Budapest: Central European University Press, 2012).

32. Eric Blanc, "Defying the Democrats: Marxists and the Lost Labor Party of 1923," John Riddell: Marxist Essays and Commentary, johnriddell.wordpress.com/2014/09/10 /defying-the-democrats-marxists-and-the-lost-labor-party-of-1923.

33. Charlie Post, "The Popular Front: Rethinking CPUSA History," *Against the Current* 63 (July–August 1996).

34. Joe Richard, "Hunters and Dogs," *Jacobin*, October 28, 2016, jacobinmag .com/2016/10/cio-unions-communist-party-socialist-party-afl.

35. Michael Kazin, *American Dreamers: How the Left Changed a Nation* (New York: Alfred A. Knopf, 2011), 171.

36. Howe, *Socialism and America*, 74.

37. Maurice Isserman, *Which Side Were You On? The American Communist Party During the Second World War* (Middletown, CT: Wesleyan University Press, 1982), 18.

38. Vivian Gornick, *The Romance of American Communism* (New York: Basic Books, 1979).

39. Howard Brick and Christopher Phelps, *Radicals in America: The US Left Since the Second World War* (New York: Cambridge University Press, 2015), 31–34.

40. Thomas W. Devine, *Henry Wallace's 1948 Presidential Campaign and the Future of Postwar Liberalism* (Chapel Hill: University of North Carolina Press, 2013), 19.

41. Brick and Phelps, *Radicals in America*, 39.

42. Maurice Isserman, *If I Had a Hammer: The Death of the Old Left and the Birth of the New Left* (New York: Basic Books, 1987).

43. Harold Meyerson, "The Socialists Who Made the March on Washington," *American Prospect*, August 23, 2013.

44. Paul Heideman, "Half the Way with Mao Zedong," *Jacobin* (Spring 2018).

45. Michael Harrington, *Fragments of the Century* (New York: Simon and Schuster, 1977), 225.

Chapter Eight: Return of the Mack

1. Indian development has been far from even, however, and rural malnutrition has actually increased in recent years.

2. Lawrence Mishel, Elise Gould, and Josh Bivens, "Wage Stagnation in Nine Charts (White Paper)," Economic Policy Institute, January 6, 2015, epi.org/files/2013 /wage-stagnation-in-nine-charts.pdf; Katie Allen and Larry Elliott, "UK Joins Greece at

Bottom of Wage Growth League," *Guardian*, July 26, 2016, theguardian.com/money/2016/jul/27/uk-joins-greece-at-bottom-of-wage-growth-league-tuc-oecd; Valentina Romei, "How Wages Fell in the UK While the Economy Grew," *Financial Times*, March 2, 2017, ft.com/content/83e7e87e-fe64-11e6-96f8-3700c5664d30.

3. Kathe Newman, "Post-Industrial Widgets: Capital Flows and the Production of the Urban," *International Journal of Urban and Regional Research* 33, no. 2 (2009).

4. Catey Hill, "Employees of Now-Defunct WaMu Sang, 'I Like Big Bucks and I Cannot Lie' at Company Retreat: Reports," *New York Daily News*, April 14, 2010, nydailynews.com/news/money/employees-now-failed-wamu-sang-big-bucks-lie-company-retreat-reports-article-1.166709; Eric Dash and Andrew Ross Sorkin, "Government Seizes WaMu and Sells Some Assets, *New York Times*, September 25, 2008, nytimes.com/2008/09/26/business/26wamu.html.

5. Lynn Adler, "Foreclosures Soar 81 Percent in 2008," Reuters, January 15, 2009, reuters.com/article/us-usa-mortgages-foreclosures/foreclosures-soar-81-percent-in-2008-idUSTRE50E1KV20090115; Louise Story and Eric Dash, "Bankers Reaped Lavish Bonuses During Bailouts," *New York Times*, July 30, 2009, nytimes.com/2009/07/31/business/31pay.html.

6. Barack Obama, *The Audacity of Hope: Thoughts on Reclaiming the American Dream* (New York: Crown, 2006), 11.

7. Lance Selfa, "What's in Store in the Obama Era," *Socialist Worker*, January 20, 2009, socialistworker.org/2009/01/20/the-obama-era.

8. Matthew Yglesias, "The Democratic Party Down-Ballot Collapse, Explained," *Vox*, January 10, 2017, vox.com/policy-and-politics/2017/1/10/14211994/obama-democrats-downballot.

9. Dave Weigel, "Poll: Occupy Wall Street Twice as Popular as the Tea Party," *Slate*, October 13, 2011, slate.com/blogs/weigel/2011/10/13/poll_occupy_wall_street_is_twice_as_popular_as_the_tea_party.html.

10. Joseph E. Stiglitz, "Of the 1%, by the 1%, for the 1%," *Vanity Fair* (May 2011), vanityfair.com/news/2011/05/top-one-percent-201105; "Trends in the Distribution of Household Income Between 1979 and 2007," US Congressional Budget Office, October 2011, cbo.gov/sites/default/files/cbofiles/attachments/10-25-HouseholdIncome.pdf.

11. Hannah Shaw and Ted Stone, "Tax Data Show Richest 1 Percent Took a Hit in 2008, But Income Remained Highly Concentrated at the Top," Center on Budget and Policy Priorities, May 25, 2011, cbo.gov/sites/default/files/cbofiles/attachments/10-25-Household Income.pdf.

12. Jo Freeman, "The Tyranny of Structurelessness," Jo Freeman personal website, jofreeman.com/joreen/tyranny.htm.

13. Keeanga-Yamahtta Taylor, *From #BlackLivesMatter to Black Liberation* (Chicago: Haymarket, 2016).

14. Bernie Sanders, *Our Revolution: A Future to Believe In* (New York: Thomas Dunne Books, 2016), 23.

15. Michael Kruse, "Bernie Sanders Has a Secret," *Politico*, July 9, 2015, politico.com/magazine/story/2015/07/bernie-sanders-vermont-119927.

16. Sanders, *Our Revolution*, 50.

17. Hillary Rodham Clinton, *What Happened* (New York: Simon & Schuster, 2017), 227.

18. Symone D. Sanders, "It's Time to End the Myth That Black Voters Don't Like Bernie Sanders," *Washington Post*, September 12, 2017, washingtonpost.com/news/posteverything/wp/2017/09/12/its-time-to-end-the-myth-that-black-voters-dont-like-bernie-sanders.

19. "Hillary Clinton's 10 Biggest Corporate Donors in the S&P 500," *Forbes*, 2016, forbes.com/pictures/emdk45ehhgg/hillary-clintons-10-big/#110cb0c13629.

20. Dana Milbank, "How Schumer and the Democrats Are Preparing to Fight," *Washington Post*, December 9, 2016.

21. "Is There a Russian Coup Underway in America? | The Resistance with Keith Olbermann | GQ" (video), December 12, 2016, youtube.com/watch?v=IAFxPXGDH4E.

22. Meghnad Desai, *Marx's Revenge: The Resurgence of Capitalism and the Death of Statist Socialism* (London: Verso, 2002), 251.

23. Julian Glover, "The Party Is Over—This Phrase Has a History," *Guardian*, September 29, 2008; Tony Benn, *Against the Tide. Diaries 1973–76* (London: Hutchinson, 1989), 301.

24. Eric Hobsbawm, "The Forward March of Labour Halted?" *Marxism Today* (September 1978): 286.

25. Ralph Miliband, "The New Revisionism in Britain," *New Left Review* (March/April 1985); Stuart Hall, "Faith, Hope or Clarity," *Marxism Today* (January 1985): 16.

26. Patrick Wintour and Sarah Hall, "Labour Membership Halved," *Guardian*, August 3, 2004, theguardian.com/politics/2004/aug/03/uk.labour.

27. Robin Blackburn, "From Ed Miliband to Jeremy Corbyn," *Jacobin*, November 12, 2015, jacobinmag.com/2015/11/from-ed-miliband-to-jeremy-corbyn.

28. Sanchez Manning, "Take Me Out? No, Jeremy Liked a Night in Eating Cold Beans with His Cat Called Harold Wilson, Corbyn's First Wife Reveals," *Daily Mail*, August 15, 2015.

Chapter Nine: How We Win

1. Sam Gindin, "Building a Mass Socialist Party," *Jacobin*, December 20, 2016, jacobinmag.com/2016/12/socialist-party-bernie-sanders-labor-capitalism.

2. Albert Hunt, "Warren Isn't Sanders, and Vice Versa," Bloomberg, April 29, 2018, bloomberg.com/view/articles/2018-04-29/elizabeth-warren-and-bernie-sanders-aren-t-the-same.

3. "Americans' Views of Immigration Marked by Widening Partisan, Generational Divides," Pew Research, April 15, 2016.

4. "A Slim Majority of Americans Support a National Government-Run Health Care Program," *Washington Post*, April 12, 2018, washingtonpost.com/page/2010-2019/WashingtonPost/2018/04/12/National-Politics/Polling/release_517.xml?tid=a_mcntx.

5. This is perfectly rational in conditions of reduced profitability or high uncertainty.

6. Vivek Chibber, "Why Do Socialists Talk So Much About Workers?" *The ABCs of Socialism*, edited by Bhaskar Sunkara (London: Verso, 2016).

7. Kim Moody, "The State of American Labor," *Jacobin*, June 20, 2016, jacobinmag .com/2016/06/precariat-labor-us-workers-uber-walmart-gig-economy.

8. See Eric Blanc's writing in *Jacobin*, including: "The Lessons of West Virginia," March 9, 2018; "Red Oklahoma," April 13, 2018; "Arizona Versus the Privatizers," April 30, 2018; "Betting on the Working Class," May 29, 2018.

9. Eric Blanc and Jane McAlevy, "A Strategy to Win," *Jacobin*, April 18, 2018, jacobinmag.com/2018/04/teachers-strikes-rank-and-file-union-socialists.

10. Carole Feldman and Emily Swanson, "More than Half of Americans Support Pay Raises for Teachers, Poll Finds," PBS News Hour, April 23, 2018, pbs.org/newshour /nation/more-than-half-of-americans-support-pay-raises-for-teachers-poll-finds.

11. See Kim Moody, *An Injury to All: The Decline of American Unionism* (London: Verso, 1988).

12. Seth Ackerman, "A Blueprint for a New Party," *Jacobin* (Fall 2016).

13. J. David Gillespie, *Challengers to Duopoly: Why Third Parties Matter in American Two-Way Politics* (Charleston: University of South Carolina Press, 2012), 1.

14. See Daniel Lazare, *The Velvet Coup: The Constitution, the Supreme Court, and the Decline of American Democracy* (London: Verso, 2001).

15. Robert Fitch, "What Is Union Democracy?" *New Politics* (Winter 2011).

16. Michael Honey, *Going Down Jericho Road* (New York: Norton, 2007), 444–445.

Chapter Ten: Stay Fly

1. Ralf Dahrendorf, *Reflections on the Revolution in Europe* (New Brunswick, NJ: Transaction, 2005), 42; Andre Gorz, *Capitalism, Socialism, Ecology* (London: Verso, 1994), vii.

2. Jeff Tollefson, "Can the World Kick Its Fossil-Fuel Addiction Fast Enough?" *Nature*, April 25, 2018.

3. "The First International: Inaugural Address of the International Working Men's Association," International Working Men's Association, 1864, marxists.org/archive/marx /works/1864/10/27.htm; Christian Parenti, "Why the State Matters," *Jacobin*, October 30, 2015, jacobinmag.com/2015/10/developmentalism-neoliberalism-climate-change-hamilton.

INDEX

Bhaskar Sunkara is the founder and editor of *Jacobin*, which he launched in 2010 as an undergraduate at George Washington University. He has written for the *New York Times*, the  *Guardian*, *VICE*, and the *Washington Post*. Sunkara is also the publisher of the UK-based *Tribune* and *Catalyst: A Journal of Theory and Strategy*. He lives in New York.